Policies for a Just Society

By the same author

The Good City (with Paul Soto)
The Politics of Poverty
A Radical Agenda

Policies for a Just Society

DAVID DONNISON

MACMILLAN

First published 1998 by
MACMILLAN PRESS LTD
Houndmills, Basingstoke, Hampshire RG21 6XS
and London
Companies and representatives
throughout the world

1994/552

ISBN 0–333–65644–X hardcover
ISBN 0–333–65645–8 paperback

A catalogue record for this book is available
from the British Library.

This book is printed on paper suitable for recycling and
made from fully managed and sustained forest sources.

10 9   8   7   6   5   4   3   2   1
07 06 05 04 03 02 01 00 99 98

Editing and origination by
Aardvark Editorial, Mendham, Suffolk

Printed in Hong Kong

Contents

List of Figures and Tables

Figures

Tables

Preface

This book was inspired by some work I did for the Commission on Social Justice set up by the late John Smith when he was leader of the Labour Party. Their first statements dealt mainly with action to be taken on a national scale. How about the local scale?, I asked. The just city or the just village? What would they be like? Can such places be created? The Commission welcomed these questions, and, with some help from the Rowntree Charitable Trust and lots more from people doing enterprising things at local levels, I eventually produced a pamphlet called *Act Local*, published for the Commission by the Institute of Public Policy Research. During the following months many other people took up issues of social justice and poverty, encouraged by reports such as those produced by the Commission and the Rowntree Foundation, and spurred on by their own experience of the growth of poverty and the strains it was imposing on people and public services. I found myself repeatedly asked to contribute to conferences and other discussions and decided it might be more helpful if I developed the ideas in my pamphlet at greater length. Meanwhile it was becoming increasingly clear that, whoever won the next general election, a movement for social justice would have to be rebuilt from the ground up. This book is my attempt to help those engaged in that cause.

Some of my readers will be busy people with urgent practical tasks, some will have a more reflective approach to these questions and others will have both. I have tried to write for all of them. Each chapter concludes with a summary of the main things I learnt by writing it, and the final chapter contains a summary of the whole work, with pointers to the chapters in which these brief statements are developed at greater length. I hope that will enable people to skip and dip their way through the study if that is all they have time for, but I would not have written a book if I did not believe the whole thing to be worth reading.

I have had generous help from many people – some working in the field and others in the academy. Since it would be impossible to name them all, I mention only those whom it would be intolerable to omit: the Gulbenkian Foundation, for covering the costs of my work; John Benington, Michael Geddes and their colleagues in the Local Government Centre at the Warwick Business School, which was my main base for this project; Ivan Turok and others in Glasgow University's Centre for Housing Research and Urban Studies, my other work base; Gerry Stoker at the University of Strathclyde for helpful comments on the whole book; Andrew McArthur and Keith Hayton in that University's Planning Centre, Neil Jameson at the Citizen Organising Foundation, Gary Craig at Humberside University, Pete Alcock at Sheffield Hallam University, Doreen Massey in her capacity as Editor of *Soundings*, Quintin Oliver and Fiona Macmillan, particularly for help in Northern Ireland. Contributions from many other friends and colleagues can be glimpsed in the references quoted throughout the book. Equally important has been the help of politicians, professional workers and community activists working in many parts of Britain and Ireland. My warmest thanks to them all.

In this book, as in everything else I do, I have constantly exchanged ideas and drafts with Kay Carmichael, my comrade and collaborator.

Acknowledgements

The author and publishers wish to thank the following for permission to use copyright material: the Controller of HMSO and the Office for National Statistics for material from *Social Focus on Ethnic Minorities*. Crown Copyright 1996 and Routledge for the use of three figures from Richard Wilkinson, *Unhealthy Societies*.

Every effort has been made to trace all the copyright holders but if any have been inadvertently overlooked the publishers will be pleased to make the necessary arrangement at the first opportunity.

Introduction

A generation ago, when the terms 'first world' and 'third world' were coined to distinguish the richest from the poorest nations, Westerners had a crude understanding of the meaning of this distinction. In third world cities they expected occasional riots and politically motivated violence, they expected to see extremes of wealth and poverty with homeless beggars on the street, and to hear of casual brutality associated with prostitution and drugs. In their own cities they were generally safe from these things.

Not any more. That description would now apply equally well to London, Belfast, New York and many other cities of the West. Here in Britain these are not the only changes which people find worrying. There appears to have been a growth in football hooliganism, and in attacks on elderly people and teachers. There are dangers for which new names have been coined: 'road rage' and 'neighbours from Hell'. There seems to be more violence against children, and more violent crime of every kind, ranging from robberies to occasional, horrific massacres. Human relationships seem to be turning brutal.

The authorities to whom people used to look for protection and leadership in times of trouble are themselves becoming corrupted. Politicians take money for asking questions in Parliament; the Prime Minister sells to tycoons the opportunity for dining with him; the bosses of big monopolies which used to be thought of as public services award themselves vast increases in pay; the perpetrators of sexual abuses against children are often priests or staff of the agencies created to care for the nation's most neglected and vulnerable youngsters. No wonder the opinion polls show declining respect for leaders of most kinds.

Whether our moral standards are decaying or not, there is certainly greater confusion than there used to be about what these standards should be. Lone parenthood, gay and lesbian weddings, the use of drugs – practices which some deplore – are enthusiastically advocated by others. This confusion extends beyond questions of right and wrong to judgements about many other things. Buildings which won prizes for their designers are pulled down a few years later because people find them impossible to live in. Piles of bricks, dead animals, human faeces and other works bought with public money for prestigious art galleries often sit there in lonely isolation because, once the first public curiosity has been satisfied, so few people want to see them. As for music, many are appalled by the incitement to violence and murder to be heard daily in some of the most widely sold 'gangsta rap' recordings.

A lot of people are dismayed by these developments. Some of them feel they should get together with their neighbours and do something to resist the drift towards social disintegration which they see all around. But what can they do? And with whom? This book is written for these people by someone who shares their dismay and bafflement, and brings to the task no confident prescriptions – only some ideas learned mainly from others who are trying to resist forces which seem to be dividing and brutalising our country.

It is upon the local scale of action – that of the neighbourhood, the town and the city – that I shall focus, but not because these local arenas are the places where divisive trends, now to be seen on a worldwide scale, can be most effectively resisted. Much of the action needed must be taken at national and, increasingly, international scales. That calls for another book. But a great deal must also be done on a local scale, for there are people and places now so excluded from the mainstream of their society that they will never find a way back into it unless special steps are taken to help them. Meanwhile the prospects for effective resistance at larger, national, scales of action are not good – for reasons which I shall explore. Political leaders will not regain a robust determination to resist the forces which are dividing our society unless they sense that they are speaking for broader popular movements. If reformers sit back and wait for their friends to gain power in Parliament nothing much will change. Resistance movements will have to be rebuilt from the ground up by people who deplore what is happening – people who rediscover traditions of local civic action, too long neglected, which used to be familiar in this and many other countries.

When and why did things go wrong? Indeed, was there ever a golden age when things were going well? It has become fashionable to describe Britain during the years following the Second World War as passing through a period of social consensus, built on the comradeship achieved during the Blitz. A 'welfare state' based on universal principles which provided the same services for everyone was founded, and a high degree of equality was achieved. Most of this story is a myth – an important myth celebrating ideals we do not want to forget – but a myth nevertheless, fashioned as a contrasting backdrop against which to portray the harsher trends of recent years.[1] There have been changes during these years which stem from the fact that Western countries are passing through a difficult time as they lose their dominant position in the world. This phase, beginning in the 1970s and gathering speed in the late 80s, has been a particularly bruising experience for the British. Until the 1970s, the more highly developed capitalist countries were gradually giving their citizens greater equality of incomes and wealth, more equal living conditions and greater civil and social rights.[2] Thanks to full employment and to the confidence created by continuing economic growth, thanks to legislation enforcing minimum wages and protecting workers' rights, and thanks to a steadily growing array of social services, a social contract was being created which provided help for the youngest and the oldest citizens that was made possible by the contributions of those in the prime of life. It was a contract between the generations which helped to protect people in need at any stage of their lives.

This contract has not been completely abandoned, but from the mid-1970s its development was first checked, then reversed. Britain led a movement, now to be seen in many other countries, towards greater inequalities. Since then, 'poverty' – the word I shall often use to summarise the trends I am talking about – has been increasing, and increasing more dramatically in Britain than elsewhere. The first chapter in this book explains the issues it deals with by considering the meanings of some of the words – poverty, inequality, exclusion – used in the debate, and by setting out the main facts which these words describe.

Do the divisive trends now at work matter? And to whom? Some people accept that poverty has been increasing but are not moved by that. They don't care. I consider their standpoint in Chapter 2. If they are right, this book should stop there.

Can anything be done to change things? If so, how much of that action can be taken at a local level? There are people who accept that poverty has increased, and that it matters, but they are sceptical about the possibility of doing anything about it – particularly at a local scale. The more pessimistic of them believe that no solution can be found for such problems – perhaps quoting from the Bible: 'The poor ye have always with you' although in fact, the prophets of the Old Testament had some more forceful and hopeful things to say about the rights of the poor. The problems, the pessimists believe, arise from human defects. The individual may escape from these, but society as a whole cannot. Meanwhile, more optimistic people believe that poverty can be reduced, but only by creating a healthy, prosperous economy. Once that has been achieved, increasing wealth will filter down to everyone. Until then, action designed to reduce poverty will only make things worse. What we need are wealth-creating policies, not poverty-reducing policies. I shall discuss both standpoints in Chapter 3. Once again, if they are right there is no point in going further.

The questions I have posed evoke the standard responses of those who have contested progressive arguments from the French Revolution onwards. Albert Hirschman reviews these responses, and their progressive counterparts, in *The Rhetoric of Reaction*.[3] I will deal with them first in Chapter 3, and then throughout the book.

If we do have a problem – a problem which matters and which can be effectively tackled ('solved' may be too optimistic a word) – the next questions to ask must be about the traditions we can draw on for that purpose. What movements, armed with what ideas, can help Britain and other Western societies to resist and reverse these divisive trends? These are the questions addressed in Chapter 4 which concludes the first part of this book.

Part II deals with action – the things which can be done at a local scale to resist the forces which are breaking up our society. To do that, we must rebuild a tradition of robust and credible civic leadership in which citizens feel they play a part. The old bureaucratic forms of government we used to rely on cannot be recreated: that kind of power has been seeping away in private and public sectors alike. People are therefore working out new ways of getting things done which involve larger numbers of citizens, call for the mobilisation of a wider range of influences, and demand new kinds of leadership. The second part of this book starts with a chapter on 'Citizens and Civic Leaders', which draws on the experience of both. Thereafter I shall assume that any major new departure in policy must start by involving the people who will be most affected by it and listening to what they say.

The following chapters address problems in the order in which they are usually posed by people living in the communities which suffer most from the trends of our times. First come 'Skills, Work and Money' in Chapter 6; then 'Safety' in Chapter 7.

Next comes a chapter – the longest in the book – on 'Mainstream Services'. It does not deal in detail with the steps which can be taken by every department of government to reduce poverty. That job has been well done in reports I shall refer to. Mine will be an essay on the main strategies required, illustrated with examples from various services and many different places.

The hardships which result from growing inequality are a central feature of the problems encountered in most fields of public policy. But they are not the only feature. The other, to which growing attention is at last being paid, is the demands which our way of life make upon the earth's resources and the sustainability of that way of life. The two debates – about social justice and sustainability – are usually carried forward in different circles and discussed in different documents. But neither issue can be tackled effectively unless they are brought together, and the contradictions between them confronted and resolved. Chapter 9, 'Egalitarians and Greens', makes a start on that task.

Although I shall try to write like a democrat in ways which anyone can understand, this book is designed mainly for people who are in some way involved in our system of governance. Whether as politicians, administrators, community activists, private sector leaders or observers of their activities, they know the ropes to some extent. If provoked to act by something that is happening in their city or neighbourhood they have some idea where to begin. But there are many other people, equally provoked, who have no idea where to begin. Chapter 10, 'For Baffled Citizens', speaks particularly to them.

That concludes this part of the book which is the engine room of the whole work. Part III begins with a pause for reflection on the nature of the task undertaken here. What kind of an enterprise is this? By what authority does anyone tell their fellow citizens how their society should be run? And how, if at all, may the answers to these philosophical questions affect the day-to-day work of those involved in local governance? These are the issues explored in Chapter 11.

That discussion provides a launching pad for the final chapter in which I summarise the main arguments of the whole book. I show where these brief statements have been developed at greater length in earlier chapters, and discuss their broader implications for those working at local scales of action to reverse the divisive tendencies now to be seen in Britain and other Western countries.

Notes

1   Howard Glennerster (in *British Social Policy Since 1945*, Oxford, Blackwell, 1995) and Nicholas Timmins (in *The Five Giants: A Biography of the Welfare State*, London, HarperCollins, 1995) present excellent histories of social policy and the welfare state in Britain.
2   For evidence about the changing distributions of income and wealth, see the Reports of the Royal Commission on the Distribution of Income and Wealth – for example, *Third Report on the Standing Reference* (Cmnd 6999, London, HMSO, 1977). For a history of the worldwide economic and political changes creating what he calls the 'golden age' of Western capitalism in the post-war years and then bringing it to an end, see Eric Hobsbawm's *Age of Extremes* (London, Michael Joseph, 1994).
3   Albert O Hirschman, *The Rhetoric of Reaction: Perversity, Futility, Jeopardy*, Cambridge, Mass., Harvard University Press, 1991.

PART I

A Disintegrating Society

Chapter 1

Hardship: Facts and Meanings

Meanings

'Poverty' is the word most often used by pressure groups in Britain to describe the trends they deplore. That leads them to say that large and growing numbers of our people are poor. But these words are not much used in this country – and least of all by poor people themselves. Most of our fellow citizens use them to describe extreme hardships, and many of them believe these are now to be found only in third world countries, so they pay no attention to the arguments of the pressure groups. It's a dialogue of the deaf. Can we find words which will at least enable us to talk to each other about these issues?

Our neighbours in the European Union have in recent years come to talk less about poverty and more about 'exclusion'. That word reminds us that people may be excluded from their society by many things besides lack of money: by the inability of people in wheelchairs to get about in a world designed without thought for their needs, by a poor education which gave them none of the qualifications they need for a job, by practices and habits of mind which deprive women or ethnic minorities of opportunities that white men take for granted, by living in remote places lacking essential commercial and public services, and by many other things. The idea of exclusion sheds the assumption, sometimes associated with poverty, that the poor are responsible for their own plight and suggests instead that they are excluded from the mainstream of their society by forces which may be beyond their control. Thus we all become part of the problem – the excluders as well as the excluded – and a natural opposite is suggested – 'integration' – which can become the aim of public policy. In meetings between governments the word also makes it easier to keep the British and the Germans on board. Their spokesmen can talk about exclusion despite being required by their masters to deny that their countries have any poverty.

But neither word distinguishes a clearly defined and countable group of people, and neither is much used by poor people themselves. In Britain, the most widely used measure of poverty has been the scales laid down by Parliament each year for the means-tested social assistance benefits paid through income support – and, before that, supplementary benefit and national assistance. These scales have the democratic authority conferred by our elected representatives who approved them in Parliament as a minimum income which the state should guarantee for those unable to support themselves. They were used by Peter Townsend in his classic work *Poverty in the United Kingdom*.[1] He added a margin to them to allow for the expenses borne by working households, and compared the results with a scale of his own invention based on a list of necessities he had compiled to show who was being excluded from the normal life of the people in this country. He concluded that people needed about 50 per cent more than the social assistance rates to keep out of poverty.

But no-one ever claimed that there was any scientific authority for the social assistance scales or for the many changes made in them since Townsend's book was written. They are only the product of contending political forces. A more systematic approach was therefore developed by Joanna Mack and Stuart Lansley who started from a third idea: 'need'. Poverty, they argued, arises when people cannot meet basic needs. In two studies, they made surveys which showed what the British people believed to be 'necessities' – things 'which you think are necessary, and which all adults should be able to afford and which they should not have to do without'.[2] Then they found out who was unwillingly deprived of these things. The proportion of people lacking these necessities was exceedingly low through successively lower income groups until a point was reached at which deprivation increased sharply. This became their poverty line – and it was about 150 per cent of the income support level, as Townsend had said.

To prove that this is genuinely a measure of poverty, we must also show that people who have to live on such low incomes eat poorer food than richer people, are less happy, and experience greater stress which shows up in poorer health, shorter life expectations, poorer attainment in school and other signs of trouble. All of which is true. I shall give some of the evidence for that later.

Meanwhile, the countries of the European Union have developed another kind of poverty line. Anyone living in a household which has less than half the average income for households of their size and type within their country is described as being in poverty. As this measure becomes more familiar, it will help people to keep track of changes which may be pushing more people, or new kinds of people, into poverty, and to compare what is happening in different countries. This, like Mack and Lansley's definition, is a measure involving the whole population. Poverty, defined in this way, could be reduced by raising the incomes of the poorest people or by lowering the incomes of the rich. It is really a measure of inequality within nations.

Where does all this leave us?: with a few useful concepts and some simple words to describe them. *Exclusion* is an idea which poses the right kinds of question. Who are excluded and who are the excluders? What factors and forces exclude people and how can these be surmounted? What are the 'mainstream' communities from which people are excluded? In what directions are these communities developing, producing what new forms of exclusion, and what new routes to integration? But exclusion is best thought of as a process, working at various scales, not a clearly defined condition. Some of the poorest people may feel excluded from opportunities in the wider society while being strongly integrated within the small communities they live in. Others with higher incomes may feel more excluded – by deafness or by race prejudice for example.

Need is another useful idea. It can be democratically defined by asking people what they regard as necessities – and that should remind us that needs are shaped by the economy and the society it supports. Thus they will change as time goes by. New necessities – and therefore new kinds of poverty or exclusion – will be created as the economy evolves.

Both these ideas call for some assessment of the whole society and the directions in which it is evolving. Both can be validated by looking at the things which happen when people are excluded and their needs are not met. Are they unhappy? Do they fall sick? Become delinquent? Both are essentially measures of *equality* and *freedom*, for only in a free and equal society would no-one be excluded or deprived of necessities.

If figures are needed to measure changes in the amount of inequality or to compare different countries, the European Union's poverty line, fixed at half-average income, is a useful device – provided we do not imagine that those falling below it are a different kind of animal from those above it. The fact that they cannot be clearly distinguished from each other is not a 'problem': it is a *finding*. Those defined as poor in this way *are* ordinary citizens – having a harder time than most. They will not all become depressed, sick, delinquent, separated from their partners, neglectful of their children... . Nor will all those above the line avoid these misfortunes. But such signs of stress will be more common below the line, which is part of the evidence showing that we are dealing with serious *hardship* – another useful term, and a word that everyone understands.

A more precise measure of inequality is the Gini coefficient, a figure showing where a population sits on a scale running from complete equality (everyone getting exactly the same income, or whatever is to be measured) to complete inequality (all the income going to one member of that population). These coefficients are useful because they are based on evidence about every member of the population. They will be frequently quoted later in this chapter, but the term is still too rarefied to be of much use in public debate.

Some people have objected to the whole argument presented here, asserting that a sharp distinction must be drawn between 'absolute' poverty, defined in some fixed, unchanging way, and 'relative' poverty, defined as exclusion from a nation's changing standards of living. For them, only 'absolute' poverty 'counts'. 'Relative' poverty amounts to no more than a failure to 'keep up with the Joneses'. Keith Joseph and Jonathan Sumption gave a robust assertion of that view in their book *Equality*, where they said, 'A family is poor if it cannot afford to eat. It is not poor if it cannot afford endless smokes and it does not become poor by the mere fact that other people can afford them'.[3] In Britain, most of the steam has gone out of this argument because, for years, relative and absolute poverty have both been increasing. Many poor people really cannot eat properly. Even if that trend were reversed, however, people are beginning to grasp that no sharp distinction can be drawn between relative and absolute poverty – as I shall show.

What many of the critics of relative definitions of poverty really want to say is that inequality is no bad thing: indeed, there should be more of it. That is a different point, to which I shall return in the next chapter. All that needs to be said about it here is that no-one is suggesting that we could – or should – create a completely equal society. While differences in talent, luck, taste and perseverance remain, there will always be differences in what happens to people. What we should be trying to create is a world in which people are treated with equal respect, and a world in which hardships and signs of stress – unemployment, illness, imprisonment, grief and the like – are randomly distributed, rather than heaped upon the same kinds of people. Meanwhile, on our journey towards that objective, we could allow plenty of scope for variations in income and wealth arising from differences in talent, luck and so on, without compelling people to live on less than half of the average income for their society. Some countries have been much more successful than we have been at preventing people from falling this far behind their fellow citizens. Moreover we should take particular care of our children who are the nation's most precious hope for the future. They have no choice about the families into which they are born, and their opportunities for making any choices in future will be shaped by the character and circumstances of those families.

The distinction between poverty and inequality is not as easy to draw as Keith Joseph and others have assumed. If poverty is a state of need, we have to ask what makes something a necessity. That question has been revealingly explored by Len Doyal and Ian Gough.[4] The essential point to bear in mind is that an advancing, changing society constantly creates new forms of poverty by turning some of the luxuries of previous generations into necessities for their successors. When most people lived in the countryside, carrying water from the stream or a village pump and digging pits in the back garden for their sewage, a piped water supply and piped sewage were luxuries: useful but not essential. Many managed happily without such things. But when they came crowding into the cities, the cholera soon taught them that these things were necessities for an urban society. When everyone lit their homes with candles, electricity was a luxury. Now that most domestic activities, from storing and cooking food to heating the home and watching television, depend on electricity, it too has become a necessity. Today, families deprived of water or electricity because they cannot pay the bills for them are in much deeper trouble than their rural predecessors would have been. The process continues. As more and more people use cars, buses are withdrawn from rural areas, and services such as shops and doctors' surgeries are centralised into fewer, larger units concentrated in the towns. A car then becomes in some places the only means of getting to work, to the doctor or the shops: a new necessity.

A society which becomes increasingly unequal cannot avoid pushing more of its people into poverty – poverty which really hurts. Unmet needs inflict pain – hardships that create stresses which show up in illness, shortened lives, failure at school and other troubles – as I shall show in the next chapter. The long love affair which the Western world has had with economic growth was based on the assumption that an economy producing more goods would eventually benefit every citizen. Thus its leaders did not have to worry about the distribution of their gross national product. Now we know that growth only benefits the whole society if its fruits are distributed in equalising ways.

Some people will object that we cannot create a pain-free world – an earthly paradise – and indeed all of us will suffer our share of trouble before we are through. But, if we are lucky, it will be no more than our share. It is when large groups of people suffer much more than their share of hardship that we know that we are in the presence of inequalities which create poverty, restrict freedom and exclude people from the mainstream of their society. There is no way in which we can draw a poverty line and assert that all who fall below it will suffer more than their fair share of hardship and all who rise above it will be spared that fate. Some people, thanks to good luck, the help of friends and relatives and their own resourceful courage, can cope with poverty without great hardship. Others are more vulnerable. It is often when things go wrong – when your home is burgled, your child becomes seriously ill or your family's main breadwinner falls out of work – that the vulnerability of the poor is revealed… . Or it may be when heavy spending is needed – for Christmas presents, a wedding, a first communion or a funeral. What would for richer people be a setback becomes for poorer people a disaster. A well-known insurance company's advertisement unwittingly makes the point: they promise that they 'will not make a drama out of a crisis' – a promise only offered to those who can afford their insurance policies.

Exclusion, poverty, hardship, inequality, loss of freedom – the dictionaries distinguish each from the others. But in real life they cannot be so clearly separated. They describe different ways of looking at the same things, not separate phenomena. We cannot understand poverty or measure it unless we understand how it is related to the other things in this list. It follows that the best measures of poverty will not be single 'poverty lines' but measures which tell us something about the whole pattern of the society concerned. Inequality and exclusion are ways of describing that pattern, rather than just the situation of the poorest people. The pattern reflects the character of the whole society. The European Union's figures showing the numbers of people having to live on less than half the average income for households of their type within their country are one such measure. Defined in this way, the numbers in poverty could be reduced by raising the incomes of the poorest people or by reducing the incomes of the richest. Gini coefficients are an even more useful measure, showing how widely scattered are a population's incomes. These are the concepts and measures on which I shall mainly rely.

Is there any poverty in Britain?

If we take the European Union's definition, it shows that, in Britain, about one person in four (24 per cent, after allowing for housing costs) was living in poverty in 1991, and these numbers had been rising – most dramatically since 1985.[5] For children the position was worse: Figure 1.1 shows that in 1991 nearly half those living in poverty were in households with dependent children. Altogether, one in three children were living in poverty.[6] This figure, which shows the kinds of family who have to live on less than half the nation's average income, gives a lower total of about one in five of the population living in poverty. That is because these figures do not take account of housing costs which had been rising particularly sharply for poorer families. The figure shows that poverty fell to a low point of 6 per cent of the population in 1977 (7 per cent, allowing for housing costs). It then rose to the present levels which are higher than at any time since the Second World War.

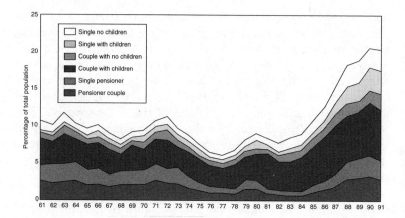

Source: Joseph Rowntree Foundation, *Inquiry Into Income and Wealth*, York, Joseph Rowntree Foundation 1995, p. 33.

FIGURE 1.1   Individuals below half-average income, 1961–91, by family type

The government's figures showing the numbers of children living in poverty are presented in Figure 1.2, as summarised in a report by the Family Policy Studies Centre.[7]

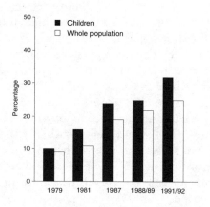

Source: Family Policy Studies Centre, *Family Report 2*, London, Family Policy Studies Centre 1995, p. 6; and Department of Social Security, *Households Below Average Income*, London, HMSO 1994.

FIGURE 1.2   Children living in poverty, 1979–1991/92

Incomes were rising strongly during this period and most people were becoming better off. Most, but not all: Figure 1.3, taken from the Rowntree Report, shows changes in real incomes for ten different income groups, after allowing for housing costs. The top three income groups made dramatically good progress – particularly during the second half of the 1980s. Those on middle incomes did reasonably well. But the bottom three income groups made practically no gains and the lowest of all actually lost ground, ending the period no richer than the equivalent group had been 24 years earlier in 1967.

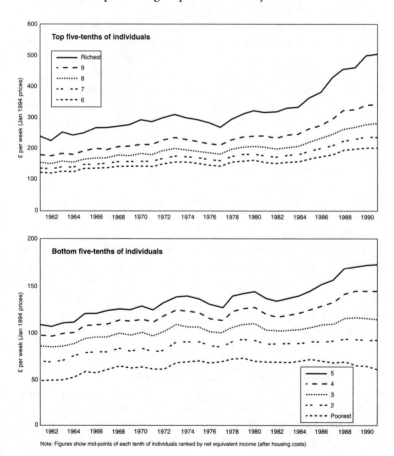

Source: Joseph Rowntree Foundation, *Inquiry into Income and Wealth op. cit.*, p. 30.

FIGURE 1.3   Real incomes, 1961–91 (after housing costs)

There are many other ways of measuring poverty and the distribution of incomes. All confirm that there has been a trend toward greater inequality and more widespread poverty, and some provide useful extra information. The Institute for Fiscal Studies has made studies of household expenditure and of the distribution of wealth.[8] These show that – to a growing extent – the people with the lowest incomes are not necessarily the lowest spenders. That is probably because more unemployed people with children, more lone parents and more of the self-employed are falling into the lowest income group. Compared with the pensioners, who have tended to move into the next higher income group but are still the lowest spenders, they are probably less good at controlling expenditure: they have outstanding hire-purchase agreements, they still have a telephone, they have not yet taught their children to turn off lights and fires… so they run more deeply into debt. They may also be more hopeful of resuming work, indeed may still be doing some on the side which does not enter into official figures for their incomes. The finding that they often spend more than their incomes is not necessarily reassuring news about the poor.

Although the details vary from one study to another, the divisive trends remain clear in all this research. Average standards of living are improving in an increasingly unequal society where the poorest people do not share in that improvement. Expenditure inequality, which used to be greater than income inequality, may now be somewhat less than income inequality, but it is still growing.

Thus far I have dealt with income and expenditure. What about wealth? Like incomes, holdings of wealth have grown larger. But they increase inequality rather than reduce it. If pension rights are included, the distribution of wealth in the United Kingdom has grown more unequal between 1976 and 1992.[9] If we adopt a very modest definition of wealth – having more than £750 in savings when pension rights are excluded – large proportions of our people attain that level only among the minority who have annual incomes of more than £17,500. This wealth is heavily concentrated among people over the age of 45, at a stage in life when the main burdens of childrearing are past. There are transfers of wealth within families which help some people out, but these are most generous among the richest and the smallest families. Thus they reduce inequality within families but increase inequality across the population as a whole.[10]

The story of recent years seems to have a simple refrain: the rich get richer, and the poor get poorer. But it is not quite as simple as that.

While the incomes of the poorest groups have indeed fallen further and further behind the average and those of the richest have gone racing ahead, the people in those groups change in the course of time. The government has used insurance and tax records to trace for the following 14 years the earnings of men who were aged between 25 and 44 on 1st January 1978. That tells us nothing about the incomes of those who had no earnings at all because they were not in jobs. They are usually the poorest people and their numbers grew massively during this period as more men became unemployed or long-term sick, and more retired early. But among those who did have some earnings the great majority gained an increase in income during these 14 years – even among the lowest paid. Since earnings tend to peak around the age of 41, then remain stable for a while and start falling when men are in their early fifties, that is not surprising. Most of the men in this sample were younger than 41 at the beginning of the study, so they tended to earn more as they moved towards the plateau of relatively high earnings achieved during their forties.[11] If the study had focused on an older age group on the declining slope of lifetime income, it would have produced very different results.

These figures should not be interpreted as unquestionably good news. They tell us that many of the lowest earners move into higher income groups, but that means that many with slightly higher earnings fall into the lowest group. Thus the anxieties associated with poverty extend well beyond the poor, afflicting large numbers who are – with good reason – worried about their future. Meanwhile, this evidence tells us nothing about the poorest people of all: those living on social security benefits. They also have another drawback. Because they deal only with the earnings of men, they tell us nothing about the growing proportion of women at work – now nearly half the labour force – or about the position of households which depend on two or more incomes. Compared with earlier generations, people's living standards now depend more upon the numbers of earners in their household and less upon the earnings of a lone 'breadwinner'.

The story I have told can be summed up in this way. Between 1979 and 1990/91, average income in the UK rose by 35 per cent, a massive improvement which never filtered down to the poorest people. Those who remained in the poorest tenth had a 1 per cent decline in real income, while those who remained in the top tenth had an increase of 58 per cent. If housing costs are taken into account, as they should be, the real incomes of the poorest fell by 14 per cent, while those of the richest rose by 62 per cent.[12] Since people often move from one income group to another, we will not be comparing the positions of exactly the same individuals when we look at the same income groups at different points in time. But they rarely move far along the income scale. What cannot be contested is that, today, more people are in poverty, and they are having a harder time than in previous generations.

In 1979 over four million families were living on supplementary benefit, the state's safety net income, and over three million others were in households with incomes which fell below that level because they were working for low wages, drawing an inadequate pension but not claiming a supplementary one, or for other reasons. Ten years later, the number living on income support – which succeeded supplementary benefit – had risen by two-thirds, and the number in households with incomes falling below that level had risen by one third. That was not because the country could not afford to be more generous to its poorest people. This increase in poverty, as defined year by year in Parliament, came about at a time when average income for the whole population increased faster than at any time over the previous 18 years. The problem, as I shall show, has economic origins, but it is essentially political in character. It is not a problem arising from lack of resources; it is a problem arising from a loss of shared concern and unity within the nation.

Trends over the years can be summarised with the help of Gini coefficients calculated in various ways which show that, in the United Kingdom, inequality remained remarkably stable between 1949 and 1963. There was then a move towards greater equality which continued with fluctuations till about 1977. After that, inequality increased – most dramatically from 1985. That increase, bringing inequality to the highest levels recorded since the Second World War, may have been checked in the early 1990s, but it is too early to be sure of that.[13]

Who are the poor?

Who are the people most likely to be having a hard time, and how have those patterns been changing? If we take the poorest fifth of the population in 1990/91, the biggest group, accounting for 27 per cent of them, were aged 60 or more, but their share of poverty was declining: a dozen years earlier, in 1979, these older people had accounted for 39 per cent of the poorest fifth. Over the same period, the share of the unemployed in these figures rose from 10 to 18 per cent.[14] Along with growing unemployment, there has been a massive increase in *non*-employment among the long-term sick, lone parents who are not working, early retirers and others. Many of these would prefer to go to work if a job were available and should be added to the figures for the unemployed.

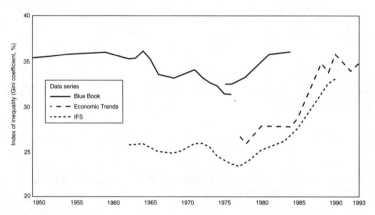

Source: Joseph Rowntree Foundation, *Inquiry Into Income and Wealth, op. cit.*, vol. 2, Figure 12, p. 26.

FIGURE 1.4   Trends in income inequality

Non-white ethnic minorities have suffered particularly severely from these trends. They are twice as likely as white people to be in the poorest fifth of incomes and less than half as likely to be in the richest fifth, and their unemployment rates are roughly double those for the white population, despite the fact that their youngsters are staying on longer at school and college than white youngsters and doing about as well in examinations.[15]

Figure 1.5 and Table 1.1 provide some of the evidence for these findings. Figure 1.5, showing unemployment in different ethnic groups between 1984 and 1995, vividly illustrates the way in which minorities form part of the reserve army of labour – their unemployment rates fluctuating through the trade cycles much more sharply than those of white workers.

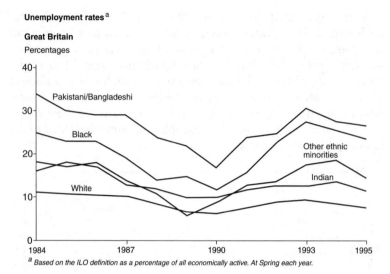

Unemployment rates[a]

Great Britain
Percentages

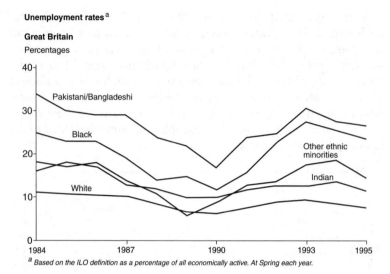

[a] *Based on the ILO definition as a percentage of all economically active. At Spring each year.*

Source: Table 4.14 of Alyson Whitmarsh and Tim Harris, *Social Focus on Ethnic Minorities*, 1996, p. 46. Reproduced by permission.

FIGURE 1.5   Unemployment rates for different ethnic groups, 1984–1995

TABLE 1.1   Participation in full-time education[a] **of different ethnic groups, by age**[b]**, spring 1994**

England and Wales	Percentages		
	16	17[c]	18
Black	86	65	50
Indian	95	77	65
Pakistani/Bangladeshi	80	80	61
Other Asian	89	83	72
Other ethnic minorities	75	74	64
White	71	55	38

[a]   In school, further or higher education
[b]   Age at 31 August 1993
[c]   Data are for Spring 1993: age at 31 August 1992

Source: Table 3.2 of Alyson Whitmarsh and Tim Harris, *Social Focus on Ethnic Minorities*, Office for National Statistics, HMSO 1996, p. 4.

Table 1.1 shows that these differences in opportunities for work are unlikely to be due to differences in education. Young people in the ethnic minorities tend to stay longer in full-time education than their white counterparts.

But the most striking feature of these trends is the growing numbers of children in poverty. Between 1979 and 1991/92, the proportion of dependent children living in households with below half the average income increased more than threefold – from 10 per cent to about 33 per cent. These children were fairly equally divided into three groups: those of low wage earners, of the unemployed and of lone parents.[16] Figures 1.2 (above) and 1.6 show how rapidly their numbers grew, particularly after 1985.

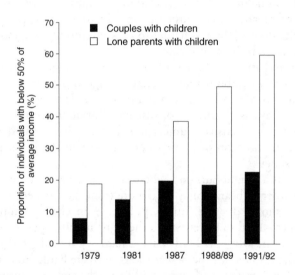

Source: Department of Social Security, *Households Below Average Income. A Statistical Analysis.* 1979–92. London, HMSO 1994, quoted in Family Policy Studies Centre, *Children in Britain* 1995, p. 7.

FIGURE 1.6   Child poverty by family type, 1979–1991/92. Percentage in households with below half-average income

Patterns which show up in studies of individual people under-estimate inequalities which would show up in a study of households. There have been increases in the numbers of households with two or more earners and in the numbers with none – both the 'job-rich' and the 'job-poor'. That is a natural result of our growing reliance on means-tested benefits as social insurance benefits have declined, coupled with the growth in low-paid, part-time and temporary jobs, particularly for women – many of them jobs which could only be taken by someone in a household where there is another person working full time. Without that full-time worker, the family, if it included children, might be better off on income support. Among married women, only 33 per cent were in work if their husbands were not working, but more than twice as many – 74 per cent – were working if their husbands were in work.[17] These patterns must affect the ways in which children are prepared for entry into the wider world. If no-one in the family is working, it must be harder to learn the role of breadwinner, harder to stay in touch with the young people who do get jobs and harder to pick up information about the opportunities which are available.

Poverty and affluence have both become increasingly concentrated in particular neighbourhoods. That change has been a steadily continuing process rather than a dramatic one. It shows up, not at the scale of towns or municipal districts, but at the much smaller scale covered by Census enumeration districts. It is related to the growing concentration of poor people in some of the larger public housing estates.[18]

To live in a neighbourhood where most people are poor makes poverty harder to bear. It may be remote from the city centre. Local services – shops, doctors, buses, pubs… even charity shops and jumble sales – tend to be fewer and their quality often poorer. Crime and squalor are worse. Schools have a harder job to do and find it more difficult to recruit the best teachers. Jobs are harder to come by because there are fewer of them within reach, and employers may discriminate against recruits from these neighbourhoods. These are some of the reasons why those who can afford to move out do so.

Conclusions

Poverty, exclusion, unmet need, loss of freedom, inequality, hardship… each provides a different lens through which to study the same central problem – a different way of looking at it and talking about it. None of them can be fully understood without taking account of the others. The central problem is hardship, and its main cause is gross and growing inequality.

Poverty arises when human needs cannot be met. But needs change as a society evolves. Candles give way to electricity, latrines set up over holes in the ground give way to water closets, and in time both inventions become necessities. Today, there are remote places where the motor car is becoming a necessity. Already, people living in centrally heated flats find they need a refrigerator and the electricity which makes it work because their homes are warm and the local corner shops have all disappeared. They may need a washing machine too if there is no safe place to hang clothes out to dry and no launderettes in the district. That's fine for those who share in the country's generally rising living standards, but those who get left behind suffer new forms of poverty which inflict real hardships. The evidence of heavy debt burdens in poverty-stricken neighbourhoods proves that. You do not borrow at the crippling interest rates charged by loan sharks who account for much of this debt or expose yourself to the attentions of the 'heavies' who police repayments to them unless you desperately need the money.

The process goes further. A neighbourhood in which most people are poor is not an attractive place for shops, banks, building societies, bus companies and other enterprises to do business. That's why there are so few of them there. Its political clout is likely to be weaker than that of a community in which everyone has telephones and is used to demanding helpful responses from public officials. So poorer people's needs for services from the private and the public sector are less likely to be met than are those of richer people living in more comfortable neighbourhoods.

Unmet need, and therefore poverty, exclude people from the mainstream of their own society. Exclusion arises from inequalities in the distribution of income, commercial and public services, and political power. Economic growth does nothing to reduce hardship unless it creates a more equal society. Increasing inequality is a sign of a failing economy, no matter how rapidly average incomes may advance.

Britain has experienced a particularly savage increase in inequality in recent years. Those worst afflicted are children and the parents who care for them in the families of low-paid workers, unemployed people and lone parents – all increasing in number. Ethnic minorities have fared worst of all. This has come about during a period when the nation has achieved great advances in income and wealth. The resources for a fairer distribution are available if we choose to use them in that way.

A clear-cut line cannot be drawn between the poor and the rest of their fellow citizens. Hardship is related to income, but only roughly. Wherever we draw a line, there will be some people above it who are having a harder time than some of those below it. Meanwhile people move in and out of poverty, for it is a condition which comes about in many different ways. Some people in the lowest income group are doing short-term, part-time jobs while passing through a period of education and training which will eventually lead them to highly paid work. Some are between jobs or suffering temporary sickness. But others have been out of work for many years and are unlikely ever to work again; or they may be lone parents who are likely to have to struggle for many years to make ends meet; or pensioners with little hope of any increase in real income.

In short, 'the poor' are not a distinct group of people. They are much like everyone else – a wide variety of ordinary folk, many of whom are having a hard time. Their worries are shared by many more people in slightly higher income groups who fear, with good reason, that they may join the poorest before long. Those conditions, as I shall show, create an anxious and ungenerous society; and that has political implications.

Notes

1   Peter Townsend, *Poverty in the United Kingdom*, Harmondsworth, Penguin, 1979.
2   Joanna Mack and Stewart Lansley, *Poor Britain*, London, George Allen & Unwin, 1985, p. 294.
3   Keith Joseph and Jonathan Sumption, *Equality*, London, John Murray, 1979, p. 27
4   Len Doyal and Ian Gough, *A Theory of Human Need*, London, Macmillan, 1991.
5   Joseph Rowntree Foundation, *Inquiry into Income and Wealth*, York, Joseph Rowntree Foundation, 1995, Chapter 3, vol. 2.
6   Department of Social Security, *Households Below Average Income. A Statistical Analysis 1979–1991/92*, London, HMSO, 1994. See also Richard Wilkinson, *Unfair Shares*, Ilford, Barnardos, 1994.
7   Family Policy Studies Centre, *Children in Britain*, Family Report 2, London, 1995, p. 6.

8   Alissa Goodman and Steven Webb, *The Distribution of UK Household Expenditure, 1979–92*, London, Institute for Fiscal Studies, 1995; and James Banks, Andrew Dilnot and Hamish Low, *The Distribution of Wealth in the UK*, London, Institute for Fiscal Studies, 1994.
9   John Hills (ed.), *New Inequalities. The Changing Distribution of Income and Wealth in the United Kingdom*, Cambridge, Cambridge University Press, 1996, p. 13.
10 Joseph Rowntree Foundation, *Inquiry into Income and Wealth op. cit.*, p. 114. See also James Banks *et al.,* 'Patterns of financial wealth-holding in the United Kingdom', in John Hills (ed.), *New Inequalities, op. cit.*, Chapter 13.
11 John Ball and Mike Marland, *Male Earnings Mobility in the Lifetime Labour Market Database*, Working paper No. 1, London: Department of Social Security, 1996.
12 Stephen Jenkins, 'Assessing income distribution trends: what lessons from the UK?', Working Papers of the ESRC Research Centre on Micro-Social Change, Paper 95–19, Colchester, University of Essex.
13 Joseph Rowntree Foundation, *Inquiry Into Income and Wealth, op. cit.*, vol. 2, p. 26. See also John Hills (ed.), *New Inequalities, op. cit.*, p. 3.
14 John Hills, *The Future of Welfare*, York, Joseph Rowntree Foundation, 1993.
15 *Employment Gazette*, May 1994; Joseph Rowntree Foundation, *Inquiry Into Income and Wealth, op. cit.*, vol. 1; Jenny Church and Carol Summerfield (eds) *Social Focus on Ethnic Minorities*, London, HMSO, 1996.
16 Family Policy Studies Centre, *Children in Britain*, Family Report 2, London, 1995.
17 John Hills, *The Future of Welfare*, York, Joseph Rowntree Foundation, 1993, p. 26. The figures are for 1991.
18 Joseph Rowntree Foundation, *Inquiry Into Income and Wealth, op. cit.*, vol.1, p. 29.

Chapter 2

Does Poverty Matter?

Why poverty matters

Only the wilfully blind now deny that poverty exists in Britain and has been growing fast. The serious debate has moved on to other questions. Does it matter? And what can be done about it? I deal with the first of them in this chapter.

Many justly angry people have responded to this question by telling harrowing stories about the experiences of people living in poverty. Year after year, on radio and television, in books, pamphlets and newspaper articles, the evidence piles up, most tellingly when the stories are told by poor people themselves. These stories will provide disturbing glimpses of our society for future historians who will wonder how any civilisation could so exploit its people and so neglect its most important asset – the children who will shape the world to be inherited by later generations. But, as one of those who has contributed to this literature and to such broadcasts, I have to recognise that they make little impact. People may be briefly moved. They may even send a donation to Shelter or Age Concern. But they are no more willing than before to take action that will reverse the growing inequality which lies at the root of poverty. That is not because they are unable to respond to calls to action, or because the action called for would be too expensive to contemplate. As I write, people all across Europe have mobilised within days to demand that steps be taken to restrict the export of potentially contaminated beef – and got their way. Last year it was the Shell oil company's plan for dumping an oil rig in the ocean which brought out the protesters.

Anyone who has read this far will probably be convinced that poverty does matter. No need to preach sermons to them. So what should we be saying to the rest of the world? Since appeals for sympathy and arguments of duty make little impact, we must focus on arguments of self-interest. These do not have to be invented. They are real and urgent.

'Ask not for whom the bell tolls', John Donne told his congregation, 'It tolls for thee.' A crippling illness, a motor accident which destroys the capacity for speech and movement, a lost job with none to replace it… if things go badly wrong for us or for those closest to us, any of us may need a safety net we can rely on: good health services, social security benefits we can survive on, an assurance that we shall not be homeless, and efficient, caring personal social services. The riskier the economy we create and the more we deprive people of secure work and predictable, full-time wages, the better the safety net we all need. As 'contracting out', 'down-sizing', 'de-layering', 'labour market flexibility' and so on become buzzwords of our society, this is a time for reaffirming the contract between the generations which created the welfare state that provides this safety net. Yet – despite an increase in national income to levels which would have astounded those who created this welfare state – we are constantly told by politicians and newspapers that we can no longer afford it.

That is a lie. Changes in our economy and society which are increasing the number of people out of work, the number of women workers and of lone parents, do indeed call for changes in the welfare state. But wholesale reductions in funding are a different matter. We have one of the cheaper, less generous welfare states in Europe. Pensions and health and welfare services for the elderly together account for a large share of its costs. It was two generations ago that we passed through the big reduction in family sizes – now being experienced by the Dutch, the Italians, the Japanese and others – which brings about the sharpest increases in the proportion of old people in the population and puts such a strain on the welfare state. Compared with these countries, we have no demographic 'time-bomb'. Our present economic growth rates and tax rates will be more than sufficient to pay for our present services for a very long time to come, even if we are foolish enough to allow unemployment to go on posing its present burdens on the system.[1] These facts are well known to anyone who wants to find out. It is time they were explained to a wider public.

Meanwhile, the hardships inflicted by growing poverty are loaded particularly onto children and those who care for them. We have multiplied by three the proportion of our children who are growing up in households living on less than half the average income. Thanks to the devotion of their families, many are doing fine, but parenting is a difficult task and poverty makes it harder.[2] The impact of poverty upon the family can be seen everywhere. There have been:

- more children whose parents have split up;
- more children who are being reared by lone parents or (which is often more difficult) with step-parents;
- a fourfold increase during the 1980s in the proportion of children on child protection registers;
- growing reports of violence against children;
- a sharp reduction in what had previously been a continuing decline in death rates in all age groups up to 45 – a levelling off which is not spread through all classes but is due to rising death rates in the poorer quarters of our cities.

Other signs show how stresses within the family are affecting children and young people. They have produced:

- a decline in reading skills among 7- and 8-year-olds (unrelated to the methods used for teaching youngsters to read) which is concentrated in the lower reaches of the ability range and the schools serving the most impoverished areas;
- probably a similar decline in mathematical attainment;
- more reports of violence against teachers by children and parents in primary and secondary schools;
- more children excluded from primary and secondary schools because their behaviour is unmanageable;
- growing numbers of young drug addicts;
- growing numbers of deaths due to glue sniffing;
- growing numbers of unemployed youngsters;
- growing numbers of homeless youngsters;
- growing numbers of suicides among young men aged 15–24,
- a long-term growth in crime – particularly violent crime – mainly committed by boys and young men;
- a rising prison population, recruited mainly from young men.

Many of these changes began, or sharply increased, after 1985, which is the point when Britain experienced a greater increase in inequality than ever before. Some of them may be due partly to a growing willingness to report and record the things which happen to children and young people, but the cumulative evidence provided by this list cannot be brushed aside. It shows that stresses within the family, due largely to growing poverty, are having destructive effects on children, young people and their parents

Data from one of the many studies quoted by Richard Wilkinson illustrate this pattern. Figure 2.1 shows the decline in reading standards in one fairly prosperous county. He summarises the general findings of research on reading thus: 'All authorities agree that there was a decline in reading standards and that it emerged particularly clearly from 1985'.[3]

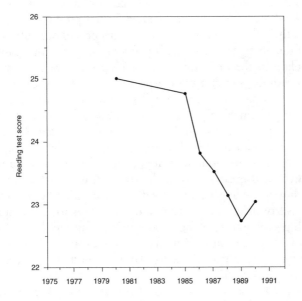

Source: Figure 8.2 in Richard Wilkinson, *Unhealthy Societies,* London, Routledge, 1996, p. 160.

FIGURE 2.1   The decline in reading standards in Buckinghamshire, 1975–91 for all 7–8-year-old schoolchildren. (Chiltern Reading Test scores)

The current fashion for attributing many of these problems to lone parenthood completely misrepresents the causal influences at work.

Children in lone parent families tend to do less well largely because they are much poorer than those in two parent families.

> When you compare children of lone parents with equally poor children brought up by both parents, most of the differences disappear. Similarly, children of the small proportion of better-off lone parents do as well as children in better-off two-parent families: almost all the educational and developmental disadvantage seems to be explained by the degree of poverty.[4]

The steps being taken by the Government, as I write, to cut the benefits of lone parents even further will make things worse.

The children who suffer from these trends are the youngsters upon whom the whole nation's future depends – the productivity of our industries, the safety of our streets, the creativeness of our culture, the rearing of the next generation.... . If many of them are unable to find a secure place in the mainstream of their society because they have few qualifications, no stable work experience, a prison record or poor health, for example, every citizen will pay the price. We are already paying that price in higher taxes to provide social security benefits, hospital care, policing, prisons and other services which would not otherwise have been needed. We are paying it in higher insurance premiums on cars and homes, greater anxiety for the safety of wives and children, and greater fear on the street. Anyone who expects a secure and predictable pension some day would do well to remember that the poverty-stricken children of today will constitute one third of the working – or non-working – population who will have to earn and pay for that pension in Britain's future industries. If we neglect them, how can we expect them to play their part in that contract between the generations?

Declining wages at the lower end of the labour market and rising unemployment are the main causes of our growing inequality, as we shall show in the next chapter. Their effects are not confined to those who are out of work. The anxiety seeps upwards and outwards. People in lower paid and less secure jobs – and many of those in better paid jobs too – fear the insecurity of the world we have created. Those worries sap the confidence and blight the hopes of the whole society. Name almost any project which reforming spirits might hope to see introduced during the coming years: more flexible retirement ages, more determined efforts to gain equal opportunities for ethnic minorities and for women, more work which would enable people with learning handicaps to support themselves, more jobs of the kinds that would enable people of all ages to work their way through college, more opportunities for people to build their own homes, more opportunities for prisoners to earn money that would compensate their victims and support their families... : every one of them can be seen as posing threats to someone's job and will therefore mobilise understandable resistance. High unemployment means that it will be harder to gain support for every kind of progressive reform.

Meanwhile, the massive costs of unemployment turn all Chancellors of the Exchequer, no matter what their political party, into enemies of any reform which costs money. Those costs average, for each unemployed worker, about £9,000 a year in social benefits and in lost revenues from the taxes which they would have been paying in work. Half the famous £50 billion deficit which compelled the Government to make drastic cuts in expenditure shortly after the last general election when the number out of work stood at around three million was due to unemployment. That arithmetic goes far to explain the reluctance of all contenders for power to make bold proposals for action on poverty. Our social divisions cripple our generosity towards fellow citizens in trouble, our confidence in the future, our capacity to take risks and to contemplate change.

For reasons which we explore in later chapters, the poorest people are rarely able to gain justice by their own efforts. Their exclusion starts and ends with exclusion from the political life of their country. There are some neighbourhoods where even the abler among them find it hard to break out and enter the mainstream. If they cannot gain justice through democratic politics and their anger is shaped and hardened by an ideology of revolt – religious, cultural, ethnic or all three – then more serious trouble follows. That is when violent crime and riots become a way of life which can lead on to organised paramilitary action, financed by increasingly elaborate rackets and extortion. In time, a whole industry of violence may develop, which eventually spills out from the ghettos to wreak havoc in the heartlands of the nation. We have gained our own experience of these dangers in Northern Ireland, the City of London, the centres of Manchester and Birmingham and elsewhere. Such conflicts cannot just be left to simmer in the confidence that the security services will keep loss of life and property to an 'acceptable' level. Sooner or later, paramilitary groups of this kind will graduate from Semtex to weapons of mass destruction, which become cheaper and more portable every year. Then it will be London itself that will be destroyed, not just a few blocks on Canary Wharf.

The equality or inequality of a society's patterns of life are not just an independent characteristic which has no effect upon other features of the society. These patterns lie at the economic and social core of a society, helping to shape its whole character. They affect family life and the burdens borne by parents, working life and relations between workers and their bosses, encounters in the street and our expectations of strangers – the health of the whole nation. Pick up any loose thread of our social relationships and you will find that it leads back to these patterns at the core. There is a correlation between the inequality of incomes within countries and the number of deaths from motor accidents. The author of the most extensive review of these patterns comments, 'Perhaps nothing is so indicative of the standards of people's behaviour towards unknown others in society than... the way people drive'.[5] When comparisons are made between nations, or between states within the USA, there are strong correlations between inequality of incomes and violent crime and homicide rates.

Correlations do not by themselves explain anything; they call for explanation. These findings do not mean that inequality is a direct and simple cause of dangerous driving or of murder. But, as more and more correlations of this kind come to light in research carried out in many different countries, they compel us to recognise that we are exploring the power of more fundamental forces, the outlines of larger structures, which shape societies and distinguish one from another.

There is evidence from many studies showing that health and life expectations in the more highly developed economies of the first world owe more to the distribution of incomes than to their average levels or their rates of growth. Countries which grow increasingly unequal, like Britain, slide down the league tables of life expectancy. Those, like Japan and – for many years – Sweden, which grow more equal climb to the top. The loss in years of life experienced by the more unequal societies is not confined to the poor or to particular causes of death. It operates through nearly all causes of death and reaches far enough up the social scale to affect those on average incomes.

The pattern can be glimpsed in Figure 2.2, taken from Wilkinson's review of this research. It shows that, in the world's richer countries, distributions of income predict how long people are likely to live. The fact that the correlation of life expectancies with income distribution emerges most strongly when the comparison is made with the proportion of income received by the poorer 70 per cent of the population is itself very interesting. Because there is always a long 'tail' at the top of the income distribution, made by a small number of very rich people, the 'average' income – meaning the arithmetic mean – usually comes close to that seventieth percentile. Everyone below this point – 70 per cent of the people – is likely to be affected by inequalities in society. Countries which are becoming more unequal are likewise those in which life expectancy is advancing most slowly. Income levels and rates of economic growth are not, in these countries, related to life expectancy in any systematic way.

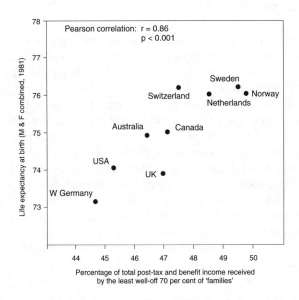

Source: Data from J.A. Bishop, J.P. Formby and W. J. Smith, International Comparisons of Income Inequality, Working Paper 26, Luxembourg Income Study, 1989, quoted from Richard Wilkinson, *Unhealthy Societies*, London, Routledge, p. 76.

FIGURE 2.2   Life expectancy and income distribution in different countries around 1981

The reasons for these patterns are disputed, but Wilkinson, drawing on research from many countries, suggests that worry, which often originates from economic insecurity and from problems within the family related to economic worries, reduces immunity to disease through psychosocial mechanisms which operate at all stages of life, but particularly among the young. The whole debate is at much the same stage as that about the link between smoking and cancer was 30 years ago when it was clear that smoking damages health but the mechanisms at work were only dimly understood. Which means that it is high time that the government warned its citizens that inequality is likely to damage their health and took action to reduce it. Perhaps the warning should be printed on our tax forms by the Inland Revenue.

Conclusions

The inequalities in British society are neither inevitable nor accidental. They are now severe enough to damage every citizen. They are most plainly damaging many of our children and young people – preparing them for exclusion from the mainstream of what should be their society. We shall all pay a heavy price for that. The price will be paid in money, in fear, in poorer health and shorter lives, in blighted hopes for the future, and in a loss of political nerve which blights a nation's capacity for creative innovation. Worse still follows when citizens unable to gain justice by constitutional means turn to violence.

Comfortable people often resent that message, feeling that it is intended to shame them. 'The politics of envy', they call it. We should rid ourselves of that misunderstanding. There is no shame in being rich when no-one is poor. It is the poverty, not the wealth, which is cause for shame. When our country becomes a fairer, juster, more equal society successful citizens will at last be free to enjoy their wealth with a clear conscience.

Notes

1   John Hills, *The Future of Welfare*, York, Joseph Rowntree Foundation, 1993, Chapter 3.
2   The data that follow were mainly gathered by Richard Wilkinson for *Unfair Shares*, Ilford, Barnardos, 1994; and *Unhealthy Societies*, London, Routledge, 1996, particularly Chapter 8.
3   Richard Wilkinson, *Unhealthy Societies, op. cit.,* p. 160.
4   Richard Wilkinson, *Unhealthy Societies, op. cit.,* p. 166.
5   Richard Wilkinson, *Unhealthy Societies, op. cit.,* p. 155.

Chapter 3

Can Anything Be Done?

Introduction

There are those who recognise that Britain is becoming a more unequal, more brutal and degraded country, but they believe nothing can be done about that. Despair offers great comfort. Once well into it, you can give up worrying about the rest of the world and cheerfully cultivate your own garden. Before looking more closely at their standpoint we should step back and reflect briefly on our times.

For a generation after the Second World War, a combination of economic and social circumstances made it possible for many Western regimes to develop policies which moved their societies in equalising and unifying directions. But those regimes also had features which seemed oppressive – some of them a necessary consequence of their search for social protection and solidarity, some of them a product of political bargains struck with major interests in society. Their rising tax rates also made people restive, although these were reluctantly tolerated as long as economic growth produced increases in income which outpaced tax increases. For a generation after the war the social settlements agreed between the central interests within these countries held together reasonably well. But there was never an untroubled consensus: there were always opponents of this settlement on the margins – Left and the Right – biding their time for an attack on the structures created by post-war reformers.

People looking for arguments with which to attack progressive reformers start on the back foot. If the reformers have an idealistic programme to bring justice to suffering humanity they have claimed the moral high ground. Thus, whether the words are actually spoken or not, their critics usually begin by saying, 'These reforms sound

31

very appealing, but… '. For two centuries and more, the next words have usually taken one of three forms which Albert Hirschman has called 'the rhetoric of reaction'.[1] They say either that the reforms, despite their good intentions, will have effects opposite to those hoped for, or that they will bring about no significant change, or that they will have fundamentally damaging effects on the whole society.

These reactionary theses of perversity, futility and jeopardy, as Hirschman calls them, are not easily reconciled. It cannot be true both that reforms will have effects opposite to those intended and that nothing will change. So the arguments are well separated in time and place. Nevertheless, these arguments have been repeatedly advanced, first among opponents of the drive for civil liberties expressed in the French Revolution and its counterparts elsewhere, then among opponents of the drive for political rights expressed in campaigns for universal suffrage and related reforms, and now among opponents of the drive for economic and social rights expressed in the struggle for full employment, the protection of workers, the creation of a 'welfare state' and – in Europe – the Maastricht programme. These are the successive reforming waves which Tom Marshall[2] claimed to discern in many Western societies and described as 'the development of citizenship' – a citizenship which conferred, first, civil rights, next political rights, and then social and economic rights. Marshall's influential but widely criticised essay failed to capture the complexity and diversity of Western experience, and did not recognise how much opposition these developments encountered and how many setbacks they suffered before they became established. Hirschman, whose book fills that gap, traces the recurring arguments against each wave of reform – arguments which were repeated through two centuries and still continue today.

The standard moves in the rhetoric of reaction are not a product of rigorous research or profound thought. They are, literally, the natural 'reactions' open to people attacking those who occupy the moral high ground. To call them rhetorical does not prove that they are wrong. One of the first assertions of the perversity thesis – Edmund Burke's warning that the French Revolutionaries' programme for achieving liberty, equality and fraternity would in fact lead to tyranny and terror – was resoundingly justified. So the arguments of reactionaries must be studied with respect. But not with awe. The human race has been here before, and we know that as civil, political and socio-economic rights gradually take root in liberal societies, the criticisms advanced by their opponents are eventually dismissed and the opponents themselves forgotten.

A better understanding of this history will not prove anyone right or wrong. But it sets the debate in a longer, cooler perspective, teaching us that the drive for social and economic rights is bound to provoke a prolonged backlash, just as earlier developments in citizenship did. Most of these attacks will take one of three predictable forms:

- the argument that social reforms will have perverse effects (well illustrated by the work of Charles Murray in the USA);[3]
- the argument that they will change nothing, making no impact on the most fundamental injustices (as advanced by Gordon Tullock[4] in the USA and by some British critics further to the Left);[5] and
- the argument that they will endanger fundamental moral values and social arrangements (repeatedly illustrated in the works of Friedrich Hayek).[6]

Despite detailed, point-by-point refutations of the critics, such as those mounted against Charles Murray by the authors of *Inequality by Design*,[7] reactionaries are undeterred by contrary evidence, because once they have assumed their chosen posture their rhetoric makes it difficult for them to adopt any other. The more extreme critics clothe their work in the trappings of scholarship, with footnotes, tables of figures and the like, but they often protect themselves from professional criticism by writing for a popular audience without first exposing their arguments to critical review by their peers in learned journals.

In this chapter, asking whether anything can be done about poverty, I deal mainly with the argument of futility. Later in the book, I shall consider the theses of perversity and jeopardy.

Is inequality unavoidable?

If nothing could be done to withstand the trend towards growing inequality it would be found in every advanced economy, which does not happen. Figure 1.4 showed that for many years after the Second World War, the United Kingdom maintained a stable level of inequality until about 1963 when, for 14 years, it followed a zigzag course towards greater equality. Then, in 1977, a trend towards greater inequality set in, which gathered speed savagely from 1985. Since 1990 our course may be changing again. If so, that will not be because the poor have done better, but probably because of the losses suffered by fairly affluent people during the recession centred around that year. It is clear that the distributional pattern has changed from time to time, and it seems likely that government policies have some influence on the outcome.

The patterns to be seen in different countries have been strikingly different too. Figure 3.1 compares Gini coefficients measuring inequality for the United Kingdom with those for other countries in the European Union. We started in 1970 as one of the most equal countries in the Union and ended in 1990 as one of the most unequal. Meanwhile France, Italy and Portugal were all growing slowly more equal.[8]

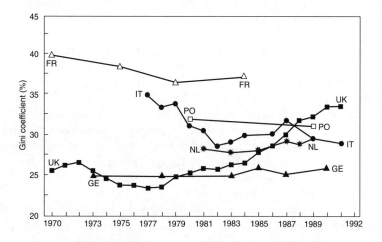

Source: AB Atkinson, 'Seeking to explain the distribution of income', in John Hills (ed.), *New Inequalities*, Cambridge, Cambridge University Press, 1996, p. 22.

FIGURE 3.1   Trends in inequality for different countries of the European Union

Unemployment has been the main factor weakening the position of all those at the lower end of the income distribution, whether in work or out of it. It holds back wages and working conditions for all in the lower paid and less secure jobs while those at the upper end of the system continue to advance. This too varies widely from country to country and from time to time. Table 3.1 shows comparable measures of unemployment prepared by the Organisation for Economic Cooperation and Development for most of the advanced capitalist economies at three points in the last 20 years. Most, but not all, of them have experienced an increase in unemployment. Other countries, not shown in this table – the Czech Republic in central Europe and others along the western Pacific rim, for example – have also kept unemployment very low. These countries are a very mixed bag. Clearly there is no particular kind of regime or type of economy which is best at keeping people in work.

TABLE 3.1   Standardised unemployment rates in OECD countries

	1974	1983	1993
United States	5.5	9.5	6.7
Japan	1.4	2.6	2.5
(West) Germany	1.6	7.7	6.1
France	2.8	8.3	11.7
Italy	5.3	8.8	10.2
United Kingdom	2.9	12.4	10.3
Canada	5.3	11.8	11.1
Australia	2.6	9.9	10.8
Belgium	3.0	12.1	9.6
Finland	1.7	5.4	17.7
Ireland	–	14.0	15.7
Netherlands	2.7	12.0	8.3
New Zealand	–	–	5.5
Norway	1.5	3.4	6.0
Portugal	–	7.8	5.5
Spain	2.6	17.0	22.4
Sweden	2.0	3.5	8.2
Total OECD	3.5	8.5	7.9

Source: Andrew Britton, *The Goal of Full Employment*, London, National Institute of Economic and Social Research, 1996, p. 14.

How do these patterns come about, and why do they change? The British Government's commitment, first given in a White Paper presented to Parliament in May 1944, to 'the maintenance of a high and stable level of employment after the war',[9] was more a political than an economic statement. Everyone understood that this commitment would call for moderation on both sides of industry, leading to informal agreements about the pace at which wages and prices advanced that would prevent inflation and economic chaos. William Beveridge, writing in the same year, said that full employment would call for 'responsibility and public spirit' from 'agencies independent of the State' – adding that he was confident that this spirit would be forthcoming.[10] The war had already compelled managers to treat their workers with respect, workers to moderate their wage demands and both to collaborate closely with the government. Everyone was aware that they were engaged in a fight to the death against Fascist regimes created by people for whom jobs had proved to be more important than freedom. In future, democracies would have to find ways of offering their people work as well as freedom if they were to survive.

An informal commitment to moderation among workers and employers, and the search for a consensus on which this could be based, continued for many years. It broke down a generation later, first at local level as managers came under growing pressure from their international competitors to reorganise and re-equip, as the state was compelled to seek economies in its services, and as militant trade union branches made increasingly aggressive demands on employers and their own national leaders. Attempts by Conservative and Labour Governments – often supported by top-level spokesmen of management and the unions – to reimpose a consensus which would control the growth of prices and incomes and help to restore full employment failed to convince the militants at the grass roots. That led, via industrial strife which brought down first Heath and then Callaghan, to the election of a new regime which turned its back on the politics of consensus and set out to destroy the power of the unions.

To make clear to his readers the fundamental character of the issues he was writing about in 1944, Beveridge placed on the title page of his book, *Full Employment in a Free Society*, a quotation: 'Misery generates hate'. The words which summarised the attitudes of Mrs Thatcher's regime to the same issues came from one of her Chancellors who described the unemployed as 'the price well worth paying' to bring the economy under control. Her government's fiscal and social policies were equally contemptuous of the principals which guided Beveridge and his contemporaries. They made changes in taxes and benefits which – far from counterbalancing the divisive impact of economic changes – hastened the country's drift towards greater inequality by taking more from the poorer half of the population and giving more to the richer half. Meanwhile the richest bosses in the land have made brutally clear their contempt for any ideas about moderation in wage demands and acceptable limits to differentials. In 1996 directors' pay is still advancing much faster than that of their employees. The example they have set encourages others to grab what they can when they can. All seem to have forgotten that misery still generates hate.

There have been massive economic changes during these years which would have made an impact of some kind, whatever the policies of governments. I come to those in a moment. Economic changes, however, have not been the main factor at work in this story. The attainment of full employment, the creation of a welfare state funded by progressive taxes taking more from the rich than the poor, moderation in wage demands – all the things which helped to create a more equal society during and after the Second World War – were not brought about by accident or by some happy change in the economic climate. They were brought about by collective decisions made possible by changes in attitudes, inside and outside government; changes which were discussed and negotiated over many years, and carried through in the face of great difficulties. The dismantling of this system has likewise come about through collective decisions, involving people at many levels of society and in all sectors of the economy over many years. To reverse these trends will be an equally lengthy and massive task.

Economic changes

Before we can embark on that task we shall need some understanding of the sources and causes of growing inequality. I will start with changes in the world's economy and their impact upon the United Kingdom; then consider the social factors which have played a part in the story before turning finally to the political repercussions of those developments.

Six changes are working their way through the world's economies, and their effects cannot be clearly distinguished. The United Kingdom is particularly exposed to most of them.

1 The replacement of labour by machines, which has been going on since the start of the industrial revolution, has been dramatically hastened by the spread of new kinds of information technology and control systems. Starting in manufacturing industries, these changes are now spreading into banking, retailing and many other services.

2 These changes have been coupled with developments in management practice which are breaking up large enterprises and bureaucracies in the private and public sectors. Production decisions, and the risks associated with them, have been shifted out to smaller units, further down the management hierarchy. Middle layers of the hierarchy are being stripped out. Workers are having to learn to combine and switch between different tasks demanding different skills. Many stable and secure jobs have disappeared, along with the pension rights and fringe benefits attached to them.

3 There has been a widespread shift in people's demands away from manufactured goods and the products of the construction industry towards services and do-it-yourself work – self-service. For men doing manual work it was the more skilled jobs in manufacturing industries which traditionally paid the best wages.

4 All three of these changes have reduced opportunities for men. Meanwhile, women have flooded into the labour market and now make up nearly half the labour force.

5 As transport costs and barriers to trade and to the movement of capital have been reduced, many production processes are being moved to countries where labour is paid less and trade unions are weaker. To survive in the battle to produce internationally traded goods, every advanced economy has had to climb continually up-market to produce the more sophisticated things with the more advanced skills in which it still has comparative advantages over less developed economies. But several of the countries which used to be regarded as less developed have learnt to compete so well in this race that they are now overtaking the old industrial leaders.

6 Punctuating these five trends, there has from time to time been a sixth kind of factor: sharp shocks to the economy inflicted by

sudden increases in oil prices, the mass closure of coal mines, the closure of military bases and defence industries and similar events. A whole generation of workers within a particular region may then be affected as large numbers lose their jobs, while youngsters leaving school in particular years find it very difficult to get started in work. People's opportunities for getting a job fade very quickly once they have been out of work for a few months. These shocks to the economy therefore leave a lasting scar in the nation's history.[11]

Together, these economic changes have brought about growing inequalities. They have greatly reduced opportunities for men in manual work, and for less skilled workers of all kinds. Unemployment has increased, and it has become much harder for people who lose their jobs to get back into work. Thus more people have been out of work for a very long time. Young men and women have suffered most severely, unless they are well qualified, and things do not improve for them as time goes by. In the past, low-paid workers earned more as they gained experience; now the lowest paid gain no real improvement in income as they grow older.[12] Self-employment has increased, but the variation in incomes for self-employed workers – always large – has grown larger still. Women's wages have grown more unequal, but their average level has risen closer to men's. That, indeed, has been the only economic change tending to create greater equality – but although it does that between individual earners it does not do so between households. Meanwhile those with the skills for which there has been growing demand and with the capacity to move to places where they are needed have done very well. Many people have had anxious times during the past 20 years, but most have prospered.

These changes in the labour market have affected the flow of many other resources which are related to work. Wages have moved further ahead of pensions and social security payments. Pensions themselves have grown more unequal as those with generous private and occupational schemes have moved ahead of those relying on state pensions for which the rate of growth has been severely cut back. Interest and dividends from private wealth have increased, but these too mainly benefit richer people.

Social and political changes

Interwoven through these economic changes there have been further
social and political changes. Women have entered the labour force in
growing numbers, and stayed there through transitions in their lives –
marriage, the birth of children, the movement of husbands to new
jobs – which in earlier generations would have compelled most of
them to give up paid work. Their growing earning capacity, coupled
with rights to legally aided divorce, social security payments,
maternity leave and subsidised housing, means that for families to
stay together the consent of both partners is now required. Men
could always opt out: growing numbers of women can now do
likewise. Indeed, they do not have to opt in. A woman sacrifices a
good deal in tying her life to a man's. When he could put a pay packet
on the table each week, there was a lot to be gained from that
contract. But in communities where there may be very few marriage-
able men with a secure job the attractions of marriage decline.[13] That
has meant a steady growth in the number of lone parents – mainly
women, three-fifths of whom live on less than half this country's
average income which is the European Union's definition of
poverty.[14] In 1971, nearly 8 per cent of British children were growing
up in lone-parent families; 20 years later that proportion had more
than doubled to over 19 per cent.[15]

Some people have said that the poverty of the unemployed has been
greatly exaggerated because they all have illicit sources of income, not
revealed to tax gatherers and social security officials, on which they live
pretty comfortably. (The origins of this story are always vague: 'My taxi
driver told me…' is the way it often begins.) Although it is notoriously
difficult to research illicit behaviour, several good studies have now
been made in places where black markets flourish.[16] They all reach
much the same conclusions. A 'black', informal or illicit economy has
always been widespread, and was probably enlarged by increases in
VAT. But it is not, in total, very big. The people who make most out of
this economy, both as suppliers and as customers, are those who do best
in the mainstream market place. These are the people with the contacts,
the tools, the skills, the cash and the confidence to do business for fivers
out of the back pocket. The poorest people and those who have been
out of work for a long time rarely benefit greatly from this economy.
They remain poor. Indeed, the amount earned by those who do get
something in this way is usually so small that it would be disregarded

under tax and social security law. There are of course a few people who earn much larger sums from drug dealing, pimping, extortion and other rackets, sometimes associated with paramilitary activities, but these are an altogether different problem.

The other bar-room story used to explain unemployment is that state benefits are so generous that they deter people from going to work. Twenty years ago that tale could usually be dismissed. Unless they had a very large family and a very high rent, no-one could get more in social security benefits than they could earn in full-time work if that included the means-tested benefits which low-paid workers could claim. But that has changed. Reductions in wage levels at the lower end of the labour market, rising rents, and the government's growing reliance on 'targeted' social security, housing and family benefits which are paid through household means tests together mean that growing numbers of people do have to calculate whether they can afford to go to work. Many of them prefer to do so even if that makes them worse off: a job can offer a great deal besides money – comradeship, status, paid holidays, pension rights... . But where wages are low, jobs are precarious and the difficulty of getting back onto benefit is daunting, some prefer to retain a low but reliable income from social security payments. In Northern Ireland, where families are larger and wages lower than elsewhere in the United Kingdom, the benefits for a family with two children come to at least 75 per cent of the wages of 25 per cent of male manual workers.[17]

This helps to explain why so many children are in poverty, for it is usually larger families which face difficult choices between work and benefits. It also helps to explain why the growing number of jobs for women – many of them part time and low paid – are usually taken by people with a partner in a full-time job. Thus the gulf between job-rich households with two or more earners and job-poor households with none grows wider.

All political parties are now aware that there is a problem here which demands attention. It is less easy to decide what kind of a problem it is. Not a problem of over-generous benefits for these have been reduced in relation to wages over the years and are now well below those of neighbouring European countries – and, indeed, below the levels which can feed, clothe and properly care for a family.[18] It would be nearer the truth to describe it as a problem of low wages, or low tax thresholds, or high rents, or over-reliance on means tested benefits. All play a part in it.

Housing is a recurring theme in our deepening social divisions. The disappearance of rented housing has, in the more crowded parts of the country, compelled many families to earn two incomes in order to pay for the homes they have to buy. In time, most families attain the incomes and the home. Those who cannot have to rely on a dwindling supply of social rented housing. As the more attractive parts of the stock have been sold off, this consists increasingly of flats in the less popular estates where job opportunities are often poor. In some of these, whole streets may be found where scarcely anyone has regular work. As those who can afford to go move out, the remaining tenants come to consist increasingly of lone parents, pensioners and people without work. Services may then deteriorate, turnover rises and morale decays. Exclusion, there, is not just an academic concept. It is real, it hurts, and the stresses that result from it show up on the streets, in schools and doctors' surgeries, and in the caseloads of social workers.

The tale of gloom which any analysis of the causes of growing inequality leads us into often suggests that we are a decaying society that is struggling to survive and unable to provide more generous help for citizens who suffer hardship. But during the last 20 years, when inequalities have been growing, most people have done very well. We are a richer nation than ever before. Our unemployment may be bad, but – at the time of writing – it is not so bad as that in neighbouring countries. This could be a success story. It is a scandal because poorer people have not shared in this success. A quarter of our people and one third of our children have been left so far behind that they have to live on less than half their nation's average income.

Other countries have been much more successful in protecting their poorest people from the impacts of economic change. Why have we failed? That question brings us to politics. Just as the struggles to achieve full employment, to create a welfare state and to build a fairer society were essentially political – that is to say, decided by power and rooted in public opinion – so too has been the decision to abandon these aspirations. Look at what has happened. If tax and benefit arrangements are left unchanged, they will normally help to check the divisive trends in a society which is growing richer in its upper reaches and poorer in its lower reaches. That is because progressive taxes, year by year, take even more from the growing numbers of rich people than they take from the poor, and benefits, year by year, give even more to the growing numbers of poor people than to the rich. In many countries that is what has happened. But in the United Kingdom the naturally equalising effects of progressive taxes were cancelled out by deliberate changes – particularly by the introduction and then the increase of value added tax and (for a while) the poll tax, and the reduction of income tax, inheritance tax and other taxes that were loaded most heavily onto the rich. Meanwhile benefit changes more than cancelled out the equalising influence of social policies. That was brought about particularly by the decisions to uprate benefits in line with changes in prices, rather than changes in earnings, and to cut out or reduce many benefits for young people, unemployed people and lone parents. The combined effect of Parliament's decisions on taxes and benefits was to make Britain much more unequal.

The influence of government is most clearly seen in taxes and benefits. These produce measurable impacts with countable effects. More important, if less easily measured, are the effects of financial, industrial, educational and employment policies. If capital is freed to roam the world in search of the cheapest labour and the least well regulated markets, if manufacturing industry is treated as of less importance than the financial centres of power in the City of London, if the best educational resources are increasingly focused upon richer families and the more talented students, if low-paid workers are stripped of their most important legal protections and the influence of their trade unions is deliberately reduced, and if people out of work are treated as of no account – the 'price well worth paying' to manage the economy – then it should not surprise anyone that the United Kingdom has grown more unequal, more quickly than any other country in Europe. That has not been an unhappy accident. Economic trends were leading in this direction, but greater inequality was the aim of a regime whose principal thinkers believed in it and were not ashamed to say so.[19]

Reviewing the history

The story of Britain's faltering route towards greater equality and the sharp turn away from that path taken in more recent years starts from changes in the economy. For many years after the Second World War this country, along with other Western democracies, sought to ensure that there would be rising incomes and work for everyone who wanted it, making possible a contract between the generations which would provide a gradually extending array of social services and benefits for those who needed them. That was easier to achieve at a time when the world was rebuilding its war-devastated economies, when Western industrial countries dominated the globe and their manufacturing industries needed growing numbers of manual workers. But the project depended on a broadly based political understanding in which employers and trade unions played their parts along with government – an understanding forged during the depression years and in the battle with Fascism. Economic trends made the project easier, but it took policy analysis and political leadership of a high order, rooted in broad popular support, to make it possible.

In the late 1960s and early 70s things began to change. Post-war reconstruction and the economic boost given first by the Korean War and then by the Vietnamese War petered out. Western dominance of the global economy began to unravel. Consumer demands, industrial structures, management methods and the skills needed by employers all began to shift. A more 'flexible' labour market developed – meaning, for many, a more precarious world demanding more highly trained workers, recruiting more women and offering less security for everyone. The new economy called for new working practices, greater investment in training, and new relationships in the workplace. The informal consensus between employers and workers which had helped to keep unemployment low for so many years disintegrated. Meanwhile the frontiers and powers of the nation state began to dissolve: capitalism was going global.

Nearly all these changes led in divisive directions. Most people did well, but they left, further and further behind them, growing numbers who fell out of work or survived on the margins of the labour force. Other sources of income depending partly on people's role in the workforce – fringe benefits, pensions and dividends – also became increasingly unequal. Struggling to pay for homes and raise families in an increasingly brutal free-for-all, the people of 'middle England' had less and less concern to spare for their fellow citizens. The contract between the generations began to disintegrate.

Then, in the 1980s, a regime came to power which embraced many of these divisive trends, and rejected ideas about social contracts and aspirations to equality. Although in four elections it never got much more than two-fifths of the votes, its opponents were unable to mobilise any effective popular resistance to its programme.

Once again, economic developments had prepared the way, eroding and undermining the settlement reached after the Second World War, but political leadership brought about the decisive change of direction. In a masterly review of the growing inequality of wages to be seen in many Western countries, Richard Freeman and his colleagues showed that political and industrial traditions make a big difference. No country is compelled to become as unequal as the British and the Americans have become.[20] These basic economic changes have in Britain developed a political life of their own. The more divided our people, the less their resistance to further divisive initiatives. People seem either to have settled for what they could get – and many got a great deal from the new kind of economy that was emerging – or they lost the courage to resist. Although support for the government in the opinion polls and at elections was often low, it faced no effective opposition.

These developments have had cruel consequences, some of which can be glimpsed in Figure 3.2 which compares death rates for different social classes in Sweden, and in England and Wales. In Sweden, where people have been determined to assure much the same living and working conditions for all classes, death rates and life expectations are much the same in all classes. But in England and Wales even the higher social classes have higher death rates than the lower classes in Sweden, and these rates rise in a steep gradient through successively lower classes. The unskilled (Class V) can expect, on average, 7 years – or about 10 per cent – less life than the managerial and professional workers in Class I. Since the timing of our deaths is determined by influences extending over a lifetime, these contrasts arise from a long history, not only from the last few years. Nevertheless they serve to show in the most concrete and practical fashion that by collective action a society can go a long way to improve everyone's life expectations, to prevent poverty, and to reduce inequalities in the life expectations of different classes.

Conclusions

The complex network of interacting economic and political changes which I have very briefly traced leads to five conclusions:

1 There is nothing inevitable about the progress of this increasingly rich country towards greater inequality, growing hardship and the social disintegration from which everyone ultimately suffers: it

could be resisted and reversed. Some countries have been much
more successful than others at doing this.

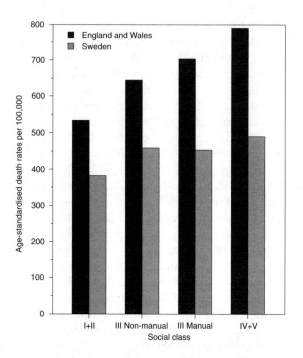

Source: Figure 5.8 in Richard Wilkinson, *Unhealthy Societies,* London, Routledge,
1996, p. 88. D. Vagaro and O. Lundberg, 'Health inequalities in Britain and
Sweden', *Lancet* 1989 **11**: 35–36.

**FIGURE 3.2   Death rates by social class in Sweden and in England
and Wales**

2   However, complex economic trends leading in divisive directions
    and the political forces now mobilised to carry these further are
    deeply entrenched. It will take a lot of hard thought and tough
    politics to bring about any major change in direction. We can
    never reinstate the settlement worked out after the Second World
    War for we now live in an entirely different world. But we can
    reformulate the basic principles of those difficult but hopeful
    years and build a new kind of contract between the generations.

3 To make any progress a healthy economy and a prosperous private sector will be needed. Although radicals of various kinds have often attacked capitalist patterns of development, they rely on a successful capitalist economy to make their reforms possible – just as successful enterprises rely on effective social policies to reproduce, house and train a healthy labour force, keep the peace and make capitalism successful. However, the private sector, left to itself, can never bring about the change of course now required. 'Economic trends' *mean* the continuation of the private sector's present trajectory, and that is now divisive and destructive. Only national and civic leaders, using the resources of the public sector, can resist and reverse these trends.

4 Much of the action required will have to be taken at a national level, and some of the most important of these things can only be done through international collaboration on a European and wider scale. I shall say something about those larger scales of action in later chapters. Something, but not much: for this book starts from the conviction that we cannot get far without mobilising civic leadership at the scale of cities and smaller neighbourhoods within them. The prospects for really effective action in larger, national arenas are not encouraging, so we have to begin wherever we can.

5 The course we have steered through successive phases of our history – our mobilisation to create a more equal society and extend social and economic rights after the Second World War, and our abandonment of many of those aspirations in recent years – has been largely due to deliberate political decisions, not to random accidents. Countries not far away chose to act differently and steered different courses. The thesis of futility – the idea that we have no control over our fate – is untrue.

Notes

1 Albert Hirschman, *The Rhetoric of Reaction. Perversity, Futility, Jeopardy,* Cambridge, Mass., Harvard University Press, 1991.

2 TH Marshall, *Citizenship and Social Class.* Cambridge, Cambridge University Press, 1950.

3 Charles Murray, *Losing Ground: America's Social Policy, 1950–1980,* New York, Basic Books, 1984.

4 Gordon Tullock, *Welfare for the Well-to-do,* Dallas, Fisher Institute, 1983; and *The Economics of Wealth and Poverty,* Brighton, Wheatsheaf, 1986.

5   For a moderate example, see Julian le Grand, *The Strategy of Equality. Redistrib-ution and the Social Services*, London, George Allen & Unwin, 1982.
6   Friedrich Hayek, *The Road to Serfdom*, London, Routledge & Kegan Paul, 1944; and *The Fatal Conceit. The Errors of Socialism*, London, Routledge, 1988.
7   Claude Fischer *et al.*, *Inequality by Design. Cracking the Bell Curve Myth*, Princeton, Princeton University Press, 1996.
8   AB Atkinson, 'Seeking to explain the distribution of income', in John Hills (ed.), *New Inequalities*, Cambridge, Cambridge University Press, 1996, p. 22.
9   *Employment Policy*, Cmd 6527, London, HMSO, May 1944.
10 William Beveridge, *Full Employment in a Free Society*, London, Allen & Unwin, 1994; quoted by Andrew Britton in *The Goal of Full Employment*, London, National Institute of Economic and Social Research, 1996, p. 5.
11 For a brief account of these changes and their impact upon the United Kingdom, see Andrew Britton, *The Goal of Full Employment, op. cit.*; and for a longer analysis, see GDN Worswick, *Unemployment: A Problem of Policy*, Cambridge, Cambridge University Press, 1991.
12 Joseph Rowntree Foundation, *Inquiry into Income and Wealth*, vol. 2, York, Joseph Rowntree Foundation, 1995, p. 47.
13 This point was first made with supporting evidence from particular urban areas by William Julius Wilson in *The Truly Disadvantaged*, Chicago, University of Chicago Press, 1987, pp. 72–92.
14 Carey Oppenheim and Lisa Harker, *Poverty: The Facts*, London, Child Poverty Action Group, 1996, p. 36.
15 Office of Population Censuses and Surveys, *Population Trends*, London, HMSO, 1993. The evidence is summarised by the Family Policy Studies Centre in *Children in Britain*, Family Report 2, London, Family Policy Studies Centre, 1995.
16 See, for example, Ray Pahl, *Divisions of Labour*, Oxford, Blackwell, 1984. For a review of evidence in many parts of Europe, see Colin Williams, 'Social and spatial inequalities in the informal economy: some evidence from the European Community', *Area*, **25**(4), 1993, p. 358; and Colin Williams and Jan Windebank, 'Black market work in the European Community: peripheral work for peripheral localities', *International Journal of Urban and Regional Research*, **19**(1), 1995, p. 23.
17 David Donnison, *Long-term Unemployment in Northern Ireland*, Belfast, Northern Ireland Council for Voluntary Action, 1996, pp. 31–2.
18 Nina Oldfield and Autumn Yu, *The Cost of a Child*, London, Child Poverty Action Group, 1993.
18 This conclusion, like much else in this chapter, owes a great deal to John Hills' report of 1995 (Joseph Rowntree Foundation, *Inquiry into Income and Wealth, op. cit.*).
19 Keith Joseph and Jonathan Sumption, *Equality*, London, John Murray, 1979.
20 Richard Freeman and Lawrence Katz (eds), *Differences and Changes in Wage Structures*, Chicago, University of Chicago Press, 1995 – see the editors' 'Introduction and summary', pp. 1–24.

Chapter 4

Traditions of Resistance

Introduction

To resist and reverse the divisive forces now flooding through the Western world will call for more than a few new policies and soundbite phrases. It will be a complex and massive task, extending through the lifetime of anyone reading these words. Political parties will have to be involved, but they respond when more fundamental movements exert sufficient pressures for change; they rarely initiate change themselves. What reforming traditions can such movements turn to for inspiration in Britain and in Europe at large? What are the groups that bear these traditions? How well equipped are they to respond to the crisis we face, and can they be helped to respond more effectively? What should be the broad priorities for reformers during the coming years? These are the questions addressed in this chapter. The answers to them set the agenda for the rest of this book.

The times we live in

This is a scoundrel time that we live in. While millions of people are out of work – far more than official figures claim – and one third of our children are growing up in poverty, while pensions fall further and further behind wages and more cuts are made in services on which the most vulnerable depend, while class sizes in the schools increase and more children are excluded from school as unmanageable, while homeless people camp out begging in the streets, our politicians try to bribe the voters with tax reductions and to curry favour by attacking foreigners, refugees, lone parents and poverty-stricken youngsters. And this is going on in a rich country where average income and wealth are rising strongly, a country which cared much better for its more vulnerable citizens when it was poorer.

Many people in Britain are disturbed about this. As I write, they are voting in by-elections for almost anyone who might help to get rid of the Conservative Government which has presided over these trends. This ought to be a great time for reformers. It is when you ask who *they* might be that you realise it is not going to be that simple. What traditions do we have to draw on which might inspire a resistance movement? As in most Western countries, other than the United States, our progressive politics are strongly marked by socialism. For many, that's still what 'the Left' means. But what does 'socialism' mean today? Progressive parties in Western countries are increasingly reluctant to use the word or the symbols connected with it. The hammer and sickle are disappearing, to be replaced by red roses and oak leaves. Some regard the whole movement as tainted by dreadful memories of Stalin. All this helps to explain the confusion among their opponents which has helped to keep the Conservatives in power for so long, and may continue to do so.

A progressive tradition

In so far as human progress is due to politics, democratic socialism has contributed more to that progress than any other system of ideas. In the countries of Western Europe and Australasia, where this tradition has been strongest, it brought working-class people into political movements and positions of power on a scale never achieved in North America, Ireland or other societies lacking a strong socialist tradition. It built for them a stronger welfare state than other regimes provided, and in many countries it came closer, for longer, to achieving full employment. It has in many countries helped to enlarge opportunities for women and to outlaw overt racism. At a time when so many write it off, it is important to recall those achievements. Socialism served the purposes of a religion (I say that with respect, not derision) explaining human suffering, providing moral principles and a guide to conduct, presenting us with a cast of saints and sinners upon whom to model our behaviour, bringing people together in comradeship to re-dedicate themselves, and promising them hope of a better future. (Economics, as a discipline, has similar functions, but for a different church – coming complete with a priesthood, schisms, arcane symbols and most of the other trappings of a religion.)

From time to time, every system of beliefs passes through a crisis which compels a reformation of some kind. Old gods and the principles they stand for are jettisoned as new times call for new ones. Karen Armstrong, in *A History of God*, tells the Christian version of this story.[1] Socialism is now going through such a crisis. Its founders were the first political thinkers who squarely asserted that morality, law and culture are products of a society's economic and social structure, and can only be changed as that structure changes. Their successors, faced with ill-comprehended changes in economic and social conditions, are uncertain how to respond to a situation for which their own thinkers should have prepared them better than most. Some stand their ideological ground and tell their comrades they should be preaching the old faith more loudly. (Brecht's comment on the East German regime's response to popular uprisings exactly describes their stance: they decided that they needed not a new programme but a new electorate.) Others engage in supermarket politics, finding out what their opponents are selling, they offer their own brand, claiming it will be better and cheaper. It took four successive defeats at the polls and 16 years of opposition to persuade these two tendencies to hold together, but that precarious alliance will not survive another defeat. If we pause to reflect on the origins of socialism we may reach a clearer understanding of the things which must be jettisoned and those which may still be of help to us.

It was radical liberals who first asserted the right of every human being to be treated with equal respect. The American and French revolutions were expressions of that hope. But towards the end of the nineteenth century more and more people came to recognise that equal rights and mutual respect between citizens could never be achieved while massive differences in wealth, status and power remained unchallenged. Socialism of various kinds inspired the movements to which they turned for a more radical assault upon privilege. But socialism had more to say about the causes of injustice and exploitation than about their cures. Marx and Engels did not explain how a socialist society might be created. Indeed, they were contemptuous of the 'utopians' who formulated constitutions and programmes of this kind. Practical prescriptions for action were only developed in detail when revolutionaries took power in what became the Soviet Union and had to decide how to use it. The policies they worked out on their feet, amidst civil war, foreign invasion, famine and crises of every kind, were for years the only practical example of what socialism meant. Others tried to apply them in various parts of the world – mainly the third world.

Long before this, radicals in the West had been formulating responses to injustice and exploitation – often without much concern for socialism or theories of any kind.[2] The German Social Democratic Party, founded in 1875, became officially Marxist in 1891. As the biggest, the best organised and electorally the most successful of these parties, its example was followed by many others in Europe. But in Britain the Scottish Labour Party, founded by Keir Hardie in 1888, did not claim to be socialist, nor did the Labour Representation Committee, founded in 1900, which formed the nucleus of the British Labour Party. The socialist label was used at that time mainly by small, radical groups led by people regarded as middle-class eccentrics. The Labour Representation Committee's aim was simple: to ensure that, just as land-owners, brewers, steel-masters and other powerful interests were represented in Parliament, so also should working men be. It was not until it prepared a manifesto in 1918 for the first post-war election that the Labour Party became frankly socialist.

The Russian revolution of the previous year was by then beginning to offer one example of what that label might mean. But as expectations of revolutions in the West faded and the Soviet example came to be viewed with growing distaste, what emerged in various countries were local responses to the things which organised working people – particularly working men – found most intolerable in their lives and most easily remediable. Trade unions, which were the engine room of the movement, were not much interested in theory: they looked for winnable issues. Since the workplace was where organisation and action were easiest, wages, working hours and conditions tended to come top of their agenda.

The labour movement was most successful where capitalism was most successful at producing the secure jobs, the organising capacity and the money needed for higher wages, for social insurance, and later for subsidised housing, medical care and other public services. Likewise capitalism needed help from the state to protect and support its operations, to smooth out the wilder fluctuations to which it was prone and to prevent ruthless competitors from driving down wages, working conditions and prices. It also needed a steadily growing investment in education, sanitation, housing, health services and social benefits if it was to grow successfully in an orderly society, to recruit healthy, trainable workers, and to shed them without trouble when they became sick or surplus to requirements: in short, capitalism, to be successful, needed the things for which the Labour movement campaigned. Thus, despite the outward signs of conflict between them – sometimes genuinely bloody and brutal conflict – capitalism and socialism each needed, and increasingly shaped, each other. But the driving force in this partnership, throwing up new problems demanding new solutions, has been capitalism. Socialism is not an independent, unchanging doctrine; it is a resistance movement seeking to shape the world in ways which will be kinder to its citizens – particularly its more vulnerable citizens – and to protect them from the dangers of that world. As the world changes, so socialism – or whatever it is now to be called – has to change too.

Until recent changes began to reshape it, the basic ideas of the British Labour Party, along with those of many related reforming groups and movements, had mainly been formulated between the wars and during the period of the Attlee Government elected in 1945. That experience led naturally to three assumptions which became part of the culture of the movement.

1 *Social class relations provoke the main conflicts in society* and create the institutions which manage these conflicts. Although socialist propaganda directed its polemics against the big bosses – the top-hatted capitalists of the cartoons, clutching their money bags – the principal frontier in the class war experienced day by day among ordinary citizens ran between manual and non-manual workers. During these years many other things came, roughly speaking, to be divided by this boundary. By the 1940s it distinguished those who hoped to buy a house one day from those who expected always to rent one, those who hoped to buy a car from those who waited in the bus queues, those who hoped to have an occupational pension of some sort from those who had to rely on the state for an income in retirement, and those who expected to pay something for education and hoped their children would go to college from those who relied on the state to provide and hoped their children would get an apprenticeship.

Class patterns were always more complex than this, but socialists – particularly those in the middle class – were often tempted to forget that. Some had a romantic hope that, in time, 'the workers' would all come to see the Labour movement as their natural spiritual home. Men were assumed to be the key people in this class system and the political allegiances growing out of it. The movement had from the start talked about the rights of women, and eventually – much, much later – it is doing things to make those rights a reality. But the language of class and much of the practice of politics were – and still are – essentially masculine: look at the times of day at which Parliament and local councils meet, the character of the buildings and the smoke-filled committee rooms in which they conduct their business, and much else.

In so far as these assumptions about class were true, we can now see that they arose from an accidental and temporary convergence of lifestyles on either side of the main class frontier. While they lasted they created, in some parts of the country, growing solidarity within the working class, and a growing conviction that the workers, being a majority, would ultimately win. Great ritual occasions, like the Durham Miners' Gala, celebrated those convictions. They were strengthened in the course of two world wars which reminded the nation's leaders that their regime would not survive unless they could persuade millions of working people to endure great suffering and risk their lives in its defence.

The worldwide turbulence of this period imposed constraints on the behaviour of political, industrial and commercial bosses. This turbulence continued right up to the fall of the Berlin Wall in 1989. Starting with strikes and threatened revolution in the early years of this century, it extended through two world wars, with the Russian revolution and the looming threat of Fascism lying between them, and then the cold war which marshalled millions of armed men on the far side of the Iron Curtain. Leaders of capitalist regimes knew there was always an alternative available if their citizens became sufficiently alienated. Since the fall of the Berlin Wall, capitalism has not 'won': rising unemployment, pollution and crime show that it is tottering towards disaster. But there is no longer any readily available alternative. And that has given leaders of the regime a brutal confidence which has led to the attack on trade unions, and encouraged the driving down of wages and working conditions at the lower end of the labour market, the steady reduction in the real value of the state pension, the greedy inflation of bosses' incomes, the re-introduction of selective secondary education, the erosion of the rights of the homeless, and the massive increase in the numbers of jails and prisoners. Meanwhile changes in the demand for labour have reduced and broken up the ranks of the organised workers.

2   *The nation state was assumed to be the principal arena for political action*, and the main stages on which the action took place were in London, and particularly in Parliament. London and the nation state likewise provided the central arenas for industrial and commercial decision-making, and for literary, artistic, religious and other activity. There was an empire which provided a worldwide framework for this economy, but it was, in a sense, London's empire – the main decisions about investment, the despatch of troops and the management of colonies being taken there.

Some people would contest this picture, arguing that the main arenas for political action were in the workplace. But although some of the struggles which went on there had a heroic and seminal character, these were essentially tactical. Strategic victories had to be won in Parliament, even though they were often partly due to influences operating on a larger scale outside – like major wars or depressions. The 1915 rent strikes in Glasgow were a classic example, leading to legislation which still affects us 80 years later. Led initially by women, they were made politically significant when these women involved their men and the unions at a time when the Government desperately needed shells for the Western Front.

The emphasis on this national, London-centred framework for action encouraged – and was in turn reinforced by – a drive to centralise power. There were many influences working in this direction: the experience of two world wars which had to be centrally planned and directed; suspicion of local government, coupled with the general trustworthiness of an efficient and reasonably neutral central government civil service; the erosion, within England, of local identities and cultures; the assumption that public ownership of industries called for monolithic, nationwide bureaucracies with headquarters in the capital and so on. Labour politicians, supported by powerful voices within the public service unions, tended to be centralisers at the local as well as the national scale. Local housing departments, originally

organised to ensure they had managers and resident staff available
in every major housing estate, withdrew them to central offices in
town halls as the estates were pushed further and further out into
distant suburbs.[3]

3 *The public service professions were to be the reformers' civilising force,*
   made accountable, from the top, through Parliament and local
   councils. They would provide solutions for a wide range of social
   and economic problems, in the nationalised industries as much as
   the public services. The British version of radical politics reaches
   back into the early years of the nineteenth century, owing a lot to
   Bentham, Chadwick and the utilitarians. They were succeeded by
   people like Morant, the Webbs, Beveridge, Keynes, Tawney and
   the whole Fabian tradition – highly educated, mainly London
   based, male and middle class. There were distinguished women
   among them too – Beatrice Webb, Eleanor Rathbone and many
   others – but in those times women were not demanding
   altogether different ways of working from those adopted by their
   male colleagues. Thus it is not surprising that the most effective of
   them were usually childless: they had to be. A growing array of
   specialists were trained to perform defined functions in the
   services which these people helped to create, and organised both
   in appropriate bureaucratic hierarchies, and in professional
   associations which helped to maintain standards of skill and
   conduct. Together, it was assumed, these professions would
   gradually oust the squirearchy, the philanthropic gentry, the
   jobbery, the profit motive and other 'archaic' forms of governance.
   In time, they also provided fairer opportunities than the private
   sector offered for women and ethnic minorities to enter their
   ranks and gain promotion.

   Spokesmen of the local gentry were sharply aware that they
   were being ousted by the new professionals. The battle can be seen
   in the pamphleteering warfare conducted shortly before the First
   World War between the Webbs, advocating the policies proposed
   in the 1909 Minority Report of the Royal Commission on the
   Poor Laws (largely written by Sidney Webb) and spokesmen of the
   Charity Organisation Society whose Secretary, C.S. Loch, had
   played a leading part in writing the opposing Majority Report.
   These Reports were classic statements of the two points of view.
   The Minority called for the abolition of a whole swathe of
   charities and relieving authorities that controlled and supported

the poor, and their replacement by specialised state services, each organised to meet a different need under the supervision of a Registrar of Public Assistance. And how, their opponents asked, would this 'enormous and apparently irresponsible bureaucracy' be controlled and coordinated? 'To whom should an official be responsible but to an official?... that bureaucrat of bureaucrats, the Registrar – peripatetic, absolute and wielding, as the sword of his spirit, nothing less than a card index'.[4]

Royal Commissions and Committees of Inquiry and the queues of expert witnesses who appeared before them over the years, the Royal Colleges of medicine (with whom Bevan had to negotiate at such length before setting up the National Health Service in 1948), the churches and their bishops (with whom Butler had to negotiate before drafting the 1944 Education Act), the senior common rooms of Oxbridge colleges, the Reform Club, the British Medical Association, the National Union of Teachers and many other professional associations – all were parts of the London-centred, professional power structure through which every reform had to be negotiated. In time, it was assumed, these procedures would provide for the working class things hitherto reserved for the middle class: security of employment, adequate wages, decent housing and health care, college education, generous pensions and so on. But although trade unions and political parties sometimes played a part in these discussions the users of the services themselves – the patients, the tenants, the schoolchildren and their parents – were rarely heard, and scarcely ever involved in managing the services which emerged from these inquiries.

More recently, writing in the aftermath of Soviet Communism, it was natural that people like Ernest Gellner[5] should celebrate the virtues of this 'civil society', with its broadly based power structures rooted in institutions independent of the state, which grew up in countries like Britain. While there were jobs with steadily rising wages for everyone, the oppressive underside of this system could easily be forgotten. But those times have come to an end.

The needs of the poorest people of all were discussed in philanthropic circles and among the liberal establishment (in the Charity Organisation Society and its successors, the Eugenics Society and the LSE), but they were not central to socialist thought. Socialists assumed that these needs would be met – indeed, until Peter Townsend and Brian Abel Smith blew away their complacency in the mid-1960s,[6] they were convinced they *had* been met – through the development of universal services which benefited everyone. Special services for the poor, they believed (and with reason) tended to become poor services.

When the first majority Labour government of 1945 and its successors began to develop and consolidate a welfare state which had its counterparts in many other Western countries, that system depended for its progress on near-full employment, a steadily expanding tax base as inflation brought more and more people into the tax net, and confidence in continuing growth – growth of population and wealth, and growth of towns and their public services.

In the early 1970s that progress faltered. The 'oil shocks' turned terms of trade sharply against countries producing no oil. Unemployment began to rise. Pre-tax, pre-benefit incomes which had, over the longer term, tended to become more equal, started – slowly at first – to grow more unequal. Commitments entered into by governments for the expansion of public services – pensions, universities, hospitals and much else – began to outpace the growth of tax revenues. Meanwhile, tax thresholds hit bottom as nearly everyone was brought into the tax net. Henceforth, increased public expenditure would call for higher tax rates. Soon Crosland was telling Labour activists that 'the party's over'. Barbara Castle, in her 'In Place of Strife' initiative, failed to persuade the unions that they had to collaborate more closely with government in managing the economy and restraining their members' demands for rising incomes. Galloping inflation and mounting international trade deficits followed, leading to the 'winter of discontent', Margaret Thatcher's first Government and an altogether different strategy for managing the economy.

Forgetting their own confused abandonment of earlier aspirations – or dismissing this as due to temporary failures of nerve under pressure from the IMF and the City – many socialists at first believed the Conservatives' own rhetoric. A new and reactionary regime had come to power, rolling back the frontiers of the state, privatising public services and attacking the working class and its institutions. To oppose it, a more robust socialism was required. The rest of the country did not accept that.

In time, after painful defeats at the polls, most of the familiar policy proposals of Labour manifestos – for higher pensions and family benefits, more public housing, more central planning and more progressive taxation – were abandoned. Similar changes have taken place in the labour movements of every other Western country. What Britain calls 'New Labour' is a worldwide orthodoxy – and very successful too. Such parties provide seven of the prime ministers in the countries of the European Union and hold a share of power in the governments of four others. But do they still speak for social justice, equality and the underdogs in their societies? What is left of 'the Left'?

Gaining a clearer view

Reformers need a more realistic grasp of this history if they are to respond more effectively to it. In Britain the three assumptions on which so many of them have relied are obsolete and damaging. I will say something about each in turn.

Class

Urban industrial society and its class system have changed. Class conflicts remain a central feature of social and political life (our television sitcoms have made an industry out of them) but they no longer run mainly along the boundary dividing manual from non-manual workers. It would now be closer to the truth to describe our country, as Will Hutton does, as a 30/30/40 society: 30 per cent struggling to survive; 30 per cent precarious; 40 per cent comfortably secure.[7] Those boundaries are not at all clear cut, but it is around these new frontiers that class conflicts now arise. Those in the poorest group are no longer rooted within social movements which speak for a majority of the population. Their position may be made even more precarious by the geography of class. As cities have become more deeply divided into rich and poor quarters, there are large neighbourhoods – and their schools – which accommodate people drawn almost entirely from one of these three groups.

Equally important are the rising barriers which exclude everyone else from the professions whose members occupy most of the top 40 per cent this hierarchy. As Figure 1.3 showed, these are the people who were much the most successful in increasing their incomes between 1979 and 1991/92. In the past, many people were able to gain entry to such jobs through apprenticeship training of various kinds: draughtsmen became architects, dental nurses became dentists, lawyers' clerks became lawyers – in their thirties and forties, after long study in evening classes. Now only managers are still being recruited in this way, and the growth of the business schools may soon close that route to social mobility. To enter other professions, people usually have to take a formal, full-time training following straight on from school or university. That may produce more highly trained professionals, but they are likely to be drawn to a greater extent than hitherto from the more privileged families whose children get the most privileged education; and their experience may give them less understanding than their predecessors had of the wide range of people who rely on their services. I am not arguing that we should go back to apprenticeships, but we urgently need to open up opportunities for people to enter professional training at all stages of life: a point to which I shall return in Chapter 8. We should also bear in mind that now, more than ever, there are, even among the poorest and most disadvantaged, very able and creative people whose talents should not be wasted.

As for the people in the least skilled jobs – the men among them seem more likely than hitherto to stick with these jobs (they probably have to: there are fewer and fewer of them to be found) while the women move around more freely and frequently betweeen short-term jobs and different industries (often because the demands of children and their husbands' work compel them to be footloose). Both find it harder than their predecessors did to move out of this kind of work into more skilled jobs.[8] These are the people who make up a large proportion of those in the poorest 30 per cent of the income distribution who, as Figure 1.3 shows, did badly during the 1980s.

The middle 30 per cent are the politically crucial group in this system. No political party can gain power without a large share of their votes. Mrs Thatcher offered them access to share ownership, home ownership, private pensions and much else, but they found that all these promises became liabilities once the essential foundation of secure employment and rising wages was withdrawn. About 70 per cent of them are buying their own homes,[9] and it is among these families that rising mortgage arrears and repossessions are most often found. They probably bought a lot of the dud private pensions too. Many, feeling that their jobs, mortgages and pensions are threatened and their children's opportunities are very uncertain, are now hostile both towards the Government and towards their fellow citizens in the bottom 30 per cent of the social structure. They are reluctant to help them if that means paying higher taxes.

Table 4.1, drawn from the latest annual Report on British Social Attitudes, shows the way people in different income groups responded in 1995 to questions about their support for extra spending on a range of public services. When asked whether higher spending would be in the national interest, there was no consistent difference between the income groups. But when asked whether it would be in their *own* interests the pattern is clearer: those I have described as the insecure and anxious middle-income group are least likely to support higher spending.

Table 4.1   Attitudes to public spending, 1995

% saying that higher spending on each programme is in...	Income group		
	Low	Middle	High
...their own interests			
Health	67	62	69
Education	55	53	59
Police/law enforcement	44	38	37
Public transport	33	24	28
Environment	30	26	30
Culture and the arts	10	5	9
Defence	17	8	5
...the national interest			
Health	69	74	79
Education	65	67	82
Police/law enforcement	41	39	39
Public transport	30	26	41
Environment	31	28	34
Culture and the arts	10	6	7
Defence	12	11	5
Base	406	328	346

Source: Table on p. 195 of Roger Jowell *et al.* (eds), *British Social Attitudes. The 13th Report*, Aldershot, Dartmouth, 1996.

The lifestyles of different classes are changing too. The average manual worker's family are now home owners, car owners, telephone owners, and drink their beer at home, rather than in the pub. Fewer people belong to trade unions. Among those who do, most did not vote Labour in recent elections. And the meaning of a union has changed: Equity, the actors' union, has more members than the National Union of Mineworkers. Union officials are more likely to be talking to their members about insurance policies than strikes. We are developing a non-political trade union system – it would scarcely be right to call it a 'movement' any more – increasingly like the Americans. Their leaders tried to do more, but when the TUC mounted nationwide demonstrations about cuts in social security benefits in 1980 they flopped, and they have not risked trying that kind of thing again. The French and German unions have recently had more success in mobilising their forces against cuts of this kind, but their benefits are more generous so they have more to lose, and trade unions play a bigger part in administering these schemes. The final outcome, however, may not be very different.

The nation state

Economic and political changes are dissolving the nation state. More power is drifting outwards to multinational enterprises, upwards to international agencies, and – in most Western countries other than Britain – downwards to regions, cities and neighbourhood levels of action. A city's economy may now be transformed, for better or for worse, by decisions taken by enterprises based in distant parts of the world. Voluntary organisations, such as Greenpeace and its associates, and groups within the women's movements, have been quicker than political parties to recognise the power to be won in these arenas. Giant enterprises like Shell can be stopped in their tracks by the petrol consumers of the world. The United Nations has only to announce some future conference on poverty or the environment and the faxes and E-mails begin to chatter, mobilising an army of voluntary activists who will come to the larger and livelier 'alternative' conference which will accompany the main event.

In more conventional political spheres the growth of networks such as those mobilised in the Anti-Poverty Unit of the Local Government Management Board, the National Local Government Forum Against Poverty and the Consortium of Local Authorities working with the Local Government Centre at the Warwick Business School shows that significant numbers of civic leaders are going back to an earlier radical tradition which saw the local, not the national, arena as the place where you have to start if you want to make the world a better place. They also see the need to work more closely with colleagues in other authorities, and with the European Union's Commission and Parliament.

Public service professions

Thatcherite Governments did not reduce taxation, roll back the state or privatise much of it. They ended up with a state and tax revenues as large as before, and far more centralised. The big change which they brought about was the dethronement of the public service professions. Kenneth Clarke, introducing the biggest reform of the National Health Service since 1948, neither consulted nor informed the British Medical Association. He then publicly insulted them before they had even opened their collective mouths – asserting on television that they had always opposed every reform of the health services and would doubtless continue to do so.[10] The universities, the schoolteachers, the lawyers, the town planners and many less prestigious professions have been treated as roughly.

They had it coming to them, we can say with hindsight if we look at the ways in which many of these professions treated the public. They achieved marvellous things, enabling many families to transform their lives. Neil Kinnock spoke for millions in his famous speech telling how the first Kinnock got a university education. But we have also alienated from education a higher proportion of youngsters than any other country at a comparable stage of development, turning many of them out into the world virtually unemployable. Nissan had to get British workers educated to somewhere near the standards expected of Japanese manual workers before it could set up a factory in Sunderland. We have built some marvellous public housing – and so neglected and mismanaged other parts of it that no-one would willingly live there. After much misery, thousands of flats are being demolished. The Warner Report, initiated in response to scandalous abuse in children's homes, showed that local authority homes were, in general, worse than voluntary homes.[11] The Health Service does marvellous things for us, but in some of the back wards it has been a different story. If the professions had treated the users of their services with greater respect and listened more carefully to them, these things would have been less likely to happen. The defects of the manual services were as disturbing – as anyone who in earlier times worked among the bin men in London's refuse collection services would confirm. Stein Ringen's review of research on welfare states around the Western world showed that, wherever the outputs resulting from their massive growth have been measured, the gains made by their staff have been more obvious than those made by their users.[12]

When demonstrators marched against Mrs Thatcher's 'cuts', the banners were carried by union members, which was a proper thing for them to do. But the patients, the pupils, the council tenants, the social workers' clients and the general body of citizens did not march at their side; and the Government drew its own conclusions from their absence.

Since then, the descendants of the gentry dethroned by the Webbs and their Fabian allies earlier in this century have struck back: managers and accountants now, many of them are brutal and bureaucratic in their own ways. Some of the reforms which were fed straight into legislation from think-tank backrooms, without consulting those most directly effected or the professions working with them, have been disastrous. The poll tax is the classic case. But much that has been done in the public services and the nationalised industries was overdue. They needed to be more efficient and made more directly accountable to their users. Could the Labour Party have done the job more constructively? It would be nice to think so – but I fear not. Look no further for a reason than the numbers of people supported by the public service unions who are Members of Parliament and candidates for the Party's National Executive. When the Supplementary Benefits Commission tried to set up local liaison groups at each social security office to represent some of the poorest people in the country, they were defeated not by reactionary politicians, nor by bureaucratic officials, but by staff unions.[13] When Labour councillors in Islington tried to decentralise their services to small neighbourhood offices where they would work in closer consultation with their users they were held up for years – not by a wicked Tory Government but by the National Association of Local Government Officers.

This is not a union-bashing statement. It is a reminder that reformers concerned about the most vulnerable citizens have to recognise whose side the unions are on. The first, and entirely proper, responsibility of trade unions and professional associations is to speak for their own members who elect and pay their leaders. Reformers, too, have an interest in the quality and vigour of these professions. If they are to enable people who have been excluded from the mainstream of their society to claim a place within it again, they will need credible public services to help in that task. We cannot do without teachers, doctors, social workers, housing managers, town planners and the rest. But we cannot – indeed, we must not – enthrone professionals in their old bureaucratic roles again or recreate the minor tyrannies which often disfigured that 'civil' society. Helping them to work in new and better ways which will make them more accountable to those who depend on their services must be one of the reformers' main priorities.

Looking ahead

What should we make of all this? The most excluded third of the population have suffered the harshest effects of recent years – victims of economic changes which are making many of them redundant or highly exploitable in the labour market. On top of this have come political changes which place them on the losing, minority, side of class conflicts that increasingly separate them from the rest of society. When unemployed workers have tried to form local groups to provide advice, recreation and advocacy for people out of work, they have often had to start by overcoming the hostility of the local politicians and trade unions. Few of these groups have lasted long. (Ireland and Finland, for different reasons, are the only countries with effective pressure groups speaking for people out of work.)[14]

The most deprived neighbourhoods, in which many of the poorest people are increasingly concentrated, generally have the lowest rates of enumeration in the census, the smallest proportions of their enumerated population appearing on the electoral registers and the lowest proportions of those registered turning out to vote. They are opting out of the statistically known world. These wards, which ought to be fiefdoms of any party claiming to speak for the underdogs, are where Labour and (in Northern Ireland) Social Democratic and Labour candidates are most likely to be defeated by the parties of anger: Militant, the British National Party, Sinn Fein and some pretty odd Liberals. Their candidates may be impractical, racist, even violent, but they are usually authentic local people who live in the area and speak for their neighbours. Labour was always ill-equipped to help the poorest people, having neither tried very hard to listen to them nor developed a fully thought-out politics of poverty.

I suggest five closely related points which will help us to resist divisive forces and seek social justice in these new times:

1   *Social class.* People's opportunities in an urban, industrial society still depend greatly on their economic status – the level and security of their income and the kinds of job they do. Specially talented or fortunate individuals can always break out of these constraints, but for people in large numbers that is impossible. Their health and life expectations are shaped by their position in this system.[15] Their chances of doing well in school, and their chances of staying out of trouble with the police show similar patterns. If we are to change these patterns we must start by getting to know the people concerned and listening to them, then, with their help, change the opportunities open to them. The simpler class conflicts of 50 years ago have given way to more complex patterns which exclude and exploit people in – roughly – the lower third of the population and make many in the middle third anxious. Conflicts between them cannot be resolved without offering greater hope and security to both groups. The people in the politically crucial middle third cannot be expected to be more generous towards people in greater need if they are constantly worried about their own future.

2   People's status cannot be changed simply by handing them larger social benefits. Nor could the state afford to provide them. Therefore, *a return to high levels of employment,* giving opportunities for decent work to all who can support themselves, must be a first priority. Full employment, Thomas Balogh wrote, 'removes the need for servility, and thus alters the way of life, the relationship between the classes. It changes the balance of forces in the economy. This is its… revolutionary consequence'.[16]

3   But getting large numbers of people back into work is going to be a slow and difficult task which the private sector will never achieve unaided. It cannot be successfully tackled unless *public sector initiatives, at the European as well as national and local levels, make that possible.* Private sector employers are reducing their demands for labour as often as increasing them and, in the present state of the labour market, have no interest whatsoever in the one and a

quarter million people who have been out of work for more than a year. There are plenty of others with more recent experience of work who are available for the jobs. To bring those people back into work, the state will have to employ them or pay others to do so. It will also have to train or retrain many of them. Although that will eventually save a great deal of public expenditure and increase tax revenues, those programmes must at first cost money. Politicians who claim that they will simultaneously bring about dramatic reductions in unemployment and taxes are lying.

Some have hoped to reduce unemployment by reducing Britain's long working hours, thereby sharing out the work more widely and fairly. But that change has to be voluntary. It is manual workers with larger families who work the longest hours – because they need the money. If we pay them better wages, and bring child benefit up to the level (in relation to wages) at which family allowances originally stood, many of them will reduce their working hours. The issues of unemployment, working hours, minimum wages and child benefits interlock and have to be tackled together.

4   We need *a more open, accountable, responsive, community-oriented array of public services*. 'Community' notoriously means whatever the speaker wants to make the word say. Its essential features for my purposes are that the people who experience a problem or have a need gain a hearing and win some power in shaping the way their society responds to their situation. Conversely, it means that people whose job is to solve social problems and meet human needs recognise that it would be incompetent and unprofessional to neglect the evidence which can be offered by those who actually experience these needs and problems. Where it works well, such a regime helps to dissolve social hierarchies, to make public services accountable and to ensure that everyone is treated with the respect that each human being deserves.

More generally, we should remember that talk about 'community' and 'giving a voice to excluded groups', although it may start from small numbers and local issues (the scale at which 'Communitarians' generally assume it will stay) must also extend to larger scales if it is to make much impact. The argument must lead to city-wide, nationwide and international action on training and jobs, on income distribution, on comprehensive education and on many other programmes which enable excluded groups to find a way back into the mainstream of their society.

5   While much that a reforming government will have to do – about employment, social security, taxation and so on – will call for action on national and international scales, it *must also give greater attention to smaller scales of action, and particularly to the civic or municipal scale.* The Germans, the French, the Dutch and the Scandinavians have all tried in recent years to devolve power in various ways to smaller, local agencies and authorities. Only the British have continued to centralise power. If we are to recreate a sense of shared citizenship and concern for our fellows, if we are to rebuild the credibility of public service and the professions responsible for it, if we are to help people who have been out of work for a long time to find a way back into the economy, if we are to help people in the precarious middle third of our social structure to feel a responsibility for those in the excluded lower third, that will mainly have to be achieved at urban and neighbourhood levels. This will call for the creation of a local government financial system which gives civic leaders more responsibility and some scope for action. The task will be difficult but not impossible: other European countries have managed it. The question is not technical but political: are Westminster politicians and their civil servants prepared to give civic leaders more power?

I have used the phrase 'civic leaders' rather frequently. Like 'community' it means many different things. Leaders are made by their followers, without whom they are powerless, and the followers they acquire depend on what they attempt to do and whom they play to. If, as appears to have happened in Stratford-upon-Avon recently, civic leaders play to the shopkeepers and tourist services of their town centre and neglect their council estates, they will become leaders of shopkeepers and publicans, and sooner or later someone gets murdered in their leaderless council estates.

We shall not get the unemployed young people who are now hanging about the housing estates back into the electoral registers and the polling booths unless we start listening to them and responding to what they say. Why *should* they show any interest in the political agenda they are being offered? Cuts in income tax? Sleaze in Parliament? Squeegee merchants? Another royal divorce...? But training that leads to real jobs, fair social benefits for young people unable to earn their own money, housing they could afford… that would begin to mean something.

Conclusions

This is not a manifesto for a future government. That would deal with many other things not touched on here. My analysis, however, may suggest how we should appraise such manifestos. We would start from a recognition that reformers are not in business to create an ultimate, perfected utopia. They should be part of an adaptable, mobile, resistance movement which has to respond to the changing world we live in by promoting and shaping the growth of its massive productive resources, civilising the operations of those forces and protecting those who would otherwise suffer from them. Socialism and capitalism – short-hand terms which each describe many different patterns of productive forces – need each other and shape each other.

To use the concepts coined by Gramsci, that widely respected Marxist, radicals cannot choose between a 'war of position' (designed to capture power) and a 'war of movement' (designed to modify the operations of power).[17] There is always the war of movement – the attempt to modify and civilise whatever regime we have. Revolution-aries who create altogether new regimes through 'wars of position' can achieve important advances – as in South Africa recently. But they also pose new, and sometimes worse, problems for those engaged in the reformers' unending 'wars of movement'.

We do not live in a classless society, but class and the conflicts between classes are changing. The emerging system is more complex than the old, and is excluding from the mainstream of society a large number of people in – roughly – the poorer third of the population. The increasingly threatened middle third hold a political balance which goes far to determine what any government can do. Policy must therefore be equally concerned with both groups.

If excluded people who are now experiencing growing hardships are to realise their full potential, the opportunities open to them must be enlarged. The preaching and whip-cracking to which politicians and moralists expose them are insulting and counterproductive. The most important opportunities of all are those which enable people to enhance their knowledge and skills, to earn a living for themselves and their families, and to contribute something to their society. No matter how successful private enterprises become, they will never, unaided, extend those opportunities to the people now most profoundly excluded from them. The state, on our behalf and funded by all of us, has to give a lead and provide much of the resources required. That will call for action on a European scale which will be briefly touched upon in this book. There is much to be done at a local scale too.

As citizens we have to rely for much of the action required for these and other social purposes on public service professions of various kinds. These professions are now in a battered condition which does no-one any good. There may have been good reasons for some features of the onslaught they have suffered, but the public and our governments now need a new relationship with them. Operating partly within the state, partly outside it, they should be more efficient, open, responsive, accountable and democratic. The dilemmas posed by those sometimes conflicting aims will play a central part in this book.

We shall also need vigorous civic leadership within a more robust and independent system of local government. Britain, almost alone among the more developed countries of the world, has been steadily centralising power within national government. That drive should be reversed. But it will not be enough simply to hand powers back to local authorities which have had too little opportunity to use them in recent years. Transfers of powers and resources should form part of a movement mobilising a commitment to create genuinely distinctive places where people have a clearer vision of the kind of community they are trying to create.

This book is written for those who are trying to do these things.

Notes

An earlier version of this Chapter appeared as an article, 'What kind of New Labour?', in *Soundings*, 3, Summer, 1996, pp. 39–54. I am grateful to the journal's editors for the opportunity of exposing these arguments in their columns and then developing them here.

1   Karen Armstrong, *A History of God*, London, Heinemann, 1993.
2   For a revealing history of movements so briefly touched on here, see Donald Sassoon, *One Hundred Years of Socialism*, London, IB Tauris, 1996.

3   Anne Power tells the story in *Property Before People*, London, Allen & Unwin, 1987.

4   T. Hancock Nunn, *The Minority Report*, London, National Poor Law Reform Association, (undated), p. 10.

5   Ernest Gellner, *Conditions of Liberty. Civil Society and its Rivals*, Harmondsworth, Penguin, 1996.

6   See, for example, Brian Abel Smith and Peter Townsend, *The Poor and the Poorest*, Welwyn, Codicote Press, 1965.

7   The point was made at a conference by Will Hutton, author of *The State We're In*, London, Jonathan Cape, 1995.

8   Jonathan Gershuny, 'Post-industrial career structures in Britain', in Gosta Esping-Andersen, *Changing Classes. Stratification and Mobility in Post-industrial Societies*, London, Sage, 1993.

9   Steve Wilcox, *Housing Review, 1996/97*, York, Joseph Rowntree Foundation, 1996, p. 126.

10 Nicholas Timmins' book, *The Five Giants: A Biography of the Welfare State* (London, HarperCollins, 1995) tells the story.

11 Norman Warner, *Choosing With Care. The Report of the Committee of Inquiry Into the Selection, Development and Management of Staff in Children's Homes*, London, HMSO, 1992.

12 Stein Ringen, *The Possibility of Politics*, Oxford, Oxford University Press, 1987.

13 David Donnison, *The Politics of Poverty*, Oxford, Martin Robertson, 1982, p. 204.

14 David Donnison, *Long Term Unemployment in Northern Ireland*, Belfast, Northern Ireland Council for Voluntary Action, 1966, Appendix.

15 Bobbie Jacobson *et al.* (eds) *The Nation's Health. A Strategy for the 1990s*, Oxford, Oxford University Press, 1991, p. 107 .

16 Thomas Balogh, *The Irrelevance of Contemporary Economics*, London, Weiden-feld & Nicolson, 1982, p. 47; quoted in Donald Sassoon, *One Hundred Years of Socialism*, London, IB Tauris, 1996, p. 448.

17 Gramsci's ideas are helpfully discussed by James Joll in *Gramsci*, London, Fontana Paperbacks, 1977.

PART II

Act Local

Chapter 5

Citizens and Civic Leaders

Introduction

The heads of the education service of a big city – the Convenor of the Education Committee and her Director of Education – are sitting in one of the committee rooms of their town hall, preparing to meet a group of local citizens who have asked to see them. The delegation which enters the room are elders of the city's principal mosque, led by their Imam. When the proper courtesies have been exchanged and the delegates are seated, the Imam begins: 'There are many publicly funded Christian schools in this city, Catholic and Protestant. We have founded an Islamic school so that we may raise our daughters in the way they should go. We believe it is time that you funded this school too.'

The Convenor is a liberal-minded and progressive woman who has tried to listen to every community in the city. She has played an active part in anti-racist and feminist movements. How should she respond to the Imam's request? The question is a real one to which various replies have been given and I will return to it at the end of this chapter. If the ideas offered here are to be useful, they should help to answer it.

'Community' has entered the jargon of governance. You can scarcely get a grant from the European Union, from the English Government's Single Regeneration Budget or its Scottish counterpart, or from the National Lottery's funds for charities without first demonstrating that 'the community' is involved in your project. What these words mean is much less clear. The main partners in community-based methods of working are usually of two kinds, as in this little story: people who speak for the public services and people – often the users of the same services – who speak for 'communities' of various kinds. There are others to be considered too, as I shall show, but let us start with these two. They need to confront each other more frankly.

Community action

By 'community action' I mean the activities of people who have no special official status but claim to speak for groups of their fellow citizens. Those citizens may be residents of a particular neighbourhood, users of a particular service, or people who have a particular problem, illness or need. If such people get sufficiently involved in the provision of public services to exert real influence upon them, we may speak of 'community-based' forms of administration, planning or government. The initiatives for setting up arrangements of this kind do not have to wait on the community; they are sometimes taken by officials responsible for the services concerned. Nor do they have to be confined only to public services: the private sector and voluntary agencies can operate in the same way.

The more enthusiastic advocates of community action sometimes seem convinced that if only they could be properly funded and empowered, and supported by consultants of their own choice, they would transform the world. The argument is attractive, but it poses a number of difficult questions.

Any form of governance – by which I mean the ways in which a society manages its collective affairs – poses problems of scale. These are both political and geographical. To make a success of running a housing cooperative, wholly owned by its residents, you would be wise to keep it small. Many people think that 200 or 300 houses can be best managed in this way. That number could perhaps be pushed up to 500 – but certainly not to 5,000. A secondary school, however, has to serve a much larger population – perhaps 10,000 people. Meanwhile a modern health centre, equipped with all the supporting services which doctors need, will probably serve about 20,000 people. A police force has to operate on a still larger scale. The task of government is to bring together and coordinate services working at these different scales. Any particular social problem – how to reduce drug addiction, or how to prevent AIDS and help the people who have it – may require action to be taken by all these services. Even the smaller problems which can be dealt with by one service make an impact on other services because they call for resources – if only of decision-makers' time and attention – which would otherwise be directed elsewhere.

Community action tends to be most effective when it works at a fairly small scale, when focused on a particular problem or service, and when tackling issues on which a negative decision is sought: stopping a rent increase or the building of a motor way for example – rather than regenerating the economy of a city which has fallen on hard times.

Next, there are problems of legitimacy. For whom exactly do community leaders speak? How were they chosen? Do they listen to those whom they claim to represent, and how effectively and frequently do they report back to them? Can they be got rid of if their followers lose confidence in them? Good answers can be given to all these questions, but that calls for careful organisation which may enmesh a project in fairly ponderous procedures.

If leaders are evicted from power, or burn out, move away or die, will their authority be smoothly transferred to convincing successors so that work continues uninterrupted? Democratic government transfers power from one leader to the next through the ritual of elections, but many splendid community projects wither or perish altogether when they lose their first inspiring leaders. There may then be no easy way to rebuild them.

What happens if customers or staff of the project feel that they have been treated unfairly? What happens if the laws about race relations or equality of opportunity are broken? What rights of appeal do aggrieved people have? – and to what independent tribunal or ombudsman? These problems too must be solved.

Can we be sure that community leaders distinguish between public money and private money, and carefully account for public funds? These problems can also be solved. In Northern Ireland, where the authorities have always been afraid that funds provided for community-based groups may find their way into paramilitary hands, their accounts are closely audited and monitored. But there is a price to be paid for that. These procedures give the state draconian powers to turn off the funding tap at short notice without any right of appeal.

More fundamentally, we should question the unspoken assumption of some enthusiasts that 'community' is necessarily a benign force, humane and democratic. 'Community' is us: *all* of us. In its name, people may act in generous, caring, courageous ways –

showing the best and most heart-warming neighbourliness. Beatrix Campbell's accounts[1] of the ways in which women living in violent neighbourhoods have struggled to maintain decent standards provide telling examples of such heroism. But community can also be brutal and bigoted – showing the dark side of relations between neighbours. When I feel myself inclined to become inspirational about it I call to mind a telephone box in West Belfast. 'That', I was told, 'is where youngsters, thought to be making trouble in this part of town, are given ten pence and told to 'phone the ambulance before they are knee-capped'. Which is also undoubtedly the work of a community.

If communities were all naturally kind, fair and equal we would not have to go to all sorts of trouble to create a kinder, fairer and more equal society. With such voters, conventional democratic politics would be enough.

Meanwhile, however kind and fair they may be, different groups within any community will have conflicting interests. How can a wise and fair balance be struck between those who demand better schools and those who demand better hospitals, those who want lower rents and those who want better housing, those concerned about children and those concerned about old people? Democratic government by elected politicians advised by well-trained officials is our attempt to strike that balance.

Some will interpret these comments as an attack on community-based action, and also as suggesting a romantic view of more conventional forms of government. But no-one claims that the normal systems of central and local government solve all these problems. Bureaucracies compete destructively against each other for influence and funds. Councillors and their officials can be as corrupt, incompetent or oppressive as any community activist. But they can at least be monitored and disciplined in all sorts of ways. Their accounts, and increasingly their general efficiency too, are audited and published. If they exceed or abuse their powers they can be surcharged – fined – very large sums, or evicted from office altogether. Officials can be run out of their professions, councillors prohibited from standing again for election. And always, every few years, the people can deprive politicians and their parties of power by using their votes.

So what should be done? We could devise complex procedures to inspect, regulate and coordinate community action. Some progress might usefully be made in this direction, but if we go too far down that road we shall end up by re-inventing local government and destroying much of the free-flowing, spontaneous creativity of communities. Which would not make the world a better place. Let us look, next, at the world on the other side of the public service counters.

Bureaucratic action

Bureaucracy is a word often used in insulting ways, but here it only means a systematic form of government in which public services are managed and delivered by officials who are accountable to their superiors within a hierarchy of some kind. They have fairly clearly defined jobs to do, and usually some training for their work. Training brings a recognised status, and often membership of a professional institute of some sort which defends and disciplines its members.

Bureaucracies were an enormous advance on previous systems. Chilly though they may seem, their impersonality was one of their advantages, replacing bribery, kinship loyalties, political jobbery and other sources of influence which people previously had to rely on in order to get anything done – and still have to rely on in many parts of southern Europe and the third world. The system had to stand on new foundations for its authority: on the law and – within democracies – on the authority conferred by elections. That authority, provided by local government committees appointed by municipal councils or by Ministers appointed by a Prime Minister who is accountable to Parliament, compels officials to look 'upwards' for their authority and their promotion – to their bosses and the people who appoint them – rather than 'outwards' to the citizens at large or 'downwards' (to adopt the form used by most organisation charts) to the people who depend on their services.

Although politicians and their officials may talk glibly about 'involving the community', many of them have a pretty cynical view of that process, so we need to look at the defects of bureaucracy as closely as those of community. The problem can be illustrated by the meeting of a steering group responsible for a major project of urban renewal. I and a colleague had been asked to help them set up procedures which would give the people who lived in the area a voice in the planning of this project – a scheme which would ultimately destroy and replace most of their homes and transform the square mile of their city which they know best.

One of the key officials involved – the head of a major service – sat silent for a long while. Eventually he blew up. 'Why are we wasting all this time talking about "community"? It's our job to get the bricks and mortar up!' The chairman looked irritably at his watch, aware that we were only half way through the agenda and all these important people would soon have to hurry on to other meetings. As I wondered how best to respond, my colleague dryly intervened: 'The Government expects you to sell most of the houses you will be building here. If their walls are scrawled with graffiti and their windows are broken you'll fail.' The point was understood: a point about giving people some commitment to the project and a sense of responsibility for it.

What more could we have said? Had there been a little more time, these are some of the points we might have made.

The people who actually experience the problems a public service sets out to solve can provide some of the most important evidence to be considered before solutions are proposed. If their voice is neglected, powerful people will get things wrong – yet again. That voice is not the only one which must be heard, but it should be the first one. To neglect it is not only a discourtesy and an act of inhumanity. It is also a mark of professional incompetence.

As more and more public services, hitherto provided by in-house staff, are contracted out or devolved to publicly funded markets where rival providers compete with each other, it becomes impossible for civic leaders to issue commands. But that does not mean that city-wide (or village-wide) policies are no longer needed. So new forms of leadership have to be invented. Talking recently with senior officials of one of Britain's biggest cities about their schools, I said: 'If more and more youngsters are being excluded from your schools as unmanageable and you cannot provide for them in other ways, shouldn't you be talking to heads and governors about this problem?'. 'That', they glumly replied, 'is only one of many problems we would like to discuss with heads and governors. But we no longer have any authority over them.' Now it was true that they could no longer order them all to come to a meeting in the town hall next Tuesday; but the future of a lot of children running wild in a big city is still a very important problem for its citizens. With the help of local newspapers and radio stations, churches, youth clubs and social services, it must be possible to get people to discuss the issue and perhaps agree on some action. Policies formulated in this way may be wiser and more effective than those decreed by the Director of Education. This example shows why civic leaders have to be able to mobilise the support of communities of many kinds if they are to do their job; why officials must learn to look 'outwards' to the public as well as 'upwards' to their bosses for the power to act; and why, in future, we have to think of governance – the collective management of public affairs – rather than government by bureaucratic command.

In some places there may, effectively, be no community. People are living in a kind of transit camp from which everyone escapes as soon as they can. The results may be violent, painful and enormously expensive both for those who remain and for the whole society. Anyone trying to create more civilised relationships between local people, and a more constructive outlook on the world at large must start by creating a community where none existed before. Community-based ways of working are an essential part of any strategy which will achieve that. They always reveal that there are some local people who have an important contribution to make, both to whatever project is in hand and to the wider society. Such people are an important asset: they have launched marvellously creative enterprises which the conventional bureaucracy would never have had the imagination or capacity to attempt. Helen Crummy's account of community action in Craigmillar[2] is one of many which tell this kind of story.

Meanwhile, if nothing is done, an increasingly divided society, in which more and more people are excluded by unemployment and poverty from the opportunities available to mainstream citizens, and in which those people are increasingly concentrated in poverty-stricken neighbourhoods, will not remain trouble-free for long. The pain and anger present in such communities lead many into depression, apathy and sickness of various kinds. Others turn to delinquency, disorder and violence. Or they mobilise their energies for more creative, constructive action which may include political protest and community-based projects of various kinds. Figure 5.1, based on perceptive observation by Kay Carmichael,[3] illustrates the options, both for individuals and for communities. Turbulent though mobilisation can sometimes be, it is more constructive for the people involved and for the wider society they live in than the other routes they may take. It will be easier for people to move in the more constructive directions if those who hold power in their society are prepared to listen to them, to take them seriously and to share responsibilities with them.

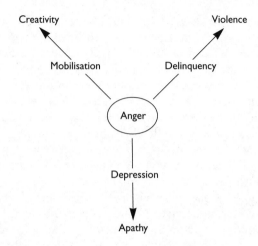

Source: Derived from Kay Carmichael, *Ceremony of Innocence*, London, Macmillan, 1991, p. 71.

FIGURE 5.1   Potential responses to prolonged poverty and hardship

If the power-holders refuse to work in these ways they may find parts of their cities slipping out of control, with housing increasingly unmanageable, workers increasingly unemployable, children increasingly difficult to educate and streets increasingly difficult to police. Anne Power has vividly described that rake's progress.[4]

The private and corporate sectors

People who talk about community-based ways of working usually assume that in this game it is the state and its agencies which are playing on the other side of the net. But markets are in general more powerful than governments. Many things which a civilised community needs can only be achieved with the help of private and corporate enterprises. The arguments for developing community-based methods of working apply with equal strength to enterprises of every kind.

Community activists are learning to confront private and corporate interests as well as the branches of the state which they have in the past more frequently dealt with. Campaigns against the use of handguns, against polluters and against inhumane methods of animal husbandry have attracted widespread attention and achieved considerable success. On a more local scale there have been many other campaigns: to persuade a Bristol building society to invest in housing for homeless people, for example, and to persuade one of Hanson's companies to convert an empty factory into workspaces instead of demolishing it – both briefly described in Chapter 10.

Agencies of the state derive legitimacy from their claim to be accountable to the citizens and must therefore pay some attention to public demands. But privately owned agencies are less obliged to concede to such pressure, unless it seems to be in their commercial interest to do so. These cases therefore invite the kinds of tactic developed long ago by trade unions to deal with employers. Later they were applied to social issues by Saul Alinsky and his colleagues in the United States.[5] They first identified 'winnable' issues. They then discovered who was responsible for dealing with them, confronted these individuals and 'unmasked' them. While they could be aggressive, their demands were usually focused on single problems, even single decisions. More recently the campaign to prevent the Shell oil company disposing of the Brent Spar oil platform by sinking it in the ocean has been a successful example of these tactics.

Activists sought no continuing influence over the enterprises involved. Since their strength lay in numbers and in mass-media coverage – for they could not win unless large numbers of people were prepared to mobilise in support of their cause – it was difficult to pursue a carefully prepared strategy with consistent long-term priorities. Perhaps community groups should get together and formulate some longer-term priorities? An example may illustrate the possibilities. Recently the posh papers and their readers were earnestly considering whether they should boycott French wines as a protest against French nuclear tests in the Pacific Ocean. At the same time it was reported that Burger King were hiring young workers on 'zero-hours contracts' which enabled managers of their bars to send these workers back to the staff room whenever there were not enough customers in the bar to require their services – and then only pay them for the two or three hours each day for which they might be working. No-one suggested that young people, who also make up most of the customers in these bars, should boycott Burger King. Since then, this firm has announced that it has abandoned this practice, but similar things happen in many other parts of their industry. There is clearly scope for a movement which would monitor employment practices, set standards in catering firms and enforce them with the help of publicity and boycotts by customers.

Another example may show how public concern could be mobilised and brought to bear on a more ambitious scale. The high street used to belong to the citizens and be maintained by their town council. But in many cities today the private sector has taken over the massive, covered shopping centres which are replacing high streets. In a world where few attend political meetings or go to church, these centres have a special significance. They are the only remaining place where most citizens regularly come together. There are towns where insurance companies and other big investors which own the main shopping centres exclude any activity that might distract customers from spending money. You may conduct a survey there which asks questions about people's preferences between soap powders, but not questions about their voting intentions. You may play music there, but not sing hymns, say prayers or hold a political meeting.

People established their rights to use public footpaths by mass trespasses back in the 1930s – and may well have to do the same thing again soon. Is it not time that we had a festival of mass pray-ins, hymn-singing and political oratory in some of our shopping centres? That should be followed by the development of some rules which would preserve our rights to use these public spaces – rules which would be enforced by regular public use of these rights.

Action principles

These are the main conclusions to which this argument leads. Many of them are given a well-researched base by Alan McGregor and his colleagues in a recent paper with helpful references to supporting studies.[6]

Civic leaders and their officials have a continuing and important job to do. They can only do it effectively if they try to work with their people, treat them with respect, listen to them, involve them and share responsibility with them. Community-based ways of working cannot replace more conventional systems of democratic governance which took hundreds of years to develop and still need to be developed further. Those systems should in future work in more open, democratic, accountable and responsive ways. Harder though that task will seem, it will give politicians and their advisers the authority which comes from a more profound knowledge than they ever had before of the problems they are dealing with and the feelings of the people whom they represent.

These more democratic ways of working cannot be confined to street level. They have to start at the top, with Ministers, committee chair-holders, senior civil servants, chief officers and chief executives. There is no point in telling junior staff to consult the public and listen to users of their service if no-one consults or listens to *them*. If they do not know the thinking which underlies their agencies' or companies' policies, they cannot respond honestly and helpfully to the questions which people ask them. The approach also has to develop in all services; it cannot be effective if confined to one of them. Most people – fortunately – are unimpressed by bureaucratic boundaries. As soon as they get a chance to speak to power they ask questions about all manner of things, extending far beyond the functions of the particular official they are talking to. The politician or official responding to them may only be able to say that their questions will be passed on to colleagues in other services whose representatives will come to the next meeting to answer them. If they cannot even say that much, their credibility will soon be destroyed.

Successful community action always depends on the help of honest mediators: politicians and officials prepared to meet the public, listen to them and deal frankly with them. That function has to be a recognised part of the job description of the officials most involved in it, so that they will themselves be listened to and not accused of 'going native' when they tell their colleagues what the community is saying. Recognition of their role has practical implications: getting time off, for example, to compensate for long hours spent in meetings held in the evenings and at weekends.

Much talk about community action deals with committee meetings of various kinds at which people are apt to get snowed under with papers full of incomprehensible official jargon. There they are compelled to sit without smoking for hours of boring talk. That may be tolerable for hardened political apparatchiks and for people who have spent years in university lectures, but most people soon get turned off by the experience. Equally important, therefore, will be the development of forms of governance which regularly expose officials and their political masters to the people they administer, in ways which encourage informal, spontaneous talk; procedures which make official faces more widely known, and give their owners a more clearly defined and better-known public to work for. Many people who are not at their best in formal meetings can be very effective in more informal settings. The decentralisation of work to small neighbourhood offices in the areas they serve can help to provide such opportunities.

If different agencies are to work well together in dealing with the public, they have to serve the same populations and areas wherever possible. Otherwise they are unable to talk to each other about the same people, or the same needs and services. Each agency usually has a different pattern of areas – or no area subdivisions at all because it divides up its work in other ways. The last thing they wish to do is to adopt some other bureaucracy's pattern. Thus changes will be needed which cannot be brought about unless civic leaders with the necessary authority insist upon them.

The private sector, and corporate bodies such as hospital trusts and universities, have as important a part to play in shaping the character of a community as does the state, and should be as open to challenge from community groups. Many community activists focus so much of their energies upon agencies of the state that they have little time for the private sector. When they do take up issues which concern private and corporate enterprises activists usually focus upon specific, one-off decisions and those responsible for them, rather than upon the continuing policies, values and standards of the bodies concerned. They should be more ambitious – more strategic – in their thinking, mobilising the help of the state when that is appropriate. The private and corporate sectors will not become most effectively involved in community-based ways of working unless local civic leaders work with them to develop a shared understanding of their cities' needs and shared hopes for their future.

'Civic leaders' is another vague term. Besides local politicians, their officials and the more effective community activists, the phrase may include business and corporate leaders, the heads of local newspapers and radio stations, church leaders, senior people in local universities and trade unions. In different cultures, different kinds of people play the part. They share a commitment to their city, county or village, they have some kind of vision of its future, and they have a capacity for working together and with grass-roots groups in the area, and speaking on their behalf to higher levels of power.[7]

Community activists and their supporters need some training and advice from supporters who are independent of the bureaucracies and enterprises they are dealing with. This help must be provided in ways which suit their needs – at times of the day and the week they can handle, perhaps with a crèche nearby to care for their children.

The people in the community with whom civic leaders have to work with include every kind of interest from the most creative and caring to the most bigoted and brutal. Many of these groups will make conflicting demands. Some will be in strife with each other. Some will be concentrated in clearly defined neighbourhoods where it is easy to find them while others will be thinly scattered across the map. Some people with urgent needs will be too depressed and apathetic or too thinly scattered to make themselves heard at all. People with disabilities may be unable to get to meetings without special help. There is nothing inherently fair or equalising about 'community'. Community-based action is unlikely to lead in fair and equalising directions unless civic leaders, armed with the authority which comes from having been elected to represent people, are prepared to commit themselves to that cause. They will then have a responsibility to ensure that the more vulnerable and less articulate groups gain a hearing, and to prevent the more aggressive from dominating proceedings. Such happy outcomes do not happen automatically. Civic leaders have to formulate their own priorities and principles, in consultation with their citizens, before they can invite people to work with them or send officials out to work with local communities. Civic leadership is about listening, but not *only* about listening: it is also about formulating visions for the future, choosing priorities and teaching standards of behaviour.

This means that civic leaders themselves have to set an example which citizens can respect about such things as declaring private interests, accounting for public funds, not accepting bribes or undeclared gifts, being easily accessible to constituents and reporting back to them, attending meetings and conducting business efficiently and regularly, and much else.

Active local communities with effective leaders will always be distributed patchily across the map, fluctuating in strength from year to year and better at doing some things than others. Thus civic leaders should always be alert to spot important unrepresented groups and forgotten issues, and to open up public debate in ways which will give them a hearing. Community politics can as easily become ossified and oppressive as the politics of more conventional political arenas.

Many experienced politicians and officials will respond to these conclusions by saying that they would be all very well if only local government had the money and the powers to respond to public demands. Without those resources, they may say, there is no point in raising public expectations. Clearly it will be most fruitful to focus public attention on areas of the city and areas of policy where things are 'going critical' – where action of some kind is feasible. But the fact that money is scarce and every demand upon it excludes other projects which may seem equally deserving is part of the reality which needs to be more frankly explained. Politicians have only themselves to blame if people are frustrated by those dilemmas because their leaders have been afraid to discuss them honestly.

If they find that the poorest people and those most excluded from their society's mainstream are apathetic, and unwilling to speak up for themselves or to support those who try to do so, questions must be asked about the character of local and national politics. What is 'politics' *about?* Do the issues debated – in local and national newspapers and broadcasts for example – deal with the forces which exclude these people, or with policies which might liberate them: with jobs, training, benefit levels and housing, for example? If not – if politicians, broadcasters and newspaper editors have chosen to speak for other interests in society – why should anyone expect them to care?

An example

It is time to reflect on the Imam's question, posed at the start of this chapter. How should the Convenor of the Education Committee reply to his request for publicly funded Islamic schools – 'so that we may raise our daughters in the way they should go'?

There is no single, 'right' answer to such questions. Each city and county, its ethnic groups and educational resources, will be different, and each has different political leaders with different priorities. So let us assume that we are dealing with a city which has a considerable Islamic population, several mosques and a Convenor of its Education Committee who wants to behave in a democratic, non-sexist, non-racist, egalitarian fashion. She might respond in these ways.

After listening carefully to their visitors and trying to understand their concerns, the Convenor and her Director of Education, assisted by the city's race relations staff, would tactfully explore feelings in other mosques and among their supporters – not to divide and rule, but because each is an independent group and they may well have differing opinions. The views of other faith communities – Sikh and Hindu, for example – should also be explored. There are likely to be integrators and separatists, liberals and fundamentalists, in every community.

It may emerge that many of the city's Muslim parents are dissatisfied with local schools. But dissatisfied for what reasons? Because they want an Islamic education?, single-sex schools?, better academic results?, better discipline?, or tighter control over their girls? Poor teaching and discipline must be put right, for everyone's sake. Single-sex education may already be found in parts of the city and could perhaps be made more widely available. But girls must be given equal opportunities with boys for doing well: the law says so.

As the answers to these questions become clearer, it may also emerge that in the Islamic community the city's schools have the precious asset of educationally ambitious families who want their children to do well, and who are prepared to tell the authorities when things are going wrong and demand a better deal for their youngsters. The presence of those youngsters in mainstream schools may help to raise standards, and teach respect for ethnic groups of every kind and for the cultural variety and vigour they bring to the city's life. If minority groups are excluded from the schools the education of all will suffer.

While it is true that the state funds separate Christian schools, that practice began because the churches founded schools long before the state took a hand, not because it is the best way of doing things. Indeed, experience in Northern Ireland and parts of Scotland leads many to believe that separate schools can be very destructive. In countries with a different educational history – such as France and the United States – schools and religion are kept well apart. All these points should be frankly discussed with those who participated in the original delegation.

It will next be helpful to look more closely at the curriculum before concluding that entirely separate schools are needed. That exploration may suggest that the work of schools falls into roughly three parts: (a) subjects which must be taught in similar ways for everyone (mathematics, much of which began in Islamic countries, modern European languages and most of the natural sciences fall into this – probably largest – category); (b) subjects in which a separate Islamic perspective, well and wisely taught, would benefit all students (music, art, history and much of religious knowledge may fall into this – probably smaller – category); and (c) subjects in which separate provision may indeed be needed (physical education for girls and religious observance may fall into this – probably smallest – category). If schools take the trouble to think these issues through, discuss them with parents and pupils, and prepare a good professional response to their needs they will provide a better education for all their pupils.

But if, at the end of the day, a demand for separation persists, arrangements may have to be made for that, subject to careful planning and monitoring of teaching which ensure that all pupils get a fair deal and are well prepared for life in modern Britain.

Conclusions

What are the main conclusions to be drawn from this imaginary scenario and the rest of this chapter?

Time-consuming though it will be, this community-based way of developing schools should produce a better education for everyone. By taking discontented people seriously, listening carefully to their concerns and not being scared by their demands, it will often be found that they have an important contribution to make to the city and the wider society. The people who insist that public buildings be accessible to wheelchair users, and houses be designed to make life easy for those with physical handicaps likewise perform a service for all of us. Any of us may be in a wheelchair before the week is out.

The best response to the demands of a minority group can only be made when the resources of the whole educational system are mobilised, not just those of individual schools. (If single-sex schools are needed, where can they be found? If minority religions and a history more sensitive to minority experiences are to be taught, where can the teachers be found and trained, and how can all schools benefit?) This is a task for civic leaders. Heads of schools and their governors can then play their part, but they cannot tackle it unaided. Indeed, the resources required are not confined to the education service: staff responsible for race relations and equal opportunities work must also play their part. The impact of community action can never be tidily confined to one agency.

Some political leaders and professional people brought up under earlier regimes may reject this approach as a 'populist' one which panders to local demagogues. Some tabloid newspapers will attack it as an example of 'loony Leftist' thinking. But in ethnically mixed, multicultural cities someone will play populist political cards sooner or later. Fascists are more likely to start that game than Muslims. If civic leaders take the initiative in fair-minded, well-informed ways they can help to ensure that positive, hopeful and constructive aspects of people's experience are brought to bear on their city's development, rather than the fear and bigotry which are always lurking beneath the surface.

Some people have talked about community action as if it will generate pressures which can be fed into a 'black box' of political decision-making from which fair, well-balanced and widely accepted decisions will normally emerge. If some groups come off best this year, others will gain a hearing next year or the year after. But there is no such black box. A more realistic symbol of the directions in which such assumptions may lead us is the telephone box where youngsters are sent to call the ambulance before they are knee-capped. Community action cannot take the place of coherent civic leadership. On the contrary, it can play a responsible and creative part in our affairs only if there are civic leaders at the centre of the process who have political principles and moral values which they are prepared to discuss, develop and defend.

A place which has people capable of giving that kind of leadership will find that by involving its people in decision-making – particularly the people who depend most heavily on public services – wiser decisions will be made. To forget that is a mark of professional incompetence.

Notes

1   Beatrix Campbell, *Goliath. Britain's Dangerous Places*, London, Methuen, 1993.
2   Helen Crummy, *Let the People Sing! A Story of Craigmillar*, Edinburgh, published by Helen Crummy, 1992.
3   Kay Carmichael, *Ceremony of Innocence*, London, Macmillan, 1991, p. 71.
4   Anne Power, *Property Before People*, London, Allen & Unwin, 1987.
5   Saul Alinsky, *Reveille for Radicals*, Chicago, Chicago University Press, 1946.
6   Alan McGregor *et al.*, 'Creating community capacity for sustainable urban regeneration', *Scottish Journal of Community Work and Development*, 1(1), 1996, pp. 55–66.
7   The workings of civic leadership operating in different countries at the scale of the big city are explored by Dennis Judd and Michael Parkinson (eds) in *Leadership and Urban Regeneration. Cities in North America and Europe*, London, Sage, 1990.

Chapter 6

Skills, Work and Money

Introduction

Anyone who listens to people who live hard lives and anyone who makes surveys of opinion in the places where a lot of them live can have no doubt about the things they most want. At or near the top of their priorities come opportunities to work and to earn the money that will enable them to support themselves and their families, and therefore opportunities also for the training which will help them to get whatever jobs are available.[1] Anyone who wants to respond to the needs of these people has to start here.

But can anything be done about these things at the local level? I will start by looking at larger scales of action before turning to the local scale. Then, at the local scale, I will consider not only the needs of those who would like a job but also a broad range of policies for increasing the incomes of the poorest people.

Larger scales of action

Much of the action required to expand opportunities for work has to be taken at national and international scales. There are more unemployed people than farmers in the European Union: nearly twenty million of them. But compare their political clout! Within weeks of the first disturbing news about mad cow disease, finance ministers around Europe were preparing to throw their budgets into disarray and to imperil their governments' chances of re-election in order to come to the aid of the beef industry – lest chances of re-election be even more imperilled by failing to do so. None of them dared publicly to ask whether the industry and its suppliers bore some responsibility for the disaster. Meanwhile, to work towards closer economic union and the creation of a single currency, the same countries adopt 'convergence criteria' – rules for the management of their economies – which make no mention of unemployment but compel them to put up interest rates and make cuts in public expenditure which are bound to increase the numbers of people out of work. 'Budgetary consolidation' is the euphemistic term for this policy.

This neglect of the unemployed – now become 'the price well worth paying' for convergence – is not an accidental oversight. In 1994 M Delors, then President of the European Commission, produced a White Paper on Employment calling for 26 special projects, to be called Trans-European Networks (or TENs) to create new jobs. Later the Commission proposed further help for small and middle-sized enterprises to enable them to create more jobs. These programmes were to be funded through the European Investment Fund – money belonging to the European Union – backed by guarantees extending the Fund's influence provided by the new European Loan Insurance Scheme for Employment. Meanwhile the European Parliament had set up a Committee to produce an Action Plan on Employment whose Reports the Parliament approved by massive majorities in December 1994 and July 1995. Thereafter, Ken Coates, the MEP who chaired the Committee, constantly lobbied the Commission and anyone else who would listen about unemployment in Europe. Yet nothing has happened. The 26 TENs were first cut down to 14, and then action on even this reduced programme was postponed – indefinitely, it seems – by the European finance ministers meeting in ECOFIN, the powerful Economics and Finance Council of the Union. In March 1996 the European Social Committee proposed eight fundamental social rights for citizens of the Union. They did not include the right to work.

The point of this brief summary of a complicated story[2] is the reminder it provides that the decision to take serious steps to reduce unemployment is always a political one. So far, those advocating decisive action have lost the battle, mainly because of the reluctance of national governments to take the problem seriously. But growing numbers of people in and around the Commission are beginning to recognise that the prospects for stable and successful development in their countries depend on ensuring that Europe's people can earn a living for themselves. Some are also recognising that economic growth, by itself, will never achieve that. Meanwhile, 'misery', as

Beveridge reminded us 50 years ago, 'breeds hate'. Racism and Fascism are not dead: in several European countries, both are gaining ground. There have been riots in Germany, major disturbances in France, and in Austria the biggest vote since the Second World War for a neo-Fascist Party. These problems are not going to go away. The Irish Government, as I write, who are taking over the Union's presidency for the coming months, have said they want to put unemployment at the head of Europe's agenda. The credibility of the Union itself is at stake. It will not find a place in the hearts of European people unless it can tackle this problem effectively.

In Britain we have a Government who believe that the main steps required to get people back to work are to develop a buoyant economy with a healthy rate of growth, and to drive down wages and create a more flexible labour market in the jobs which are already lowest paid. More money is being invested in training, but still on a scale which is quite modest when compared with that of neighbouring countries. Most of the training, however, is for people who already have some qualifications. More recently, growing attention has also been paid to the social security system which is thought to deter people from taking jobs. Insurance benefits and income support for the unemployed are being replaced by the job-seekers' allowance, paid on much more restricted terms. With most of this the opposition agrees.

In short, the assumptions of those responsible for policy in this field are that the massive increase in unemployment which has come about over the past 20 years is due to economic changes, complicated by excessive wages and rigidity in work practices at the lower end of the labour market, and the effects of a social security system devised to meet the needs of earlier times when everyone who wanted to work could get a job. It follows that the country needs investment in new industries which will replace the old ones; training services to provide the skills which new employers demand; lower wages and a more 'flexible' labour market for those who are already low paid; and reforms of social security leading us towards something more like the American workfare system. That leaves little for local authorities and civic leaders to do about employment other than smooth the way for foreign investors who may be persuaded to locate their plants in Britain, and contract out their own services to entrepreneurs who will get this work done more cheaply by paying lower wages to the people who do it.

Local action

Taken one by one, there is a lot of truth in these assumptions. The long-term increase in unemployment levels *was* set going by worldwide economic trends. Our heavy reliance on social benefits provided through a household means-test *is* one of the factors making it difficult for people with several children to accept low-paid jobs. We *do* need an expanding economy offering rising incomes if we are to bring unemployment down. Otherwise we can at best only churn growing numbers of people on the margins of the labour force in and out of work. But this story is incomplete.

The people who believe that unemployment will disappear if only we have a growing, mainstream, private sector economy and some sharper goads to drive the unemployed back to work are often the same people who believe that homelessness will disappear if only we build some more houses and drive the dossers off the street, and that poor educational standards will disappear if only we put more money into the schools which get the best results and take a tougher line with those which do badly. They are less likely to say, however, that if only we promote the general health of the nation we can close all our hospitals, although that would be consistent with their views on other matters. The beliefs I have crudely summarised are most often found among people, secure in the mainstream of their society, who are looking out at those who have been excluded from it. Nice people, many of them; unaware that they speak the language of class war. They use words and phrases – 'the underclass', 'dossers', '*the* unemployed' (not 'people who are out of work') – which convey their sense that the excluded are animals of a different kind whose misfortune may well be their own fault.

To help people back into work we do indeed need a healthy, growing economy – just as we cannot do much for the homeless if there are severe, general scarcities of housing. Local civic leaders can work towards these broader objectives, but more must be done before the most excluded people can gain much from any of these policies; and that presents political difficulties. For, painful though everyone finds it to contemplate the plight of those who are out of work, this army of people conscripted to solve the problems of the economy suits the rest of us pretty well – at least in the short term. For other people, they really are a 'price worth paying' to bring the economy under control and to protect their jobs. The political arithmetic behind that statement is stark. The Dublin-based Economic and Social Research Institute calculated that in that country '50 per cent of the unemployment in the... ten years prior to 1987 had been carried by only 4 per cent of the population. The figure for the ten years to 1997 is likely to be worse' – or 'better', one might add, from the point of view of the employed.[3] The pattern in other countries of the European Union will not be very different.

The first thing needed, therefore, is to give people who are out of work a voice, at both national and local levels, which cannot be disregarded when policies and programmes of action for employment are being worked out. If that voice had been heard earlier and more loudly, we would not be suffering from the kinds of illusion I have briefly summarised and would not have made so many mistakes. This is not easy. The exclusion of unemployed people from the mainstream of their society starts with the political weaknesses which exclude them from the country's power structure.

In this chapter I turn first to people who are out of work, assuming that economic policies benefiting people in the mainstream of the economy are also being developed. I will then look at people in low-paid or precarious jobs, and finally at people who are unable to work.

People out of work

The people with the most difficult problems of all can be briefly described. They are those who have been out of work for a long time. These tend to be men – often younger men whose opportunities were devastated by earlier mass closures of manufacturing enterprises. Some of them never got a decent job. They tend to be heavily concentrated in areas where many others have no work – areas often regarded with fear and disapproval by the rest of the community. They usually have no marketable qualifications and will therefore need training of some sort if they are to stand a chance of finding work in the future. They may have several dependent children and they probably live in a household where no-one is working. This description does not provide an explanation of the causes of unemployment – they reach much further back into the history of our economy – but it provides an outline of the difficulties which must be surmounted by its victims and those who would help them.

Long-term unemployment is entered from a pool of people who have been more briefly out of work. They first fell into that pool from school, a training course, a sick bed or a job. They escape from long-term unemployment by getting a job, retiring, entering a training course, getting themselves reclassified as sick, or dying. Thus, to reduce long-term unemployment, we must help school-leavers, people who lose their jobs and people who have never been employed to move promptly into appropriate training or jobs. We must also provide extra support for people with caring responsibilities or special handicaps of various kinds to help them do this.

The cautionary word 'appropriate' is important. Training courses should offer prospects of suitable work to those who do well on them – which means they will not be cheap or brief. The work should provide skills, self-respect, a decent wage and opportunities to join a trade union. Employers, even if required to recruit from particular areas or groups of people, must be able to choose which individual to hire and have the authority to get rid of them if things go wrong.

Other solutions are more problematic. Should unemployed people be encouraged to retire? Only if the choice is a free one, not dictated by lack of alternatives. Should they be helped to emigrate? Only if they set off with good qualifications for work; it is a harsh world out there for ethnic minorities unless they can look after themselves in unwelcoming labour and housing markets.

To anyone who has been out of work for a long time in an area of widespread unemployment – in big public housing estates, for example, on the fringes of Glasgow, Sunderland, Liverpool and many other cities formerly described as industrial, or the more impoverished inner-city neighbourhoods of Manchester, and West and North Belfast – the most striking obstacle to finding a job is that there are very few of them within reach: that is to say, in places which they can afford to travel to, feel safe in and are likely to hear about. No matter what is done about training and other measures to improve the supply of labour, many people in such neighbourhoods will remain out of work unless we can get a lot more jobs into them, or into places within safe and easy reach of them.

It should be obvious that low-paid workers cannot afford to travel far. It may be less widely known that employers hiring low-paid workers rarely advertise in newspapers or job centres. They or their foremen need only let it be known that they will be taking people on and queues form, attracted through local gossip. People who live in families and in streets where few are working are unlikely to hear about these jobs. Such neighbourhoods get a bad reputation and employers who are able to take on only a few of those waiting in the queue may use an address in that area as a handy way of excluding people. Those who work comfortably behind desks may be unaware that youngsters in rougher areas – particularly young men – learn very early in life that they will not be safe if they venture beyond their own familiar streets. Such dangers are brutally obvious in Northern Ireland's working class Catholic and Protestant communities. But they are familiar too in many parts of Britain where people may be attacked because they are the wrong colour or regarded as intruders from the territory of another gang or group.[4]

The departments of central and local government responsible for economic development are prepared to spend millions attracting major investors who set up new factories in this country but, although they may try to attract them to the regions most in need of this help, they rarely ask investors to go to smaller-scale neighbourhoods where a lot of people are out of work or to recruit workers from these neighbourhoods. If they think about that question they probably assume that growing prosperity, wherever it begins, will eventually filter down to the poorest. Which is untrue. The unemployment trap closes pretty quickly on its victims. The longer people stay out of work, the less likely they are to get a job. In Northern Ireland in 1992, 44 per cent of those out of work for no more than 3 months moved out of the trap – back into work or training, or into retirement or some other status. But among those who had been out of work for 3–6 months, only 16 per cent left the unemployment register. By the time people had been out of work for 15 months or more, only 3 or 4 per cent were escaping from the trap.[5] Throughout the UK, those who have been out of work for more than a year are no longer of interest to employers unless they happen to have valuable qualifications. Meanwhile, people excluded from work are becoming increasingly concentrated in deprived ghettos where jobs are scarce. More must be done if they are to stand a chance of escaping from this trap.

Urban renewal

Cities in Western Europe and North America which have recently passed through difficult times often pin their hopes for recovery on property-led renewal schemes for the regeneration of their economies, mounting great rebuilding projects in long-neglected inner-city areas. The experience gained in places such as London's Isle of Dogs, where Britain's most ambitious scheme of this kind collapsed along with the demand for office space, has warned everyone against 'flagship projects' and the rhetoric of gung-ho politicians who promised 'cranes in the sky – jobs on the ground'. Those that live by the market shall perish by the market. Win or lose, these projects have often done little for the residents upon whom they have been dropped from a great height.[6] But more modest renewal programmes, conducted in close consultation with local residents, in which housing plays a central part have been more successful – as the experience of Belfast, Manchester and several Scottish cities shows.

Some people have tried to negotiate contracts with construction firms which oblige them to hire local labour. With careful preparation by someone who knows the industry well, opportunities for unemployed people can be won in that way. But the new-build end of construction is one of the hardest industries for people who have been out of work for a long time to gain a foothold in. The work is often brutally hard, and each trade stays on one site only for a few weeks – sometimes a few days. After that, the workers have to move to another which may be many miles away. The repair and maintenance branches of the industry offer more secure and steadily paced employment. It may be easier for local people to get this kind of work if community-based housing cooperatives are created, run by residents living in the houses concerned.

Renewal projects open up other possibilities too. Their housing, it should go without saying, must first meet the needs of the people who live in the areas to be renewed. But if, in addition, a larger or richer population is brought into the area, it should be remembered that they will need services which local people may be able to provide. It has been estimated that an economically active population of 1,000 people in the UK generates a demand for services, in the public and private sectors combined, which will employ on average about 400 people: doctors, teachers, hairdressers, television repair workers, panel beaters, refuse collectors and many more.[7] Regional planners are not much interested in that because demands for these services will fall somewhere in their region and they are content to let the market decide where. But, for those concerned with the prosperity and civility of life in small areas undergoing renewal, the capture of a few hundred jobs for a population including many unemployed people may be crucial. That will not be achieved unless these demands are foreseen, employers are approached, and unemployed people are trained and alerted to bid for the jobs. All this calls for skills in small-scale economic and social planning which are hard to find.

Small and middle-sized enterprises can be persuaded to set up in, and move to, even the least attractive areas, as repeated experiments have shown; and they do recruit some workers who were previously unemployed. But rarely have these recruits been unemployed for long. For readily understandable reasons, small enterprises employing only a handful of workers tend to pick people they know and trust: relatives and people who have worked with them before.[8]

Urban renewal should serve more extensive purposes too. If jobs are taken by people living in a dreary, run-down neighbourhood where few would choose to stay, then as soon as the newly enrolled workers have got on their feet and paid off their debts they move out, leaving an even more impoverished community behind them. To retain them and rebuild a self-sustaining local economy, jobs are not enough. They also need decent housing, good schools, attractive parks, well-stocked shops and lively places of entertainment.

Low pay

Many of the poorest people are in work for which low wages are paid. Their needs deserve equal attention with those of people who have no work. Those responsible for local economic development policies have usually regarded the attraction of large new plants built by foreign investors as their greatest triumphs. That should not lead us to forget that long-established local enterprises are more likely to employ local people with modest skills. The newcomers often demand higher skills and bring key staff with them – which contributes vigour to the mainstream economy and the society built on it, but may be less helpful for people with more limited prospects. For the less skilled, timely efforts to help local businesses to survive will often be more useful.

Civic leaders should also be asking whether the low wages which cause so much poverty should be tolerated. That question may prove embarrassing – revealing that some of the lowest paid workers are providing public services, often now contracted out to private enterprises. European law requires these employers to maintain the wages and contracts of workers transferred with the enterprise – a requirement sometimes flouted and now being challenged in the courts. But it does not prevent them from replacing their staff, when they leave, with lower-paid people who get lower pensions, shorter holidays, and less sick pay, maternity leave and other fringe benefits. These are often the workers who care for children, the old and the sick in homes, hospitals and similar settings. They cannot in the long run give more care than they receive. If they are neglected and exploited, the vulnerable people we ask them to look after will ultimately suffer. Civic leaders – politicians, officials, trade unionists, local media and business people – must find ways of tackling this problem. They will find it easier to do so if there are branches of independent, critical bodies such as the Low Pay Unit, Age Concern and the Child Poverty Action Group active in their region. If these are lacking, they should help to set them up.

Local authorities, hospitals and other public services have no power to require their contractors to pay any particular wage rate. If exploitation affects standards of care in visible ways, they can decline to use the services of the contractor concerned and ultimately drive him out of business. But that may take a long time. In the more flagrant cases it may become the duty of local citizens to do what some trade unions in the United States have done: to tell the neighbours and associates of employers who exploit their workers just what the offenders are doing – by demonstrating and leafleting in their streets, and at the doors of their churches and clubs. Market places provide opportunities for more than buying and selling.

Complementary economies

Wise doctors no longer talk about 'alternative medicine'. Accepting that the services provided by acupuncturists, aromatherapists and many others are often very helpful to their patients, they call them 'complementary medicine'. In the same way, non-profit community enterprises, credit unions, housing and food cooperatives, LETS systems which enable people to trade in currencies of their own invention, and similar projects should be thought of as a complementary economy and developed in conjunction with the mainstream economy.

Community enterprises have probably not been as successful as conventional businesses at surviving and prospering, but they have done more to bring people who have been out of work for a long time back into jobs. Some of these people then move on into mainstream employment.[9] They may find niches, neglected by mainstream enterprises, where they provide valuable services and create useful opportunities for work. Starting in Glasgow and now extending to many other places, the Wise Group of enterprises recruits people who have been out of work for a long time to training courses which enable them to provide insulation, landscaping, maintenance and other services. The 6-month training costs about £14,000 per worker, and only about half of the trainees gain lasting jobs. But that is a better score than most such projects achieve. Savings in benefits, coupled with reduced fuel costs for people whose homes have been insulated and less quantifiable social benefits (an improved environment, less crime, fewer people in prisons and hospitals…) make the programme worthwhile for some kinds of worker in some kinds of places.[10]

Money saved in a credit union and borrowed from it is usually spent in the mainstream economy. Other services often develop around these unions – food cooperatives, babysitting circles and so on. Their social contribution to life in some fairly bleak neighbourhoods has been as important as their economic contribution.[11]

Bargains struck in LETS currencies often include an element of conventional cash. Even if they do not, the practice of producing and exchanging goods and services and setting a value on their own labour helps to keep people in touch with the mainstream economy and makes it a bit easier to return to it when opportunities arise.[12] All these systems help to create local networks which are valuable in an increasingly private urban society where there are fewer and fewer activities that bring people together with their neighbours and fellow citizens.

Women, men and local planning

When people talk about getting more opportunities for work into a city, these jobs are often assumed to be for men. Any policy relying on the construction industry for jobs will have a bias of that kind, for it is an industry that mainly employs men. Unemployment rates recorded for women tend to be lower than those for men, but that may be only because so many women have no reason to record themselves as being unemployed, having no benefits to claim and little chance of finding work. Is there a conflict here between the interests of men and women?

At the lower end of the labour market there are families which must get two people into work – at least one of them in a reasonably secure job – if they are to be sure that they will be better off in work.[13] Any strategy for helping large numbers of men back into work must also create more jobs for women in the same places – and therefore more childcare to enable both to take up jobs and training courses.

The supply side

Some people familiar with local initiatives to help people into work will be surprised that I have said nothing so far about most of the things which they have done: providing education more closely linked to employers' needs and arranging 'compacts' with local employers prepared to recruit from selected schools, creating better training schemes, setting up 'job clubs' and other confidence-building projects which help people to write CVs and secure interviews, providing temporary work through grants to voluntary associations and others capable of taking on extra workers… and so on. All these measures are useful if there are more jobs available and if such initiatives are planned in ways which help people move into these jobs. But the evidence shows that in the places where unemployment is highest the people out of work already have more skills to offer and strive harder to find work than do their counterparts in places where fewer are unemployed.[14] When the Second World War created massive demands for labour throughout the United Kingdom, all the people who had been described a year or two before as irredeemably discouraged and unemployable went back to work without special confidence-building initiatives or help with the writing of CVs.

Although supply-side initiatives of these kinds do not tackle the root cause of unemployment, which is the lack of demand for less-skilled workers, they become very useful once progress is made in solving that problem. Even when jobs are available, there will be some people who need special help and support in dealing with employers before they can get work. They will include people who have disabilities of various kinds, and people who suffer discrimination because of their ethnic origin or because they have been in prison. But until the basic lack of jobs has been corrected, schemes of these kinds can only get a few extra people into jobs which would otherwise have been taken by their neighbours. That may spread fear of unemployment more widely through the lower reaches of the labour market and provoke hostility towards the people such schemes were intended to help.

Welfare rights

Many of the poorest people are unable, temporarily or permanently, to go to work: pensioners, people with severe disabilities and lone parents for example. For them, welfare rights will be of greater help than jobs. Several studies have shown that, if the aim is to raise incomes in a poverty-stricken area, the most effective way of spending public money for that purpose is to hire another welfare rights worker. In Scotland's more deprived neighbourhoods, such a person, working full time on advice and advocacy, will increase the incomes of local people by about £150,000 a year – nearly ten times the cost of employing the worker concerned. This money comes in the form of benefits to which people are already legally entitled (pensions, disability benefits, bus passes, free school meals, housing benefit and so on), funded mainly by national, rather than local, tax-payers. It is a concrete demonstration of a commitment to help poor people which confers credibility on civic leaders. A high proportion of the extra income secured in this way is spent on locally supplied goods and services – paying off debts, reducing rent arrears, buying food and clothing for children, and so on. Thus the multiplier effects are significant for local shopkeepers, landlords and other service industries.[15] More recent research shows that as discretion has been gradually squeezed out of the social security system and the take-up of disability benefits has improved, the real value of the benefits secured by welfare rights work has fallen but their money value remains much the same.

Rights mean more than money. Anyone who talks with people who have been out of work for a long time and others who are having a hard time will know that they are too often treated in off-hand or humiliating ways by the public service professions, their telephonists, receptionists and other officials. If they look defeated, that may be because they have been. Defeated and angry: 'What would you call a thousand dead housing officers?' goes a joke told on bleak housing estates: 'A start?' Doctors, teachers, social security officials, housing visitors and many others must learn to treat these people with courtesy and respect. In some services that will call for retraining programmes, much like those which have been required to improve race relations.

Conclusions

This chapter has dealt mainly with jobs and money. That is where the people who are having the hardest time would expect us to begin. They fall into three groups: those depending on low-paid jobs, those unable to work who depend mainly on social benefits from the state, and those who would like to work but have not got a job. I have dealt briefly with the first two groups, saying something about local action on low pay and on welfare rights.

Most of the chapter has focused on the third group – particularly those who have been out of work for a long time. Policies to create a healthy, expanding local economy are an essential foundation for any programmes to help those most severely excluded from the mainstream. By themselves, however, they will never bring everyone into work. Those who have been out of work for more than a year are completely excluded from the mainstream unless they have good qualifications. Unemployment among qualified workers goes up and down with the trade cycle. Among those without qualifications it is much less responsive to the economic climate, and among older unqualified workers it hardly responds at all.[16] That is partly due to the growing concentration of these people in deprived neighbourhoods which are of no interest to private investors.

Only the state, either as employer or as subsidiser of employers, can make an impact on this problem. A healthy private sector is important for many reasons: to attract people and investment, to develop skills and self-confidence throughout the mainstream economy, to generate tax revenues and general prosperity, to give life to the local community... but it will not bring those who have been out of work for a long time into jobs. Those who believe that we live in a 'trickle-down' economy in which any kind of activity will ultimately benefit the poorest people have failed to notice what is going on around them. We live in a 'trickle-*up*' economy which works in the opposite way. The Republic of Ireland has the fastest rate of economic growth in the

European Union. It also has the highest rate of really long-term unemployment. Its economic success has not solved this problem.

There is plenty of work to be done without trespassing on private sector businesses and driving other people out of their jobs – particularly in the places where jobs are most needed. Helping in the schools; providing nursery care, and many activities for youngsters during evenings, weekends and school holidays; cleaning and repairing streets, parks and buildings; caring for the aged and for people with physical and mental handicaps; running day centres for old people and people with handicaps of various kinds; developing sports, and mounting pop concerts and cultural occasions of various kinds: all can help to make to make the world a better place.[17]

Economic regeneration should be treated not as a separate strategy, but as a process firmly embedded within a broader, community-based programme of urban renewal. Women's needs for work deserve as much attention as those of men, partly because there are many families who cannot afford to leave the low but reasonably secure safety net of benefits unless there are to be two earners in the household.

I have stressed the importance of the complementary economy, or 'third sector', of community enterprises, credit unions, cooperatives and LETS, arguing that these projects should form a recognised part of economic development policies and should be particularly designed to help the more excluded people.

To develop programmes of all these kinds successfully we shall need capacities for social and economic planning at smaller scales than those at which planners and development workers usually operate. The local universities should play their part in the research and teaching required to train people for that task.

Employment, unemployment and the generation of jobs should figure in the performance standards which local authorities are now adopting as a measure of their achievements. Civic leaders who have built these measures into their own practice will be in a stronger position to tell their colleagues in national and European Parliaments that they should do likewise.

Technical expertise will not be sufficient to make a success of these programmes. For that we shall also need the expertise of those who actually experience unemployment and poverty. Unless their representatives play a recognised part in formulating and applying policies at national and local levels, we shall continue to misunderstand the problems and lack the necessary determination to act.

Many civic leaders will say that these proposals could work well if only they had the funds and the powers to do anything about them. And they would be more than half right. However, they can already do *something*: my proposals are all drawn from practice already to be seen somewhere in the United Kingdom. The resources for a more ambitious programme will only be found if those who know what is going on at grass-roots level and know what could be done about it continue to bombard the national and international leaders of their parties and anyone else who will listen with this information. Some day, the people trying to mobilise action that will bring down unemployment will gain a hearing. The European Union and many democratic regimes within it will fall apart if they fail. Much of the action then needed will have to be taken at the local scale by people who understand the infinite variety of local problems and possibilities.

The costs of such policies, although massive, are no heavier than those which already arise from neglecting the problem. It has been calculated that to get people off benefits in large numbers calls for a wage that is £50 a week more than their benefits.[18] (I am sceptical about that reasoning: if the jobs offer self-respect, worthwhile work and reasonable security, I believe most of those out of work would seize such opportunities, even for lower pay. But the argument can be rephrased thus. Our social benefits are so low that a wage for a full-time job which was not at least £50 higher would be outrageously exploitative – so let us accept the figure.) Making realistic allowances for the costs of materials and administration, this suggests that it would be possible to get 10,000 people back to work for £80 or £90 million a year – which would be no more than the average sum spent on social security payments for these people, together with tax lost when they are not earning wages – about £9,000 a year each.

Such calculations do not solve the problem, but they do make clear that it is essentially a political, not an economic, problem. It is a question about how to reach agreement within our society that the task must be tackled, not a question of whether we have the resources to tackle it.

Notes

1   Surveys producing such findings in which I and my colleagues have been involved were made in Glasgow's East End and the Gorbals, in Manchester's

Hulme estate, and elsewhere. See, for example, David Donnison and Alan Middleton (eds), *Regenerating the Inner City*, London, Routledge, 1987.

2   For a fuller account, see Ken Coates *et al.*, *Dear Commissioner. An Exchange of Letters*, London, Spokesman, 1996.

3   Quoted in *If You Think the Economy is Working – Ask Someone Who Isn't*, Dublin, Irish National Organisation of the Unemployed, 1996.

4   For an account of the ways in which young people's sense of territory develops, see Simon Anderson *et al.*, *Cautionary Tales*, Edinburgh, University of Edinburgh Centre for Criminology, 1990.

5   Graham Gudgin and Geraldine O'Shea (eds), *Unemployment for Ever?*, Belfast, Northern Ireland Economic Research Centre, 1993, p. 91.

6   For an account of property-led renewal, and the Isle of Dogs' experience in particular, see Nicholas Deakin and John Edwards, *The Enterprise Culture and the Inner City*, London, Routledge, 1993.

7   Nick Buck *et al.*, *The London Employment Problem*, Oxford, Clarendon Press, 1986, pp. 52 and 97.

8   For evidence on these points, see Andrew McArthur, 'Jobs and incomes', in David Donnison and Alan Middleton (eds), *Regenerating the Inner City*, London, Routledge, 1987, p. 88.

9   Andrew McArthur, 'An unconventional approach to local economic development: the role of community business', *Town Planning Review*, **57**(1), 1986, pp. 87–100.

10 Alastair Grimes, *Unemployment: A Modest Proposal*, London, Employment Policy Institute, Economic Report 10, May 1996. See also Dan Finn *et al.*, 'Making benefits work', *Local Work*, **69**, 1996, Manchester, Centre for Local Economic Strategies.

11 Andrew McArthur *et al.*, 'Credit unions and low-income communities', *Urban Studies*, **30**(2),1993, pp. 399–416.

12 See Peter Lang, *LETS Work*, Warminster, LETSLINK UK, 1994.

13 The problem is discussed by David Donnison in *Long-Term Unemployment in Northern Ireland*, Belfast, Northern Ireland Council for Voluntary Action, 1996, p. 31.

14 For a review of this evidence and the arguments for getting jobs into the right places, see David Webster, *Home and Workplace in the Glasgow Conurbation*, Glasgow, Glasgow City Housing, 1994.

15 David Donnison and Alan Middleton (eds), *Regenerating the Inner City*, London, Routledge, 1987, p. 281. Since this study was made, the Chief Welfare Rights Officers of the Strathclyde and Lothian Regions, shortly before their authorities' demise, made studies producing closely similar figures.

16 For Northern Ireland data on unemployment rates by age and qualification, 1981–93, see Northern Ireland Economic Council, *Employment Creation in Northern Ireland*, Belfast, 1994, p. 20.

17 For further information on local demands for labour in public services see C. Trinder, *Full Employment. The Role of the Public Sector*, London, TUC/Employment Policy Institute, 1994; and Mike Geddes and Madeleine Wahlberg, *The Value of Public Employment*, Coventry, Local Government Centre, Warwick Business School, 1996.

18 David Donnison, *Long-Term Unemployment in Northern Ireland*, Belfast, Northern Ireland Council for Voluntary Action, 1996, p 64.

Chapter 7

Safety

Introduction

In places where a lot of people are having a hard time, surveys questioning them about their hopes for the future show that safety for themselves and their families usually comes second only to opportunities for earning a living in a decent job. That may not always have been so. National surveys made over a long period show that anxiety about crime has probably increased more than crime itself. The proportion of people in Britain saying they feel 'very worried' about various kinds of crime increased significantly between 1992 and 1994.[1] I shall explore briefly the reasons for that important change in public feeling and its implications. It compels anyone who plays a part in public affairs to say where they stand on these matters.

Next I shall consider who suffers most anxiety, and what threats to their security people are most worried about. This is a chapter about safety, not only about crime. Different dangers call for different responses.

Turning to crime, which is a source of many of those dangers, I consider its relationship to the conditions in which people live, and the responses which can be made to it at a local scale of action. The whole argument is then very briefly summarised in the concluding section of the chapter. But, first of all, we should pause to reflect on the extraordinary things happening in the United States.

The American disaster

More people seem to be growing more worried about their safety. If their concern helped politicians to mount effective policies for improving matters, that would be no bad thing. But in the United States these anxieties have led to mounting anger against offenders – a veritable demonisation of them – and to savagely punitive policies which send growing numbers of people to prison for very long periods. That has led the Americans into a major disaster: a very expensive policy which is devastating other more valuable programmes, a policy which has failed but is now very difficult to reverse; too many people have staked too much of their credibility on it. Britain frequently follows American trends a decade or so later, and there are signs that this is happening again over crime, as Figure 7.1, showing imprisonment rates in different European countries, suggests. So it is very important to note the key facts before we go further down this road.

- No experiment in public policy has ever been so vigorously and completely carried through as the American adoption of tougher penal policies – and particularly their growing use of imprisonment. The numbers of prisoners in Federal and State prisons in the United States rose from 196,000 in 1974 to 1,100,000 in 1995 – more than a fivefold increase. Together with those in local prisons, the Americans have now incarcerated more than one and a half million people. This and most of the following points come from Elliott Currie, one of the USA's most distinguished criminologists.[2]
- The policy has massive implications for race relations: the increase in the numbers of prisoners has been most rapid among black and Hispanic men and is focused upon places where their communities are most heavily concentrated.
- Federal and State spending on prisons and other 'correctional activities' has increased enormously, and most of this money has, in effect, been taken from training schemes, schools, welfare and other services, which were among America's most effective crime-prevention programmes.
- 'The prison boom has... changed what we mean by government. It has made the prison a looming presence in the lives of America's poor... '.[3] What has sometimes been called the 'war against crime' is also a war of oppression against ethnic minorities. In Baltimore – to take one example – a majority of young men are black and a majority of those are now in prison, on probation or on parole. Yet, between 1970 and 1994, the city's

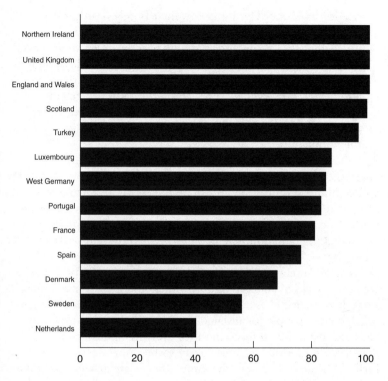

Source: Taken from p. 61 of Gordon Barclay (ed.), *A Digest of Information on the Criminal Justice System*, London, Home Office, 1991.

FIGURE 7.1   Prison populations: an international comparison. Rate per 100,000 recorded crimes.

homicide rate had increased by 75 per cent since this experiment began.

- These policies are not intended to work towards closer understanding, integration, reconciliation or mutual respect between offenders and the rest of the community – the traditional objectives of a liberal democratic penal policy. They are intended to punish, to frighten, to deter, and generally to distance and distinguish offenders from others who are regarded as law-abiding citizens. They are archaic.
- These policies have not succeeded in reducing crime. There is no link between trends in crime and high rates of imprisonment in

relation to crime. The argument, increasingly heard in Britain, that American experience shows that 'prison works' is not true. It is usually based on data for carefully selected cities, time periods and types of offence, and on a highly imaginative use of figures for the costs and savings resulting from changes in crime rates. It also neglects the evidence of 'victimisation' studies, relying instead on dubious official statistics of reported crime rather than the less encouraging experience of representative samples of the population.

Yet there can be no doubt that these policies are popular in the United States and probably in Britain too. With so much evidence to show that they do not prevent crime there must be other motives at work. They are, in effect, America's main – and very expensive – way of managing unemployment and providing support for the unemployed. The scale of the programme needs to be stressed. Two per cent of American males of working age are now in prison. There are more blacks in jail than in universities, and it costs much more to keep them there. These policies also satisfy the widespread demands of frightened people for revenge. For white people disturbed by the advances made by ethnic minorities over the last 25 years, the fact that these minorities are most likely to be imprisoned may provide further reassurance. Much the same motives are at work in Britain, and some of those who should know better – politicians on both sides, newspaper editors and journalists – are playing to them. When our Prime Minister, paving the way for his Home Secretary to go down this road, said, 'It is time to understand a little less and to condemn a little more', he was warmly applauded in many quarters.

Why do we worry?

So why are people frightened and vengeful? There has indeed been a long-term increase in crime – for many rather obvious reasons. There is far more to steal: television sets and videos in homes which, 60 years ago, had little in them that would have been worth taking; cheque books and credit cards in handbags and pockets which would once have scarcely been worth rifling. Things worth stealing are far more accessible than they used to be: cars left on the street with mobile phones and radios in them, and goods displayed, unsupervised, in self-service shops. There are more laws to break: about parking, speed limits, insurance contributions and much else. An increasingly mobile, urban society offers greater privacy and independence, but also more anonymity, less pressure for conventional behaviour and greater uncertainty about moral standards. The liberation of women from restrictive conventions of the past – their greater freedom to work, to speak to strangers, to go to pubs and to go on holiday alone – may have deprived them of some of the protection once conferred by seclusion and male inhibition.

Some of the rising trend in crime figures is due to increased reporting rather than a real growth in crime. People are prepared to protest and to seek the help of the police about many things – theft and burglary, rape and sexual abuse, violence and drunkenness – which used to be concealed, disregarded or dealt with in other ways: not necessarily better ways. The spread of insurance obliges many to report losses, not because they expect redress through the law but in order to make an insurance claim. The rising figures of reported crime may nevertheless alarm people. The fear of crime has increased faster than crime itself, and this has sometimes been attributed to the sensational treatment given to frightening forms of crime by the media. But the media operate in a market. If they devote space to news of this kind, their readers and viewers presumably want them to do so.

That may be because we live in an increasingly private society in which we are less likely than our predecessors to get to know our neighbours. We drive to work, to school and to the shops in our cars instead of walking or queuing for the bus; we shop once a week in vast, impersonal supermarkets instead of making more frequent visits to gossip with neighbours in the local corner shop; we shelter behind front doors and garden fences instead of meeting our neighbours on the tenement stairs; and we are more likely to bring beer home in a six-pack to drink in front of the television set, and less likely to drink with friends in the pub. Traffic hazards and other dangers mean that our children are much less likely than their parents were to be allowed to roam the streets, and we have all become less likely to go to church, to political meetings, to street markets, cinemas, music halls and other public places where we might get to know our fellow citizens, or at least to feel at home in their presence. The characters in television programmes like *Neighbours* become more familiar to us than our real neighbours, and the sense that we are members of some larger civic society fades. The sense that there is a growing social distance between the average car-driving, house-buying citizen and the people without cars and with no opportunity to buy their own homes is real – and well founded – at least in terms of income differences and the growing tendency of these people to live in separate neighbourhoods.

Paradoxically, the barriers we have erected between us and the rest of the world mean that we feel more exposed to strangers. In country places it may be different, but in the cities where most of us live the people in the street, the supermarket, the next car fuming at the traffic lights and the queues in the social security office are all likely to be completely unknown to us. And strangers are potentially menacing. Fear then becomes cumulative: if others fear us, they are more likely to behave in ways which make us fear them.

The growing number of elderly people in the population may also increase anxiety levels because it is older people – and particularly those living in inner city areas – who are most likely to feel unsafe. That is not because they are most likely to be attacked – it is young men in these neighbourhoods who are most likely to become victims of violence – but because they feel most vulnerable. Ethnic minorities – particularly Asians – feel more worried about crime and more unsafe in the streets at night than do white people, as Figure 7.2 shows.

Findings like these led many to believe that fear of crime is a problem in itself, only loosely related to the real risks involved. Those most afraid of it tend to be worried about a lot of other things too. Perhaps they are just anxious people, needing reassurance rather than protection? But more recent studies tend to discredit this rather paternalistic view. They show that anxiety is fairly closely linked to vulnerability, which is different from risk; they show that a lot of disturbing things happen to women owing to male behaviour which often falls short of recordable crime; and they show that worried people often have a lot to worry about – poverty, insecure jobs, illness in the family, and responsibilities for children, as well as living in rather intimidating neighbourhoods. So people's feelings must be taken seriously.

Moral standards

Before considering how to respond to them, we should frankly confront John Major's admonition to understand less and confront more. What should we make of that? Crime is behaviour which damages other people, showing no respect for fellow human beings.

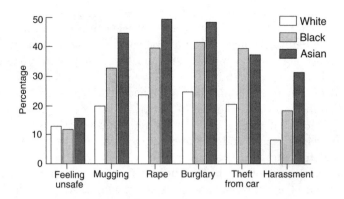

Source: Figure 2.9 from Michael Hough, *Anxiety About Crime: Findings from the 1994 British Crime Survey,* London, Home Office Research Study 147, 1995, p. 18.

FIGURE 7.2 **Variations in anxiety by ethnic origin.**
Percentage feeling 'very worried' or 'very unsafe'.

So it should of course be condemned and – more important – reduced. But that means we also need to understand it. We cannot choose between the two reactions: they have to advance together.

If my analysis in the previous paragraphs is correct, any response to crime and the fear of it must include an attempt to rebuild a stronger sense of community – greater confidence between citizens of the same town, and the people living in the same street or block of flats. This is the setting which creates and sustains the culture within which moral standards take root and evolve.

Any initiative of that kind must include action which returns powers to a democratically accountable local government. The systematic transfer of local government functions and powers to nominated, unaccountable, specialist bodies with no responsibility for the welfare of a city as a whole has been a major obstacle for anyone trying to strengthen civic culture and identity. I come back to that point in a later chapter.

People's places of work have been a major influence on behaviour. If their employers treat them as expendable labour, to be casually hired and fired as demand fluctuates, we should not expect them to feel much loyalty to the enterprises in which they work. If people have no work at all, they have no opportunity to participate in one of the principal settings where standards of behaviour have in the past been forged and passed on to succeeding generations. Secure jobs with good employers are a basic requirement for crime prevention.

We must deflate the pomposity of so much talk about crime. Moral standards are important, but we are all involved in them. Crime is not 'out there', among an 'underclass' of menacing strangers. In Britain, one man in three is found guilty of a 'standard list offence' before the age of 35, and, if driving offences are added, the great majority of men have been found guilty of offences by then.[4] For every transaction in the 'informal' economy where goods and services are exchanged for cash out of the back pocket, there are customers as well as suppliers. For many illicit workers concealing earnings from the social security and tax offices there are illicit employers – probably paying low wages and no insurance contributions. Surveys show that most people believe that most people steal things from work – and since making occasional telephone calls on private matters from your employer's phone is theft, that is certainly true of most university teachers, civil servants and other office workers. Most people say they would keep money picked up in the street if there were no danger of being found out.[5] We all live in a grey world of uncertain virtue.

How we behave in that world depends heavily on the culture in which we live, the opportunities it affords and the pressures it imposes on us. There are always a few individuals who carve out their own destiny without much regard to others' expectations. But for most of us it is harder to keep to the speed limit when every other driver around us is exceeding it, to stay sober in a drunken party, to protest at racist or sexist jokes when everyone else is roaring with laughter at them. When your infant child comes tearfully home saying, 'I don't want to go to school any more: there's a boy in the playground who keeps hitting me', how do you respond? Do you say, 'Keep away from him, and if he does it again talk to the teacher. I'm sure she'll sort it out'? Or do you say, 'If he does it again, roll your fingers up into a hard ball like this, and hit him so hard that he leaves you alone'? Your choice will probably depend on your guesses about the community in which he has to survive, and about the character of its leaders, the teachers. It is hard to be non-violent in a violent world.

Take a more complex example. I once worked in a housing estate where the flats had underfloor electric heating systems so expensive to use that no mother living on income support payments could keep her child warm, healthily fed and clothed without running into debt.

Most of the mothers living in these flats were lone parents living on income support. Some of them, thanks to the help of friends and relatives and to their own remarkable house-keeping skills, cared beautifully for their children and kept within the law. But it is not surprising that the estate had a rather large number of illicitly bypassed electricity meters, a lot of women who were concealing part-time earnings – and part-time men – from social security officials, a thriving market in drugs, and, in the shopping centre, a good deal of shoplifting. All of which is crime. And all of it will tend to increase as the recently announced reduction in benefits for lone parents begins to bite. This estate also had a lot of children with bronchial troubles, running ears and other signs of poverty. Since even the families who avoided all these things depended on friends and neighbours who were involved in crime, few people in these streets were prepared to speak to police officers or anyone else in authority. They would lose their friends if they did so. Thus what could be called a criminal subculture developed. It was criminal for sure: but was it as wicked as that kind of jargon suggests? If the alternative to this lifestyle is to see your child underfed or freezing cold, would that be better? For whom?

Morality in this neighbourhood was not being abandoned; it was changing. These were resolute and loyal women – honest in their fashion. Keeping their children healthy and happy became their first obligation – an obligation well understood by their friends and neighbours. If we deplore such a life – as these women certainly did – then we must change the circumstances which create it. If we do nothing, we are not entitled to preach sermons at those involved in it. Nor would there be any point in doing so.

This does not mean that personal choices are impossible or personal example unimportant. They can exert a big influence – particularly when they come from the top. In the United States the Treadway Commission, reporting on financial fraud, stated that the 'most important factor' reducing fraud is 'a visible interest by management and directors in ethical behaviour and strong controls', which will 'permeate the organisation and limit the risk that fraud will occur'.[6] The Nolan Committee had similar things to say about Standards in Public Life.

Towards a strategy

Before turning to consider action we must clarify aims and purposes. This is a book about social divisions, inequality and hardship. So why write a chapter about safety and crime? Not because 'the perishing and dangerous classes' – as our Victorian forebears used to call the poor – are mainly responsible for crime. But because people having a hard time say they are worried about these things and want something done about them; because poorer people and ethnic minorities are more often victims of crime and 'incivility' of various kinds than richer white people are, and such things happen more often in the neighbourhoods where they live; because crime and the fear of it play important parts in dividing society by encouraging hostile, uncaring, punitive feeling between groups, neighbourhoods and social classes. And because influential people in this country are already tempted to follow the American lead which excludes and demonises poorer people, lone parents and ethnic minorities, and diverts resources from the services on which they depend to programmes which oppress and humiliate them.

When, a few years ago, Scotland's Central Regional Council asked their citizens what they most wanted of their local government, greater security came high among the responses. Other authorities which had found the same pattern of opinion had focused at once upon crime, but the Region made another survey asking questions about safety. What were people most worried about? The answers showed a wide variety of fears, varying from place to place. In some a polluting industry was the main source of anxiety. In others it was traffic dangers. 'Galloping horses' was the answer given in one village. 'You're pulling our leg!' was the Region's first response to this – but no: there was a riding school down the road. Crime and 'incivilities' – noise, graffiti, litter and so on – often ranked high, but these problems, too, varied from place to place. A conference was called to discuss the problems of each area, and to mobilise the support of local communities and the help of services best equipped to tackle these problems – public health, traffic management, schools, housing, parks, refuse collection and so on.

I tell this story as a reminder that we must never assume, when people worry about their safety, that we know what the problem is. We must start by listening to them and gaining their help in working out solutions. Listening to the people who are said to be the source of the problem is as important as listening to those who feel themselves to be innocent victims. Another example from this Region may help.

The police were receiving a steadily growing number of telephone calls from people complaining about disturbances on the streets. The callers were typically old people, living in the less popular public housing estates, who complained about young people drinking, shouting, breaking down garden fences, obstructing entry to local shops and generally behaving in intimidating ways. The police responded to all these calls but usually found that no offence was being committed, so they could only tell the youngsters to move on – which set telephones ringing from further down the road. When these calls reached 5,000 a year they resolved to look for more constructive responses.

One of these was called the Crosstalk project. First the complainers are invited to a meeting with their local councillor, a local police officer and a community worker from the Chief Executive's department. The three listen for about half an hour to a torrent of anger: the youngsters are 'animals', 'disgusting', should be 'kicked out'. There should be 'a policeman on the beat' all the time. Then the official visitors say, each in their own words, that they understand how angry these elderly people must be, but they can offer them no extra police, no new resources... the problem is *theirs*. But they may be able to help them to work on it, as others have done in similar places. Another meeting is then arranged. This brings older residents and youngsters together with the same councillor and officials, led by a young actor from a well-known Scottish drama company who has been brought in to help. He plays lively party games with them which compel the old and the young to give up sitting on opposite sides of a circle glowering at each other, to get thoroughly mixed up and to learn the first names of everyone around the circle. There's a good deal of laughter and everyone gradually relaxes. Then old and young are put together again in small groups of their own age and told to form 'living statues' – clustered figures representing 'youth' and 'old age' – each portraying the other age group. Next they are asked to 'turn the volume up' and talk about their stereotypes of the other age group. Questions posed in this way are discussed: 'Who thinks cannabis should be legal?', 'Why?'

After an hour of this, the councillor and officials, who have been vigorously playing these games along with everyone else, begin talking to the whole group, reminding them that in future the youngsters will still be on the streets and some of them will still get drunk. But they will know the old people and appreciate how intimidating their behaviour can seem to them; and the old people will know the youngsters and appreciate that no-one is going to hurt them. 'Shall we see how things go?'

These meetings have brought the numbers of telephone calls a long way down. The police recognise that they will have to do the same thing again from time to time but believe this will be a more efficient way of using their time than chasing telephoned complaints. Similar mediation schemes have been developed in many other places, with help from NACRO, SACRO (its Scottish counterpart), Crime Concern, the Safe Neighbourhoods Unit and other bodies. The most successful of them call for the training of well-respected local people as mediators, so that when the immediate problems have been resolved the community is left better equipped to tackle such problems in future.

Different tactics will be needed in different places, but the principles of the Crosstalk strategy may still have something to offer. Listen to the people who are frightened. Get to those who make the trouble and listen to them too: unless their behaviour begins to change, the problems can only be shifted from street to street. Bring both groups together in ways which defuse tension and make it easier for them to talk honestly to each other. Where community has broken down, help local people to recreate it. When things go wrong, help them to recognise that the problem is theirs. Others can help them to tackle it, but there is no big daddy in the wings who can stride in and tell everyone to be good boys. Civic leaders wise and brave enough to tell their constituents these things play a crucial part in the story. But it is not every kind of conflict which can be addressed in this way: party games with an actor will not prevent knee-capping in Belfast or battles for drug-dealing territory in Manchester's Moss Side.

We should try to understand what life is like in places where there is a lot of crime, and a lot of poor people who have been excluded from the mainstream of their society. A diffuse kind of anger washes around many of these neighbourhoods – and with good reason. If you doubt that, imagine yourself to be an 18-year-old with no qualifications that count for anything, no prospects of ever getting a decent job, little prospect of being able to support a family or of finding a mate capable of doing so, no prospect of ever driving your own car or motor bike or even your employer's van, unable even to walk to the other end of the housing estate without exposing yourself to the danger of abuse and attack from the youngsters who live beyond the frontiers of your territory. Exclusion is not just a figure of speech.

People cannot go on being angry for long. As individuals and as whole communities they tend to move out of anger in one of three directions, as illustrated in Figure 5.1. Many become depressed and eventually sink into apathy. Nothing matters much any more. Knock on their doors and invite them to meetings about the future of their estate, invite them to their doctor's surgeries for free screening tests to protect them from life-threatening disease, invite them to the local school pageant... they don't come. They may sink further into dependency on alcohol, into mental breakdown and domestic violence, which tends to rise when incomes fall. They may become very expensive to their city through the costs of illness, family break-up and child neglect. But they do not make trouble for those who manage the city's affairs. They don't turn out for demonstrations and sit-ins or ask rude questions from the back of the hall. And they certainly don't riot.

Others move out of anger into minor delinquency and may eventually go on to more serious crime and violence. They may steal from shops, and break into cars, homes and local workshops; if they become seriously hooked on expensive drugs they may have to work harder at these things to feed their habit; they may begin to deal in drugs and to fight over territory for that purpose. They may find a place in criminal 'industries' – money-lending and the policing of repayments to lenders, extortion, pimping... . These people cause a lot of trouble to their neighbours, to local enterprises and the authorities responsible for law enforcement, and many of them eventually become residents of our very expensive prisons. But they don't disturb the power structure in any way. Indeed, for politicians who gain a reputation – deserved or not – for being 'tough on crime', they may be an electoral asset.

A third group mobilise and organise themselves – and sometimes their communities too – for purposeful action. They may get some training, find jobs and eventually move out to more attractive neighbourhoods. They may, with their neighbours, protest, march, sit-in and nominate candidates for local elections. They may set up tenants' associations, housing cooperatives, drama groups, youth clubs... . Some of these people are a thorn in the flesh for those who hold power. They compel them to come to meetings, held at unsocial hours, which go on much too long, and expose them to aggressive questioning and noisy protests. But they may also set going all sorts of creative things which would never have found a place within the conventional bureaucratic system. There are many examples. The Women's College and its offshoots, set up in Castleford by miners' wives after the collapse of the miners' strike, was a celebration of the human capacity to mobilise in face of disaster. The marvellous mosaic, made by local people, which is spread along two walls in Glasgow's Easterhouse estate is another. The credit unions, now being set up at a rate of about one a week in many of the poorest neighbourhoods of Britain, provide further examples.[7]

These are not the only responses available. In Belfast and other neighbourhoods of Northern Ireland, where people are united by culture and an ideology of revolt, exclusion from the wider society has produced what amounts to a rising which provokes counter-risings in other communities within the same cities. These share some of the characteristics of more creative mobilisations (the political ideology, the mutual support, the community enterprises and gaelic classes) and some of the characteristics of the delinquent option (extortion, robbery, money laundering, knee-capping, terror), but they should not be equated with either. Riots elsewhere in the United Kingdom have occasionally had a brief flash of the same purposeful anger – but very brief.

Sometimes it is difficult to decide which of these responses is the dominant one. When tenants in the Hulme housing estate threw bags of cockroaches across the counters of the Housing Department which had failed, despite all their protests, to get the vermin out of their flats, some said that it was protest and others called it delinquency – depending on which side of the counter they were standing.[8]

These are some of the conclusions I draw from this analysis. We need to understand individual and collective motives, and the interaction between them. By themselves, neither psychology nor sociology are enough. People do not only respond in negative ways to hardship. They may also respond bravely and creatively. Their capacity to seize creative options depends both on the character of the local community – its traditions, stability, leadership and much else – and on the response they get from people in the power structure. I have been moved by the number of community activists who have, somewhere in their family, a radical tradition to draw on – a father who was an active trade unionist, an uncle who fought in Spain – and concerned that the spread of unemployment, and the decay of trade unions and radical movements mean that these traditions of solidarity and collective action may be dying. Meanwhile, unless they are given continuing advice and support by one or two politicians and officials, community-based projects in deprived areas rarely prosper for long. If civic leaders respond destructively – giving no straight answers, postponing meetings, sending to each one a different official who never has authority to decide anything – they can drive people back into angry cynicism and depression from which it will be harder, next time, to escape. Civic leaders and their officials play vital roles. They need to understand that anger and delinquency are only two responses within a larger array of reactions to exclusion, and not the most destructive ones. People cannot move out of depression and apathy except through anger. Once angry, they may be capable of moving on to more hopeful things. Delinquency is painful for a lot of people, but its perpetrators are at least alive – capable of doing something for themselves – and if people with something more constructive to offer can get alongside them they may move on to more creative things.

Local action

Faced with crime and frightening behaviour, people tend – individually, collectively and in our Parliament – to call for the police. (It probably goes back to childhood: 'Dad, Dad – there's a boy hitting me! Come and help me!') Public debate about crime leads quickly to discussion of policing, courts, prisons and the whole clanking penal apparatus. That debate is often couched in terms of a militaristic kind which distance us from the criminals and make it impossible to consider the causes of their behaviour. Ministers, opposition spokesmen, editors, pundits of every kind, call for 'crack-downs' in the 'war against crime', more police 'in the front line', 'toughness' of every kind, to be directed against enemies demonised as 'squeegee merchants', 'aggressive beggars', 'muggers', 'animals', 'beasts' – a rising scream of hate.

Before engaging in this Victorian war dance of vengeance, let us reflect on one figure. Of all the offences committed in the United Kingdom this year, only three in a hundred will lead to a conviction in court.[9] Figure 7.3, derived from the British Crime Survey, which starts by seeking the experience of victims of crime, shows how few offences resulted in police cautions or court convictions. The average criminal tends to have a rather poorly developed capacity for planning his future and great confidence that he will escape the consequences of his actions. At this rate of conviction he will probably be justified – at least for a long time. Police and the whole criminal justice system play very important parts in helping our society to manage crime and its consequences, after it has taken place, but they do very little to prevent it. Those who argue that higher conviction rates would be a more effective deterrent than harsher punishments are right – but only because harsher punishment is so ineffective. We can scarcely expect these rates to double. Even if that impossible feat was achieved, a 6 per cent chance of conviction would not deter many of those undeterred by the present rate. So, to reduce crime, other strategies are needed.

The next chapter deals with the parts that mainstream services of every kind can play in resisting and reducing the social divisions which play major parts in causing many kinds of crime. Here I lay out a broad strategy which provides a framework for that discussion. It deals briefly with: (a) the labour market, (b) urban regeneration, (c) policies for family support, (d) opportunities for ex-offenders, and (e) support for potential and actual victims of crime.

The strategy must start with the labour market. Nine out of ten crimes deal with property – burglary, theft, stealing from cars and so on.[10] These crimes have, since 1970, been related to long-term unemployment among young men. The relationship is not a simple matter of cause and effect. High unemployment erodes stability, social order and family life in many ways. Property crimes are also related to changes in consumption: as consumption falls, people are more likely to steal. The quality of jobs matters too; poor-quality jobs are not much better than unemployment as preventers of crime, and there are more of them about when unemployment is high. Before 1970, when there was less long-term unemployment and fewer people without hope for the future, the relationship between crime and unemployment was less clearly marked.[11] Crimes of violence account for only 6 per cent of British crimes. Those related to alcohol increase in more prosperous times, but domestic violence moves in the opposite direction, rising when incomes are falling.

The strategies for improving economic opportunities which were discussed in the previous chapter will exert the most powerful immediate influence on crime rates. People who claim to be working to reduce crime without doing anything about unemploy-

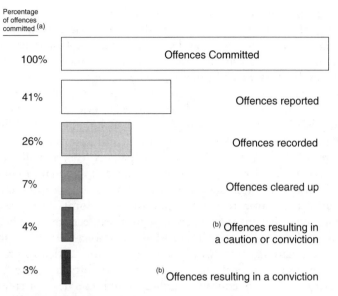

Percentage of offences committed (a)

100%   Offences Committed

41%   Offences reported

26%   Offences recorded

7%   Offences cleared up

4%   (b) Offences resulting in a caution or conviction

3%   (b) Offences resulting in a conviction

(a) Criminal damage; theft of a motor vehicle; theft from a motor vehicle; theft in a dwelling; bicycle theft; burglary; wounding; robbery; sexual offences; and theft from the person

(b) Estimates include additional findings of guilt at any court appearance and offences taken into consideration

Source: P. Mayhew *et al.*, *The 1988 British Crime Survey*, Home Office Research Study No. 111, London, Home Office, 1989; and *Criminal Statistics, England and Wales*, London, HMSO, 1989.

FIGURE 7.3   What happens to offenders. Attrition within the Criminal Justice System

ment or the quality of jobs at the lower end of the labour market are, at best, ignorant.

Policies which help to stabilise life and improve services in hard-pressed communities with high crime rates can exert an important influence on safety and crime. The programmes mounted for these purposes under the Single Regeneration Budget and the Scottish Partnership Schemes are an advance on previous schemes of this kind – the Estate Action projects, Housing Action Trusts, Enterprise Zones, Educational Priority Areas and so on – because they involve more services and a somewhat more determined attempt has been made to involve local people. But they still focus on a few fairly small patches of the map for limited periods of time. More extensive and lasting programmes will be needed. They should include steps, taken in consultation with local people, to make neighbourhoods safer. I shall develop this theme further in the next chapter.

The quality of family life plays a major part in determining how safe our society will be. There is a great deal of evidence to show that family breakdown is related to delinquency, but the relationship is not a simple one: breakdown is apt to be related to unemployment and poverty which make it harder for parents to cope with crises. Lone parents are far more likely to be poor, but children in families with step-parents often do less well than those in lone parent families. Some of the action to which these findings point – such as the restoration of benefit cuts which have penalised teenagers and helped to bring about an increase in homelessness among them – has to be taken at a national level. But local action will be needed to provide the consistent support for families in difficulty and the good childcare, pre-school education and community services for children and young people which have proved cost-effective in reducing crime. This theme, too, will be taken up again in the next chapter.

Probation, prison and penal services in general do not have a very encouraging record as preventers of crime. Meanwhile, parts of the prison experience which do seem to offer hope – such as the education service – are being squeezed out by a system compelled, as numbers increase, to focus on quantity rather than quality. More important still are the opportunities open to prisoners when they have completed their sentences. Training and placement schemes for ex-offenders are difficult to extend while jobs are scarce for so many other people. But they must be given high priority by employers and by any administration – central or local – which is seriously determined to reduce crime. Northern Ireland has the most urgent version of this problem. More than half its large prison population now consists of people sentenced for 'political' offences related to the troubles of the last quarter century. If the peace process is resumed, all of these prisoners will be hoping for release. The opportunities for work and a normal life then open to them will go far to determine how long the process lasts.

This analysis, like most discussion of crime, has dealt mainly with offenders – potential, current and recent – so it is important to remember that the victims of crime need help too. Prompt action may be needed to provide support for victims – but not in the fairly insensitive ways which have been reported after the recent disaster in Dunblane. People suffering shock and injury need comfort offered in ways which help them to retain control of their situation.

Mediation and restitution schemes which bring offender and victim face to face, where each agrees to that, have helped victims by giving them a stronger sense that justice has been done. People who feel particularly vulnerable should be put in touch with support groups or helped to form them where they do not exist. Women exposed to domestic violence, children suffering from sexual abuse at home or from bullying at school, people living in old people's homes or in homes for those with learning difficulties – each needs expert help from resolute groups familiar with their situation. Neighbourhood groups living in places particularly vulnerable to crime can be given greater safety and confidence through schemes which seek their help in redesigning buildings and public places, and organising mutually supportive collective action.

Conclusions

Many people feel that the world has become a more dangerous place than it used to be. Whether that is true or not, the feelings are real enough and political leaders must respond to them in some way if they are to retain credibility. But they will not be trusted for long unless they can respond effectively and honestly. The assumptions that these fears arise only from crime, that criminals are an alien, hostile form of life, not human beings much like everyone else, that they will be deterred from crime by punishment and that imprisonment is the most effective of these punishments... every one of these is mistaken. When offered to us by government ministers and senior spokesmen for the opposition, who are advised by some of the best research groups in the land, these assumptions are also dishonest – for the politicians know very well that they are untrue. Truth – and indeed crime prevention – are not the names of the games they are playing.

This is a hard message for civic leaders. It calls for a wiser understanding of the threats to our security and a capacity sometimes to challenge senior people in their own parties. We must condemn behaviour which shows no respect for other people, but we shall not stop it unless we also try to understand why it happens. Understanding and effective action, theory and practice, have to go together.

That compels us, first, to explore the threats to their safety which most worry people. They vary from place to place and from group to group. The first task of the security services is to mobilise from the community, the private sector and the public services the best response they can collectively muster to these dangers – and that will be a different response in each place.

Turning to crime, which will certainly be one of the sources of danger, our response must start by recognising that only 3 per cent of the offences committed in Britain this year will lead to a conviction in court. Police, prisons, judges – all the 'forces' of law and order – play important parts in every society's procedures for managing crime after it has occurred. They do not – they cannot, by themselves – prevent it. To do that we must:

- recognise that crime, like law-abiding behaviour, arises from the circumstances in which people live, the kinds of community they participate in at home and at work, and the kinds of family life which these communities support;
- involve those most likely to be victims of crime, listen to what they say, and do our best to offer them greater security and better ways of protecting themselves;
- offer potential offenders and their parents a better start in life which helps to set good moral standards and makes it easier for them to live by these standards;
- ensure that everyone can find legitimate ways of making an honest and decent living;
- treat convicted offenders in ways which make it easier, not harder, for them to find a way back into law-abiding lives – particularly by ensuring they have oportunities for work; and
- call upon leading politicians and others who should be among the most respected figures in the land to set standards of behaviour which all can follow.

That is a formidable agenda. But nothing less will make an adequate response to the fears of an increasingly anxious society.

Notes

Much of the evidence and many of the proposals briefly deployed in this chapter are set out at greater length in the NACRO Report on *Crime and Social Policy*, London, National Association for the Care and Resettlement of Offenders, 1995, and in the Morgan Report on *Safer Communities: The Local Delivery of Crime Prevention through the Partnership Approach*, London, Standing Conference on Crime Prevention, Home Office, 1991.

1 Michael Hough, *Anxiety About Crime: Findings from the 1994 British Crime Survey*, Home Office Research Study 147, London, Home Office, 1995.
2 Elliott Currie, *Is America Really Winning the War on Crime and Should Britain Follow its Example?*, London, National Association for the Care and Resettlement of Offenders, 1996.
3 Elliott Currie, *Is America Really Winning the War on Crime and Should Britain Follow its Example?, op. cit.*, p. 7.
4 GC Barclay *et al.* (eds) *Information on the Criminal Justice System in England and Wales*, London, Home Office, 1993.
5 NACRO, *Crime and Social Policy, op. cit.*, p. 8.
6 *The Report of the Treadway Commission on Fraudulent Financial Reporting*, Washington, US Federal Government, 1987; quoted in NACRO, *Crime and Social Policy, op. cit.*, p. 10.
7 See Barry Hugill's report in *The Observer*, 11 August 1996, p. 18.
8 This categorisation of responses to exclusion is developed from an analysis by Kay Carmichael in *Ceremony of Innocence*, London, Macmillan, 1991, p. 71.
9 Gordon Barclay (ed.) *A Digest of Information on the Criminal Justice System*, London, Home Office, 1991, p. 31.
10 Home Office *Criminal Statistics: England and Wales*, HMSO annual.
11 For a discussion of the relationship between crime, employment and unemployment, see David Downes, *Employment Opportunities for Offenders*, London, Home Office, 1993.

Chapter 8

Mainstream Services

Introduction

Not long ago, a book about local strategies to combat poverty would have been like a voice crying in the wilderness – and unlikely to find a publisher. But all that has changed. Spokesmen of our central government may continue to deny that there is any poverty in this country. Peter Lilley, Secretary of State for Social Security, loftily commented that the calls for national Programmes of Action to eradicate poverty, which emerged from the Copenhagen summit meeting of 1995, 'relate principally to the needs of developing countries...' , not to 'well-developed industrial nations such as the UK'. The Prime Minister's office, responding to the same inquiry, endorsed Lilley's statement.[1] But politicians working closer to the ground are now well aware that poverty and social breakdown are spreading to a point at which they threaten, in some cities, to destroy public services, public order and investors' confidence; and they are determined to do something about it. By 1996, well over a hundred local authorities claimed to have 'anti-poverty strategies' or to be developing them – more than twice the number making this claim 18 months earlier.[2]

These authorities are supported by an increasingly effective network of small think-tanks, pressure groups and academic researchers operating at local, national and international scales. The English local government associations – of metropolitan authorities, county councils and district councils – together set up the Local Government Anti-Poverty Unit which sends out excellent newsletters and pamphlets, and runs conferences and study groups.[3] It speaks mainly to, and for, local officials. So councillors have formed the National Local Government Forum Against Poverty[4] which employs regional officers throughout the country to provide similar help for local politicians. The Office for Public Management has set up a unit to do the same kind of work,[4] and the Local Government Management Board and the Audit Commission have also begun to commission research in this field.

Similar initiatives are taking shape on a European scale. The Commission of the European Union has, over past years, launched three major poverty programmes, each consisting mainly of local experimental projects. A fourth series has been postponed, but voluntary agencies in many countries of the Union have joined forces to create the European Anti-Poverty Network which is researching, lobbying, publishing, and organising study groups and seminars. Operating on a wider scale, the Council of Europe has a Directorate of Social and Economic Affairs which has developed a programme of work on social rights serving countries from Ireland to the Pacific coast of Russia.[5]

British pressure groups and voluntary agencies contribute to the flow of information and advice for those involved in local anti-poverty work. Some of them are also deeply involved in practical projects set up in collaboration with local authorities. They include the Low Pay Unit, with branches in many cities around the country; the Priority Estates Project, Save the Children, the Child Poverty Action Group, the Citizens Advice Bureaux, the Scottish Poverty Alliance, Energy Action Scotland (concerned with fuel poverty), LETS Solutions (promoting LETS systems), Action with Communities in Rural England (ACRE) and many others. Mainstream professional associations representing housing managers, public health workers, community workers, social workers, community safety officers and others have in recent years devoted more of their conferences to questions about poverty and what their members should be doing about it.

Meanwhile research workers in many parts of the country are studying local anti-poverty policies, urban regeneration, difficult housing estates, local 'healthy cities' projects and other poverty-related themes, and spending more of their time writing reports for those responsible for this kind of work.[6]

All this may only show that it is easier to write reports and make speeches about poverty than to do anything about it. But at least it is clear that there is no point in writing the kind of handbook for those engaged in anti-poverty work which would have been useful two years ago. The job has been done – many times.[7] Instead, I shall take the argument further. So, after briefly summarising where local anti-poverty strategies stand, this chapter goes on to consider what must be done next. This leads to a brief discussion of the action needed from central government, particularly in the fields of education and housing. But I shall continue to focus mainly on the local scale, ending finally with some briefly sketched conclusions, which will be developed further in the final chapter of this book.

Because it has to cover so much ground, this chapter is bound to be the longest in the book. I hope its subheadings will help to signpost readers through it.

State of the art

The will to do something about poverty in one's own community has sprung from many different quarters: a housing committee's recognition that some of their estates are slipping right out of control, and something must be done before they are wrecked and abandoned; police concern about the violence growing up around illicit money-lending that develops in neighbourhoods where there are many poor people and no banks or building societies; an energetic welfare rights officer who points out that there is a lot of money out there which local citizens are entitled to claim if they only know how; a scandal in the local paper about an old lady, unable to pay her fuel bills, who was left to freeze in her home; a public health official who points out that government departments with a bit of money to spend are allowed to discuss ill-health even if they are not allowed to mention the poverty from which most of it springs; the tourism committee's distaste for homeless beggars in the high street who deter their town's paying customers... these and other motives have set things going, and people who want to reduce hardship and social injustice are right to seize whatever opportunities they may be given by local events and personalities.

Although the opening moves and the lead roles for an anti-poverty strategy vary from place to place, people start working towards the same broad priorities before long. These can be summarised under six headings:

1. *Reduce the cost of living for poor people* and make it easier for them to get by. Under this heading come reduced charges and fares for swimming baths, sports centres, public transport and other services. These have in some places been provided through a general purpose plastic card with the holder's number and photograph on it which can give access to a gradually extending array of discounts and privileges in the private sector as well as the public services. Rotherham Council's 'Rothercard' is probably the best known example of this device.

   Poor people tend to live in homes which cost more to keep warm than those of richer people. Projects for insulating these homes more efficiently can both bring about reductions in their fuel bills and provide jobs for the unemployed. The Wise Group, mentioned in the previous chapter, has been a pioneer in developing programmes which achieve both these objectives. For those who still have difficulty in paying their bills, more careful attention to methods for billing poor consumers, more sensitive procedures for collecting debts, advice about the management of money and debts, and better support for families in which someone may be using money for drink, drugs and other addictions can all be helpful. Such action has to involve the public utilities, and the private and public sectors, and it calls for close collaboration between the courts and their bailiffs, the housing department and housing associations, social workers, welfare rights officers and others.

   Goods tend to cost more in poor neighbourhoods than in richer ones nearby where turnover is higher and there is keener competition among retailers. It may be possible to modify that by attracting new retailers to poorer places, by improving public transport and reducing bus fares, or by supporting the development of LETS systems and food cooperatives run by volunteers who buy in bulk. That will call for much negotiation. Do not assume, for example, that the local Co-operative store which originated from similar ideals will necessarily welcome these developments.

2. *Make it easier for poor people to get the services which can help them.* Under this heading come welfare rights work, the rewriting of leaflets and posters in clearer language, and the development of multipurpose claims forms enabling people to claim benefits from

several different services at once. Some councils have sent 'benefits buses' around more remote areas to help people make claims. Others have set up widely dispersed local offices which provide a base for several services that work in the surrounding neighbourhood. These may be designed in an open-plan fashion, with a playroom for children and a meeting place for local community groups – altogether more welcoming and comprehensible than the usual public office. Islington, Tower Hamlets, Walsall and Manchester are among the authorities which have developed these local neighbourhood offices to the fullest extent.[8]

3. *Involve the people who suffer the hardships of poverty and give them a voice in policy-making.* This has been tried in various ways. Public forums have been set up to discuss poverty and social justice, or the needs of particular hard-pressed areas. Groups with particular needs and interests – lone parents and people with disabilities for example – have been helped to establish a continuing foothold in local policy-making. Meetings of the council and its committees have been thrown more freely open to the public, and local committees of service users have been set up at neighbourhood offices. Public housing has been transferred to cooperatives and housing associations run by the residents, and training courses have been devised to help them take on these responsibilities.

4. *Improve the opportunities of poor people to earn a decent wage in a decent job.* Under this heading come another range of initiatives, explored in Chapter 6. They include better opportunities for training, and for the childcare which enables people to take training and jobs; the creation of new jobs and the moving of new enterprises into areas where unemployment is high; negotiations with employers to persuade them to recruit workers from areas and groups with few opportunities for work; and pressure for higher wages and more secure jobs at the bottom end of the labour market – some of them jobs in the public services or their contractors.

5. *Improve safety and reduce crime in hard-pressed areas.* Action of this kind will soon be demanded by their residents if they are given a say in policy. That will call for responses not only from the police but also from the schools and those who run youth services, those

who design and maintain buildings, parks and public spaces, those providing mediation services, and doing social work with families and young people, and all concerned with improving opportunities for work. These initiatives were discussed in the previous chapter of this book.

6. *Focus investment and professional staff on regenerating particularly impoverished neighbourhoods.* Projects of this kind go back nearly 30 years, before anyone thought of anti-poverty policies, to the beginnings of the urban programme launched by the Home Office in 1968 and the educational priority areas called for by the Plowden Committee in 1967. Community development projects, enterprise zones, estate action schemes, urban development corporations, housing action trusts, city challenge projects and other versions of the same basic ideas followed. As professional opinion and political ideologies evolved, the emphasis laid on different departments of government – Education, Home Office, Environment, Employment – varied from time to time, as did the priority given to involving the residents, the local authorities and private investors. But all these projects were designed to focus extra resources temporarily on particular bits of the map, long starved of investment, where many poor people live.

These area-focused regeneration projects have generally been supported by central government funds which put them into a different league from local government's anti-poverty policies: sometimes larger in scale but usually more tightly focused on particular neighbourhoods and tasks. Where they exist – which means in nearly all the larger industrial towns – they account for an important part of the publicly funded efforts devoted to reducing poverty. The Single Regeneration Budget, which brings together all the resources provided by central government departments for such purposes, channelled through the regional offices of central government – now with a government minister attached to each of them – is the latest product of this thinking. To get money from this budget, competitive bids can be made by any agency – not necessarily a local authority, although that is where the successful ones have usually come from. These bids must involve the private sector and local people living in the area concerned. In Scotland and Northern Ireland similar policies have been pursued under different arrangements. The four

Scottish Partnership schemes and the Belfast Area Teams have as much to teach the English as to learn from them. The Report of the Labour Party's 'City 20/20' Committee, chaired by Keith Vaz MP shows that this line of policy will continue to evolve, whoever wins the next election.

These six priorities cannot be sharply distinguished from each other. Any attempt to reduce living costs and debts leads into a concern for welfare rights and access to services. That concern has led people to decentralise services to neighbourhood offices and to base their work more firmly in the communities served. Meanwhile area regeneration projects cannot be separated from city-wide concerns about economic development, public safety, and the involvement of the private sector and local citizens.

The common feature of all six of these priorities is that they cannot be effectively pursued by giving orders from the top down, within the framework of one profession or one department of government, central or local. They call for a capacity to work together among a lot of people in different agencies in all three sectors of the economy – private, public and voluntary. That demands strong civic leadership to which influential local politicians have a vital contribution to make. It also calls for good corporate planning and constructive collaboration between central and local government: in short, a form of governance – a regime rather than an authority – capable of giving a sense of direction to a place, be it a city, county or village.

People have set about this task in various ways. Sometimes the Department of the Environment or one of its quangos takes the lead – which can prove effective within the area allocated to them but does not compel civic leaders to formulate a broader corporate strategy involving all their services. Some local authorities appoint an anti-poverty committee, led by a senior politician and supported by officials in their chief executive's department. This committee may be given a budget to spend on anti-poverty initiatives. Others have feared that this approach will encourage mainstream departments, their chief officers and committees, to get on with their 'proper' jobs of running the schools, housing, libraries or whatever, and to forget about poverty – whereas all departments must learn that poverty *is* part of their proper job. A school which is given help enabling it to teach even its most difficult pupils without having to expel them will be a better school for everyone. A housing service ensuring that, thanks to efficient heating and insulation of buildings and convenient payment systems, poor people do not run into debt and rent arrears will provide a better service for everyone. A librarian who offers people reliable information about the benefits they can claim and where they can get them will bring new people into the library and some of them will stay to read the books. How best to involve all its own services in anti-poverty policies, and to make productive links with other public services and the private sector must be for each authority to decide for itself – provided it is clear that this is what they have to do. There is no single formula or best model for this purpose.

Since this is a very difficult task, no authority would claim to have got very far with it. Those working seriously on it are rediscovering an old tradition of civic leadership which used to be strong in this country. It is rooted in the conviction which Victorian reformers had that if you are to create a city that people can be proud of you have to start where you are, in your own place, without waiting for your political friends to gain power in Westminster. Today it is much harder to do this because the central government has captured most of the taxes which people are prepared to pay and tightly controls local government spending; and because it channels more and more of our money through local quangos, concerned with economic development, training, housing and so on, whose directors are not obliged to listen to local people. But it is also clear that central government – even if we get a new one – will be neither well equipped nor deeply motivated to tackle local problems of poverty and injustice. Civic leaders concerned about the growing social divisions which are tearing their communities apart must therefore start from where they are, doing their best with what they have got. They must call upon their colleagues in central government for local help and for nationwide action when they need it, but they will do that with greater authority if they are already making sufficiently good progress to show that they know what they are talking about.

So what more can they do?

What are we trying to do?

First a sombre thought must be kept in mind. The projects which I have described as the present state of the anti-poverty art are mainly designed to make the present system work better and to treat poor people in kinder ways. Travel concessions and cheap swims at off-peak hours, gentler debt collection procedures, forms which are easier to understand, offices which are easier to reach, public landlords who repair their houses more promptly, a bureaucracy which tries to listen to you... together, these things amount to a massive exercise in courtesy towards people who have received too little of it. It was overdue; but there will be just as many people falling into poverty next month, next year... although they may not feel quite so bad about it and may be less likely to riot.

There's nothing wrong with that. It's the proper place to start, provided we recognise that we have to go much further. Part I of this book showed that although the growing inequalities in British society originated from economic causes, they have now gained a political momentum of their own which drives them onwards. A large part of the growth in poverty which gathered pace after 1985 was due to changes in taxes and benefits that took more from the poorer half of the population and gave more to the richer half: due, that is, to political decisions which could have been – and in some countries were – made differently. Those political influences are not confined to taxes and benefits. They just happen to be more easily measured in these fields where the state records money transfers. Even more divisive changes are working their way through the laws which govern wages and the labour market, and through our education system. It follows that to resist and reverse social exclusion we must be prepared to challenge the systems we live under and the power structures which sustain them. That is an essentially political task, not just a matter of better administration. I do not welcome that; it makes the road harder and longer. But we shall get nowhere unless we understand what has to be done.

What exactly are local anti-poverty policies *for?* There are good reasons why people are reluctant to answer that question clearly: to do so might be divisive and would expose them to the danger of failure. The first documents prepared for council committees and working parties often start by discussing the various ways in which poverty can be defined, followed by a lot of figures suggesting that bad things are happening in their area. They show the numbers out of work, the numbers living on income support payments, the numbers of lone parents, children getting free school meals, tenants getting housing benefit, and so on. Then there may be maps of the city or county showing where these people are most and least heavily concentrated. (There's nothing wrong with that: this book started in much the same way.) The paper then moves directly to proposals for action. The figures may be revealing and the proposals sensible, but the link between them is not clear.

That link should be explained. Policies cannot be evaluated unless we know what they are intended to achieve. Let us take an average city in the United Kingdom and start by finding out which of its people are in poverty – measured in any ways that seem feasible and helpful. Next, show how those patterns have been changing and explore their consequences. If the city is indeed typical of this country, this exercise will show that the deepest poverty is still often experienced by old people living alone, but the most rapid growth of poverty in recent years has occurred among children, young people and those who care for them – in three overlapping groups: the families of low wage earners, families in which parents are out of work, and families with lone parents. Some of the city's ethnic minorities and some neighbourhoods – often the less popular council estates – suffer particularly severely. Other vulnerable people with mental and physical disabilities are scattered more widely through the city, and many of them are having a hard time too.

The big and growing problem is family poverty. There is also likely to be plenty of evidence showing that the consequences of family poverty are destructive for children, their parents, and ultimately for everyone: evidence of declining school performance in the lower reaches of the ability range, growing numbers excluded from schools as unmanageable, growing numbers of people heavily in debt, poor health among parents and their children, a growth in crime, an increase in addiction and so on – the kind of evidence summarised in the early chapters of this book.

Armed with this analysis of stress and its consequences, choices can be made about policies. These call for political decisions, but at least they will be better-informed decisions. In a city like the one I have described as typical of Britain there should be a concern to make the lives of pensioners and people with disabilities – particularly those of them who live alone – as comfortable as resources permit: to ensure, for example, that they get all the benefits and concessions to which they are entitled, to provide good caring services for those who need them and support for those who care for them at home. That is no easy task but it does not call for major changes to the present system, only a determination to make it work as well as possible.

That, nevertheless, demands a great deal of determination and ingenuity. Some very encouraging things have been achieved, showing that the public services can be as enterprising and innovative as any other sector of the economy. Among many examples quoted in a recent study,[9] I particularly admired these:

- Bradford City Council's scheme, worked out in collaboration with the local Training and Enterprise Council, for helping older people back into work after redundancy or illness.
- Bury Borough Council's purchase of community education time to conduct outreach work with younger people to combat discrimination against older people.
- The support offered by Lewisham Borough Council, Leicester City Council and many others for groups of elders from ethnic minorities; Redbridge Borough Council funds a support service for holocaust survivors.
- Warwickshire County Council's provision of a cheap 'help on call' service (paid for by the Social Services department) for old people who have emergency telephones which, outside office hours, communicate with the fire service. Through this they can get help and advice or simply a call for a plumber.
- Redbridge Borough Council's reorganisation of its annual procedures for claiming housing benefits, which enables housing officers to call on pensioners, block by block through the year, armed with benefits advice literature and a small photocopier with which they take copies of pension books or other evidence of incomes required to ensure that housing benefits are promptly updated and paid.

These and many other examples show a capacity to get different services and departments working together in a common cause, with help from quangos and voluntary groups in their area. That capacity will be needed to an even greater degree for the more challenging task of transforming opportunities for families in poverty. Old people provide a cause which attracts more public sympathy than children. But to neglect its children is to squander the city's most precious asset – its own youngsters, whose health, skills, confidence and affections will go far to shape the kind of place the city will become and the future generations who will eventually succeed its present citizens.

What exactly should civic leaders be trying to achieve in this cause? Every city – and many smaller places too – should record and regularly report on what is happening to its children and young people: infant and maternal mortality, birth weights, the housing conditions of families, school attainments, results of school medical examinations, the qualifications children get and the ages at which they leave school, the number who are excluded from school or brought before the courts or children's panels, the number going on to further education, training, jobs or universities, the number whose families break up, the number of families in arrears with rent, the number of youngsters becoming homeless and so on. It will be the spread – the distributions – of these figures which need to be most carefully studied. Are the most vulnerable youngsters being left further behind, or are they catching up? Most of these figures are to be found in the files of various official agencies and call for no new research. If they were brought together and interpreted in a regular report which could be discussed in the local press, this would show whether things were getting better or worse for these most precious citizens, which neighbourhoods and groups are doing best and worst, and whether the city is treating its youngsters better or worse than other cities of a similar economic and social character.

With this measure of progress or the lack of it regularly before them, civic leaders, their officials and local citizens could make wiser choices about what to do and more wisely evaluate the results. Do better job opportunities reduce crime, addiction and homelessness? If not, that poses questions about the quality of the jobs, who gets them and who is excluded from them, and how the excluded can be given fairer treatment. Do educational programmes about healthy diets improve the health of mothers and their children? If not, perhaps it is more money they need to enable them to get the better food they already know they should have. Schools, now under pressure to show that their more favoured pupils get good examination results, would also have to think about what is happening at the bottom of the class, and how exclusions can be avoided by timely preventive action, rather than encouraging the departure of pupils they would be glad to see the back of. Courts tempted to believe that 'prison works' by keeping young burglars locked up for a while would be reminded that prisons are expensive and miserable places, and one of their city's aims is to keep young people out of them. (Why do we regard a prisoner as a 'solved' criminal problem? Are hospital patients likewise to be regarded as 'solved' health problems? It was reasoning of this kind which led the Nazis to their 'final solution': the grave solves all problems.)

The difference which this kind of monitoring could make can be seen in an impressive report recently made on 15 years work in 20 unpopular housing estates. These were classic examples of area-focused regeneration projects. The report shows that intensive, locally based management, carried out in consultation with residents, left people feeling that these neighbourhoods were nicer than they had been at the start of the project – better managed, better equipped and less stigmatised. There had indeed been a decline in the number of empty properties, better maintenance, more prompt repairs, and an increase in clubs and facilities of various kinds. However, the authors frankly concede that unemployment, poverty and crime were worse than before. Meanwhile, although these estates were no longer at the bottom of the 'pecking order' in their cities, we are told nothing about the condition of others, even more deprived, which have taken their place there.[10] The work was worth doing and the report on it is an excellent one. It makes frankly clear that this was an exercise – overdue and badly needed – in treating vulnerable people with greater respect and courtesy. It was not a policy for reducing poverty.

Where next?

So what more must be done if the forces dividing a society are to be resisted at local level? The decay of some neighbourhoods and the exclusion of their people from the mainstream of what should be their society has in some cities reached a point at which massive, area-focused projects are needed if they are ever to be reintegrated. There are so few jobs there, so many people without work, so many without the skills and qualifications that workers are going to need, and so many signs of squalor, decay and the collapse of public services – these communities, if they remain neglected, will be left further and further behind, no matter how well the rest of the economy does. To reintegrate them there must be more work within easy reach, more skills and confidence, and better services to support lone parents and others with heavy burdens to bear, together with housing and a social and physical environment which will encourage people who have got on their feet again to stick with the neighbourhood and strengthen its communities. Projects mounted through the Single Regeneration Budget and its Scottish and Ulster counterparts now seek to involve local people, and to combine the efforts of many professions in the public, private and voluntary sectors. More can be done to make this kind of area-focused work effective, but after 30 years of development the learning curve is flattening out.

Henceforth it will be increasingly important to recognise the limitations of this strategy. By focusing on small areas and mounting special projects there which can break out of the usual public service culture, we have created a framework within which it has been easier to work with local people in a community-based way, and easier to develop collaboration between different public services and between the public, private and voluntary sectors. But profound and increasing inequalities are not confined to these small bits of the map, and they are not reversed by special, one-off, temporary projects which make no long-term impact on mainstream services. We have demonstrated that with skilled and determined effort it is possible to get jobs and private investment (particularly in housing) into even the most unlikely areas, and to transform their appearance and the way people feel about them. That is an important achievement and we shall have to go on working at it. But the main task must henceforth be to apply the lessons learnt in these projects on a wider scale. We have to transform the culture of mainstream services and the private sector so that they, too, recognise that they have an obligation to help in creating less divided communities in which all can share in the benefits of growth and progress. That will pose formidable problems which can only be really effectively tackled when central government also puts its shoulder to the wheel. Here I shall only pose some of the more important of them.

Education

The schools are the biggest locally administered public service, if scale is measured in expenditure and the numbers employed and served. In a world where people without qualifications find they are increasingly unemployable, they provide the first experiences which either open the way to the continuing opportunities for learning that everyone will need throughout life, or deter them and thereby make their exclusion from the mainstream of society increasingly likely. Yet practically nothing is said about schools and teachers in the rapidly growing literature on urban regeneration and anti-poverty policies.

All political parties now promise that there will be more nursery education. Nurseries can do a lot for children, but most of them close during the school holidays and do not cover the full working day so they are not of great help to working mothers. Unless their work is extended, and backed up by other groups involving parents as well as children, they cannot be major players in policies to prevent poverty.

Until recently, the barriers between schools and the communities they serve were slowly being dismantled. The Plowden Report made the case for that with extensive evidence showing that education is something which happens – or fails to happen – to whole families and the communities in which they live.[11] Parents have become increasingly involved in the work of schools, and not only as helpers, governors and fund-raisers. In cities such as Glasgow, adult students have been welcomed into schools, and people who thought they had finished with education have been helped to carry their learning further into the local colleges. But the growing fear of violence in schools, coupled with tragedies like the Dunblane disaster, may reverse these trends. Meanwhile the pressures imposed on them to demonstrate academic success will encourage many heads to neglect their wider social obligations towards the cities in which they work; and the transfer of many schools to locally managed or grant-maintained status makes it harder for directors of education and their committees to formulate city-wide policies of any kind.

The measures of a school's success must be developed to include evidence about what happens to less successful students, and that should lead to action which rewards schools for educating those who find it hardest to learn, and mobilises for them the help they need from parents, remedial teachers, home teachers, social workers and youth workers in order to do that.

There are many cities which will have to recast the whole organisation of their education if they are to give everyone a fair chance. As with all Messianic faiths, the principles preached by the first advocates of change eventually harden into institutional forms: the vision dies and faith decays into idolatry. When comprehensive reorganisation of secondary education was first advocated its prophets showed that the all-through secondary school for pupils between the ages of 11 and 18 was only one of half a dozen ways in which to work towards the aim of opening up opportunities for all to take their learning as far as possible. This version would best suit big cities. Some of the pioneers – like Leicestershire and Anglesey – adopted quite different patterns, as did other countries grappling with the same dilemmas.[12] But the prestige of the grammar schools which were firmly rooted in our system led most authorities to adopt their all-through 11–18 pattern for the new comprehensive schools. This has become what everyone means by 'comprehensive education', a fiercely defended idolatry.

In big cities where there are large areas where the people are increasingly deprived, this kind of school has to be huge if it is to provide decent opportunities for the minority of pupils who stay to the end: a minimum of ten forms of entry (300 first-year pupils) was the estimate made by those planning the London County Council's transition to comprehensive schooling. Now that more youngsters are staying longer at school, that figure is coming down. But where the population is declining, as it is in the inner parts of London and most of our bigger cities, this prescription is impossible to adhere to without constantly closing smaller schools – which is politically impossible. So we have developed a pattern of secondary education in many of our poorer urban areas, which provides schools too small to do their increasingly difficult job. Thus they cannot avoid cheating working-class children of the educational opportunities they would get in more fortunate neighbourhoods.

Their difficulties are exacerbated by the gradual drift back into academic and social selection, now being encouraged by the Government, which enables more popular schools to cream off the more privileged children from their less popular neighbours. Northern Ireland has not got far enough to confront this problem: it retains selection at 11-plus for grammar schools. Scotland has done somewhat better because it has a long-accepted and reasonably effective comprehensive system. Most of the bigger English cities – Birmingham, Manchester, Newcastle and many others – conceal the problem because their more affluent families move out to the suburbs where they can choose between good local schools and the good private day schools which keep going in the city centre. Working-class families left in the inner city are cheated but are less likely to protest effectively.

London is the big exception. Here the middle class are firmly rooted in inner areas where, nearby, there are great deprivation, declining populations and many children who speak languages other than

English at home. When politicians like Tony Blair and Harriet Harman take the escape routes which other parents, less exposed to the media's attentions, also follow – sending their children to selective schools far from home – the chattering classes scream with rage: against them or against 'comprehensive schools'. No-one confronts the real problems which can only be solved by new systems of comprehensive education which transfer youngsters from middle schools at the age of 14 or 16 to senior secondary schools, colleges of further education or sixth-form colleges, as happens in other countries which face similar dilemmas.[13]

An education authority which was seriously concerned about the poverty and social divisions it helps to create would be as concerned about adults as about children. The rapid growth in the numbers of young people staying on at school and going to universities and colleges has been one of the great British success stories of recent years. It is a change which was long overdue and needs to go much further in a country that has excluded more of its youngsters from full-time education sooner than any other country at a comparable stage of development. The determination of these young people and their parents to stick with full-time education is well judged. Chapter 4 of this book shows that social mobility enabling people to move in middle life from the declining number of manual and junior non-manual jobs into the growing professions is being closed off in Britain, and in other countries where education and training are 'front-loaded', demanding continuous full-time attendance which is completed before people start work.

A city which is to prevent growing numbers of its people from getting trapped in shrinking sections of its labour market and drifting eventually into precarious, low-paid work or long-term unemployment must keep opportunities for full-time and part-time learning open to everyone throughout life, no matter what standard they start from. It is widely assumed that unemployed men are not greatly interested in education, but studies of people who have been out of work for a considerable time show that many of them do enquire about courses which could help them, but they are too often brushed off by gate-keepers of the system who tell them there is nothing for people who did not gain the necessary entrance qualifications when they were at school. The colleges and courses which provide the opportunities these men want must then be recognised by mainstream university departments so that their successful students can easily move into higher education. We have a lot to learn from other countries: the Americans and the Danes have always been much better at keeping opportunities for education open to all.

Housing

Housing is another field in which central government will have to play its part before big changes can be expected. This is a disaster area of public policy. A brief review of its history explains why, and suggests what needs to be done.

Political parties choose a few issues on which to stage the battles which define their differences. In Britian, through the interwar period and for a generation or more after the Second World War, housing was one of the main battlefields chosen for this purpose. It was not so in most of the other countries of the European Union where housing, though a critical issue, was rarely a politically contentious one.

Here, successive governments tacked back and forth, constantly changing course. Although this precluded consistent, long-term policy-making and wasted a lot of time and energy, it did not prove disastrous so long as the parties alternated in power. But since 1979 we have had a regime which has held to the same course through four successive terms: watering down planning powers in the interests of private developers, destroying the Metropolitan authorities and the Scottish Regions which were the main bearers of strategic planning responsibilities, forcing up rents for tenants of all kinds and relaxing rent controls and security of tenure, breaking up and selling off the stock of council housing and deploying heavy subsidies to promote owner occupation and to revive the private landlord, switching funds from general subsidies for bricks and mortar to means-tested housing benefits for households in need, dismantling the rights of the homeless, breaking off the long-standing alliance between the local housing authorities and the Minister who spoke for them in cabinet, and steadily depriving local civic leaders of power and confidence. Throughout these years, public housing has been the main victim of the recurring cuts in public expenditure imposed by the Government. Thus a disaster has unfolded.

Increasing the number of owner-occupiers has become a political obsession. This has been achieved through a system of loans and subsidies for house purchase which stokes up booms, prolongs slumps and helps to destabilise the whole British economy.[14]

We rely increasingly on social security benefits and housing benefits administered through household means tests. When coupled with rising rents and falling wages at the bottom of the labour market, this makes it much harder than it used to be for people to move back into work if they have several children or live in places where housing costs are high.

Massive mortgage arrears and repossessions, and growing problems of decay and disrepair have built up at the lower end of the market for owner-occupied housing. These difficulties add to the worries of thousands of anxious people in the middle reaches of society whose jobs have become increasingly precarious.

There are growing concentrations of deprived and vulnerable people in the sections of council housing which are most difficult to live in, leading in some places to serious breakdowns in public order.

Meanwhile everyone is aware of the most visible, and thus the most politically salient, sign of trouble. As the most vulnerable people are ground down and finally excluded from shelter altogether by this system, we have seen a dramatic increase in homeless beggars on the streets of every big city – a sight which we once thought we would only encounter in the poorer cities of the third world.[15]

These policies are now reaching a dead end. Their contradictions make that clear. Claiming that it would roll back the state and lift its tax burdens from a long-suffering people, the Government has had to pour public funds into private pockets to persuade home-buyers, landlords and developers to move into sectors of the housing market and neighbourhoods of our cities hitherto occupied mainly by local government. Claiming that it would cut back the state and its quangos and return power to the people, the Government has created more quangos than any of its predecessors and the most centralised State in Europe – all to oversee and enforce its privatisation programmes. Clearly the time has come to think again.

What needs to be done is now widely agreed by most authorities other than the Government itself.

First, after a devastatingly long slump in building, more houses are urgently needed, both for social renting and for low-cost home ownership.

Second, the main flow of subsidies for rented housing must swing back from means-tested, household-focused payments to bring about more general reductions in rent levels. With 70 per cent of council tenants drawing housing benefit in many places, a subsidy to all of them would be a fairer and more efficient way of 'targeting' those in need.

Third, for house-buyers, we need the opposite kind of switch – swinging funds away from indiscriminate mortgage interest tax relief to more selective support for first-time buyers, and for home owners who cannot afford badly needed repairs to their homes or adaptations which could help disabled members of their households to stay put.

Fourth, the scandal of homelessness must be more effectively tackled. That will call for action not only on housing but also on social benefits, on training and jobs, and on various forms of support for vulnerable youngsters and for people of all ages leaving institutional care of various kinds.

Fifth, the long war between Labour governments and the private landlord must end. The party itself is now asserting that landlords have a limited but important role, no longer as mass providers of housing for ordinary families, but to meet the needs of the growing numbers of mobile workers, students, foreign visitors and others who want promptly available, short-term, transitional housing.

Each of these themes deserves – and has been given – book-length treatment. Here I have time only to stress their central, shared aims. Those who created for this country a nationwide stock of public housing sought to provide decent homes for all our people at rents which they could afford. In doing that they were also weaving an essential strand into the safety net of the welfare state which sustained people in old age and in times of sickness, unemployment or family breakdown. In time, they broke the link, still to be seen in every market economy, between housing conditions and incomes. As that ideal has in more recent years been abandoned, public housing is in many places no longer a part of the safety net but a part of the poverty trap which excludes people from the mainstream of their society, exacerbating and perpetuating our social divisions. The link between housing and incomes has reappeared. Meanwhile, across the Atlantic, the violent and poverty-stricken ghettos of a society far richer than ours forewarn us of the fate towards which we are heading if we allow present trends to continue.

Celebration

Public support for culture and the arts – music, drama, galleries, museums and the visual arts – goes back to the dawn of government itself. The ancient Greeks were unsurpassed pioneers. The galleries, museums and theatres bequeathed to us by our Victorian forbears are still some of the best in the world. In recent years there has been a revival of interest in the contribution that the arts can make to the development of our communities, both urban and rural. In the 1980s research focused on their economic impact which was presented in figures showing the people employed, money earned and tourists attracted.[16] In the 1990s attention has turned to their social and cultural impacts: words like 'inspiration', 'identity', 'reconciliation', 'self-confidence' and 'vision' appear in the literature.[17]

How much does all this have to do with inequality and hardship? Some say that public support for the more expensive 'high' art forms is a subsidy for the middle-class people who make up the majority of the audiences for them – people who often live in the leafy suburbs where they contribute nothing to the revenues of the central cities providing the subsidy. (Expenditure on roads, parks and public transport presents similar dilemmas.) I can only offer some speculative comments derived from observation and from discussion with people who have a great deal of experience of these things.

It would trivialise the policy problems in this field to pose them merely as a choice between investing in 'high' art for posh people and 'low' art for the plebs. The aim should be to build and strengthen a range of art forms, bridging and linking the communities and classes, much as every stage of an educational system needs to be fostered and integrated. Better school plays and carol concerts will in time encourage more youngsters and their parents to go and hear Pavarotti on the rare occasion when he comes to town; and the opportunity to hear him will help to lift standards in the schools. The important choice to be made is between good and bad performers at every level.

Marvellously creative people are to be found everywhere – in remote rural areas, in the poorest city neighbourhoods, in the jails, and among people with physical and mental handicaps. Yet educated people often forget this, although they may know that John Bunyan wrote some of his best work in prison, that John Milton wrote poetry when blind, that John Clare wrote poems in a lunatic asylum and Vincent Van Gogh did his best painting in one, and that Charlie Chaplin scarcely ever went to school and was partly raised in a workhouse.

Talent can be found everywhere, but it does not spring into being fully formed. It has to be nurtured, disciplined and introduced to a wider world – usually by teachers, sometimes by relatives, often by both – by people who stay for years working in the same schools and neighbourhoods. Experts who are parachuted in for two or three years and then move on rarely leave a lasting mark behind them.

Where this kind of cultural development is wisely supported it helps people to explore and celebrate their past, to come to terms with whatever conflict and anger it has bequeathed them, and to look ahead with greater confidence in themselves and their communities. Where there is a history of conflict and humiliation within a society, the arts can help to reconcile enemies and heal battered identities. If they are any good, music, drama, painting – museums too – are always about the future as well as the past.

For these reasons the arts should play a central part in any programme of action concerned with social justice. Helen Crummy's book, *Let the People Sing!* provides telling arguments for this view.[18] Yet politicians, officials and academics concerned with poverty have too seldom worked closely with those concerned with the arts.

This may explain why teachers capable of developing art, music and drama are being lost in many of the places where they are most badly needed. Recent cuts in local expenditure, coupled with the 'marketisation' of education and the arts, mean that the Arts Councils are reducing their support for local projects, and education authorities and schools are reducing the number of part-time and peripatetic teachers (which is how most music teachers have to work). Meanwhile schools grow less willing to seek help from advisory services for drama, music and art, because they have to pay for them. They close earlier to save fuel, and are more likely to make charges for extra-curricular activities. In short, it is becoming harder to mount and sustain a coherent programme of visual and performing arts which welcomes children and young people from all social classes and enables the most excluded people to make their own contributions to local culture. There is no sign yet that the opposition parties have a more imaginative policy in view. Local civic leaders have a responsibility to challenge and reverse these trends. No-one else has the local experience and the political authority to argue that case so convincingly.

Conclusions

There has been an impressive growth in the number of local authorities claiming to have an anti-poverty strategy. The work they have done so far has mainly been designed to make existing services work better and to treat poor people with greater courtesy and kindness. That task can be approached in highly innovative ways and is well worth doing, provided it is recognised as being no more than a beginning. Poor people may feel slightly better about their poverty – may be less likely to make trouble – but there will be just as many of them next year and the year after. So we have to go much further.

The evidence which many authorities have got together about poverty in their own cities and counties needs to be better used to answer questions about the 'who', the 'where' and the 'why' of poverty, the trends now at work and their consequences. That analysis will often show that the worst and most rapidly growing hardships afflict children, young people and those who care for them. If these trends are not resisted and reversed our communities' future health, economic viability and quality of life will be threatened. Big words – but this is the biggest challenge of our times.

Special renewal projects, funded in special ways and focused for a limited number of years on small areas, will be needed to rescue some of the most excluded neighbourhoods. But poverty is not confined to those neighbourhoods nor mainly concentrated in them. In the longer run, the most important contribution of such projects may be that they teach us to talk with the people who experience the problems and to listen to what they say, to formulate clearer priorities, and to mobilise a wide range of services in various public authorities to work towards these priorities in collaboration with the private sector and voluntary agencies. But these lessons need to be applied across the board within mainstream public services if we are to respond effectively to the main challenge.

In most places the central aim of anti-poverty policies should be to improve life chances for children and young people, and thus for their parents too – to demonstrate that the figures monitoring their progress through life are moving in the right direction, particularly for those who are now having the hardest time. We need targets, not because the task will be complete once they have been attained, but because all services should be more sharply aware of these priorities. They have plenty of other targets to worry about: examination successes in the schools, rent arrears and vacant dwellings in the housing departments, air and water pollution levels for the environmental services, reductions in smoking and heart disease for the public health services. The health and school attainments of children from poorer families, their chances of getting jobs and of avoiding incarceration and homelessness are no less important.

There is no single formula or model for anti-poverty policies. To make progress towards their objectives demands a capacity to challenge long-established power structures – political and professional – posing problems which civic leaders have to tackle as best they can.

Many of those who have been out of work for a long time in areas where there are few jobs will never be employed again if we leave it to the private sector; one way or another, the state has to take the lead. That will ultimately call for more purposeful intervention by central government. But civic leaders, who will then have to take much of the action required, should already be analysing their local problems, preparing employment plans and making the case for these interventions.

The British education system is deeply divisive. If the present enthusiasm for expanding it is pursued without worrying about who benefits, these divisive influences will persist. That has been our usual pattern. Even when new colleges are set up to provide opportunities for working people they are taken over by the middle class when they succeed: Eton itself was originally a school for the poor. It is the standards of Britain's average and weaker performers which are an international scandal; our top 20 per cent do as well as any in the world. The whole structure needs to be reappraised if working-class children in poorer neighbourhoods are not to be cheated of their rights, and if adults working in the shrinking pool of manual jobs are to have a chance of entering the growing and more affluent reaches of the economy. Central government will have to play a major part in making that possible. Housing policies also need radical reappraisal. Here too national resources and strategies will be required, but there is already widespread agreement about what needs to be done. The visual and performing arts have an important contribution to make to policies designed to reduce inequality and injustice – a contribution which comes very cheaply when it is compared with the much bigger budgets for other services. Despite that, money for the work that is essential for supporting the arts is in many cities drying up.

The restrictions now imposed on local authorities make it very difficult for them to tackle these tasks. One of the jobs of civic leaders – a category which includes politicians but extends well beyond them – is to demonstrate from their own experience what needs to be done and, in collaboration with their colleagues in other places, to press national and European centres of power to act.

Already they are achieving important things. All across Britain, more and more of them, drawing on their own experience of what is going on in their wards, are talking about poverty. That may seem little enough. But after many years during which government ministers have done their best to eliminate the word from public discourse and the necessary data from public records, that itself is an important achievement.[19] They are resisting the thought police.

They will do that more effectively if they ensure that groups speaking with authentic experience of hardship are also given a voice and enabled to support each other in addressing power-holders at local, national and international scales. That is not an easy message for politicians and senior officials who are aware that this voice may threaten their own positions. The massive public funds which backed the Scottish Partnership projects – which were all to be conducted in collaboration with people living in the areas concerned – did not extend to helping these people meet and talk with community groups in other projects. Likewise, the European Commission's third poverty programme did not help community spokesmen involved in its projects to meet, to share ideas and experiences, or to press collectively for further action.[20] It is the voices of those who are actually living the problems which often compel most attention from the mass media, and eventually, therefore, from power-holders too.

The people working in this cause are rediscovering the conviction that those who want to make the world a better place must be prepared to start wherever they are, without waiting for their political friends to capture power in Parliament. Because they no longer have the powers they used to have to command and control, they are having to create forms of governance which mobilise shared concerns among interdependent agencies, enterprises and community activists. It is a harder task, but one which gives those who succeed in it greater authority than the old bureaucratic system ever conferred.

Notes

1 A letter quoted by Mona Patel in 'International year for the eradication of poverty gains momentum', *Anti-Poverty Matters*, **9**, 1996, p. 14.
2 *Anti-Poverty Matters*, **9**, 1996, Editorial.

3 The unit is now based at the Local Government Management Board, Layden House, 76–86 Turnmill Street, London EC1M 5QU.

4 The forum is based at 2 Nightingale Court, Nightingale Close, Moorgate, Rotherham S60 2HZ. The office for Public Management can be found at 252b Grays Inn Road, London WC1X 8JT.

5 Based at Council of Europe, F–67075 Strasbourg, Cedex, France.

6 Contributors to this locally focused social science are too numerous to list here, but many will be found in the Research Reports of the Rowntree Foundation. Pete Alcock, at Sheffield Hallam University, Gary Craig at the University of Humberside, John Benington and Mike Geddes, at the Local Government Centre, Warwick University, Alan McGregor at the University of Glasgow and Anne Power at the London School of Economics have been among the ablest and most frequent contributors to it.

7 See, for example, Pete Alcock *et al.*, *Combating Local Poverty*, Luton, Local Government Management Board, 1995; Gary Craig, *Poverty and Anti-Poverty Work in Scotland*, Glasgow, Strathclyde Poverty Alliance; and the Local Government Anti-Poverty Unit's regular newsletter, *Anti-Poverty Matters*.

8 Lucy Gaster, *Quality at the Front Line*, Bristol, Bristol University School of Advanced Urban Studies, 1991.

9 John Benington *et al.*, *Local Strategies and Initiatives for an Ageing Population*, Warwick University, Local Authorities Research Consortium, 1997.

10 Anne Power and Rebecca Tunstall, *Swimming Against the Tide*, York, Joseph Rowntree Foundation, 1995.

11 Central Advisory Council for Education (England), *Children and Their Primary Schools*, London, HMSO, 1967, Chapters 3 and 4.

12 The most widely cited early advocate of comprehensive education was Robin Pedley, with his book, *The Comprehensive School*, London, Pelican, 1963. The policy implications of this debate are reviewed in the *Second Report* of the Public Schools Commission, London, HMSO, 1970, Chapter 7.

13 Some of these issues are discussed in a useful book by Teresa Smith and Michael Noble, *Education Divides*, London, Child Poverty Action Group, 1995.

14 Gavin McCrone and Mark Stephens, *Housing Policy in Britain and Europe*, London, University College, 1995.

15 Data supporting the assertions in these paragraphs can be found in Steve Wilcox (ed.), *Housing Review, 1996/97*, York, Joseph Rowntree Foundation, 1996. The argument is developed more fully in David Donnison, *Housing Policy: From Catastrophe to Consensus?* Stamp Memorial Lecture, University of London, 1997.

16 John Myerscough, *The Economic Importance of the Arts in Britain*, London, Policy Studies Institute, 1988.

17 Charles Landry *et al.*, *The Art of Regeneration. Urban Renewal through Cultural Activity*, Stroud, Comedia, 1996.

18 Helen Crummy, *Let the People Sing! A Story of Craigmillar*, Edinburgh, published by Helen Crummy, 1992.

19 The Government's attempt to drive the very idea of poverty out of public discussion is well described by Gary Craig in *Poverty and Anti-Poverty Work in Scotland, op. cit.*, p. 31.

20 Gary Craig, *Poverty and Anti-Poverty Work in Scotland, op. cit.*, p. 32.

Chapter 9

Egalitarians and Greens

Introduction

This book deals with poverty and inequality which together pose many of the biggest problems running through the politics of the more highly developed economies. Most of our current public debates, whether they be about crime, health, education, unemployment, social benefits or taxes, deal with subheadings of this fundamental issue. The problems which these debates deal with are, in large part, causes of poverty or effects of poverty, or both. They would not all disappear if we lived in a society of equals, but we cannot get far in solving these problems unless we also make progress in reducing poverty and the divisive drift into deepening social inequality which excludes growing numbers of our people from the mainstream of their society.

But inequality is not the only fundamental issue running through our political debates. The other, which ranks in importance with it if we are to create a civilised society, is the threat to the world's natural resources and the very survival of our own species arising from our present lifestyles and future aspirations. This has become a worldwide issue, addressed in the work programmes called for by member states of the United Nations under Agenda 21 at the meeting of the Earth Summit held in Rio in 1992 ('Agenda 21' because the action it calls for will shape the twenty-first century). That initiative was preceded, and later reinforced, by many other international agreements and reports.[1] Many of today's political debates – about town and country planning, roads and transport, energy and water supplies, housing, health, farming and food supplies – deal with subheadings of these more fundamental 'green' issues. They can only be effectively tackled within the framework of a sustainable national and global economy.

The fundamental questions about growing inequality and growing degradation of the environment cannot be evaded. If we choose to disregard either of them we shall find that we have answered it by default – and in destructive ways. This book is one of many which demonstrate why we have to resist the drift towards deepening social divisions. But there is another shelf of books which demonstrate why we have to find less destructive ways of living if our grandchildren are not to be poisoned by the wastes poured forth in the course of economic development. International authorities are calling upon every nation to play its part in a worldwide attempt to address these problems, and on this front Britain's performance has been better than most countries. Whereas more than a hundred local authorities in Britain claimed to be working on anti-poverty policies by the spring of 1996, six months earlier more than 400 authorities in England and Wales appeared on the Environmental Coordinators Database of the Local Government Management Board, and more than 50 per cent of local authorities had committed themselves to developing a local Agenda 21 of some kind. Some of these are beginning to place the more measurable aims of such a policy – reduced levels of water pollution, for example – into their performance review systems which lay down the criteria for evaluating the general quality of their work. These standards can then be incorporated in the performance expected of the agencies contracting to provide services for the authority. Meanwhile the Audit Commission is beginning to build such standards into a nationwide system for assessing and comparing the performance of local authorities.[2] Those concerned with poverty have a great deal to learn from their colleagues working in the environmental field. There is no reason why similar standards dealing with the outcomes of policies to reduce poverty cannot be added to measures of local government performance.

How much collaboration is there likely to be between the two groups? Different agencies and different kinds of people have usually taken the lead in drawing these two fundamental issues to the attention of the world. Social justice questions have generally been taken up most vigorously by people concerned with social conditions and economic development. 'Green' questions have generally been taken up most vigorously by people concerned with environmental health and the management of natural resources. Each have their allies within the academy, where students of social policy and economics tend to work with the poverty lobby while students of the natural sciences and geography – and economists of other kinds – tend to work with the environmental lobby.

The two issues have been taken up with varying degrees of conviction in different kinds of places. While there are exceptions to the rule on both sides, anti-poverty measures have often gained most support where poverty itself is most obvious – in urban, industrial centres stricken by economic changes such as Strathclyde, Rotherham and Islington. Meanwhile Agenda 21 programmes have tended to develop first in beautiful places where people can see that they have a lot to lose: Mendip, Sutton and Bristol for example.

Some people have grasped that the two issues must be worked on together. The United Nations' Agenda 21 itself insists that workers, trade unions, women, children, old people and disadvantaged groups must be involved and consulted. The United Kingdom's admirable list of 24 'best practice suggestions', prepared for the United Nations City Summit held in June 1996, includes projects in many places where there is a lot of poverty.[3] But these are exceptions. Meanwhile, in the other camp, those working on problems of poverty have generally paid scant attention to environmental questions.

Politicians, both central and local, find it difficult to focus public attention and their own efforts upon two major initiatives at once. Time, energy, funds and innovative officials are all scarce. Thus egalitarians and greens can too easily find themselves competing for policy-makers' attention. They may also demand conflicting policies. Some advocates of green policies welcomed the Government's plan to impose value added tax on fuel: by reducing consumption it would also reduce a major source of pollution. Meanwhile those concerned about elderly people trying to keep warm on low incomes were horrified by the proposal. In places like the Hebrides, where the views are beautiful but jobs are scarce, proposals to build new bridges and quarries provoke the fiercest controversy between those who worry about jobs and those who worry about the environment.

This is not the place to give a detailed account of the local action required to create a more sustainable world. There are many other places where that can be found, as my footnotes show. But a book about inequality must consider the links between these two causes. I will start by explaining why. Next I shall show where a recognition of the common ground between them may lead. Finally I draw some broader conclusions.

Sustainability and justice: the links

Much of the literature about environmental policies suggests, either that they are a technocratic matter, properly understood only by scientists, or the kind of thing that any boy scout would be good at – making compost, recycling bottles and going to work on a bicycle. Neither approach poses contentious political questions. One of the earliest and best books on the subject began in a simpler and more brutal way:

> People can't change the way they use resources without changing their relations with one another. For example there are dozens of ways to economise energy: some would stop the rich wasting it, others would freeze the poor to death. Forests or beaches or country landscapes can be conserved to be enjoyed by many, by few or by nobody.[4]

Policies to create a more sustainable world, like policies to reduce poverty, are essentially contentious. Both call for changes in relationships between people. The changes called for by each may be complementary and easily reconciled, or contradictory and irreconcilable, or they may fall somewhere between these extremes. Both sides had better know where they stand.

In a place where a lot of people are having a hard struggle to survive, it is difficult to persuade anyone to think about conservation: that – their leaders often say – is a luxury which can be left to richer people to worry about. Opinion polls show that working-class people do indeed give higher priority to policies which create jobs or raise incomes. Policies for improving the environment are of greater concern to richer and more educated people.[5] Growing inequality and poverty therefore kill off support for environmental policies in poorer communities. In this respect the two causes can be reconciled: a more equal society in which no-one is poor would care more about its environment, other things being equal.

The link is more complex and more deeply rooted than this statement suggests. Planners in the public sector and managers of the private sector both like to have some slack in their systems. It makes their jobs easier. Everyone knows that as demand fluctuates and technologies change, employers want a reserve army of labour – workers who can be hired when needed and shed when no longer needed. This is not a motive that is declining in strength. As the pace of economic change has sharpened in recent years, the numbers of workers in temporary and part-time jobs, who are more easily shed without any rights to redundancy payments, have increased. (This used to be called 'casual labour' which was regarded as a bad thing. Similar patterns are now called 'flexibility' by those who regard them as a good thing.) It is less widely understood that the same principle applies in every part of the economy. Developers and town planners find it useful to have reserve land and buildings which can be brought into use when they are needed, and neglected – sometimes for many years – when demand is slack. Education directors like to have schools which can be brought forward for rebuilding and extension when they have secured a budget for that, and neglected or closed down in times of contraction. People running railways and telephone systems have similar needs.[6] It is in the neglected margins of these systems that poor people tend to live – in decaying buildings standing amidst unkempt, litter-strewn spaces, where the schools are closing down and the telephones don't work. Thus neglect of human beings and of urban capital often go together. Then, if neglected buildings have to be demolished before their lives would normally come to an end, resources will be wasted on a massive scale, for a building embodies very large amounts of energy.

If, in communities increasingly divided by extremes of wealth and poverty, the more successful people are driven out of the inner city by squalor, poor schools and fear of crime to distant, leafy suburbs, that too makes a heavy impact on global resources through the building and extension of the new suburbs and the increasingly long, car-borne journeys which commuters make to the city for work, shopping and entertainment. As more affluent tax-payers escape the central city's taxes by withdrawing to the suburbs, while still using many central services, it becomes harder for central councils to maintain these services and the fabric of their cities. That may hasten their decay and the flight of the affluent.

Within the neighbourhoods where poor people congregate, many households cannot afford to heat their homes properly. If their landlords installed cheap central heating systems which are very expensive to run – as too many British local authorities did – they are forced to economise even more. Dampness spreads, buildings decay, and people may be compelled to use ineffectual and wasteful heating equipment. Poverty and environmental degradation increase together.[7]

There will be occasions when the classic conflicts between development and conservation, jobs and sustainability, the needs of people living in deprived and densely built districts and the hopes of those who cry 'Not in my back yard' will set egalitarians against 'greens'. But enough has been said to show that common cause can often be made between them. What are the basic principles on which that alliance can be built?

Joint action

My aim is to introduce good people working in both causes to each other by drawing on the experience of those who are already working together and noting some of their shared concerns. I will start with immediate, practical matters before turning to more strategic issues.

Some of the most expensive disasters which have gone far to discredit local government in Britain arose from a combined neglect of social and environmental needs, and are now being put right by attending to both. The monster concrete crescents of the Hulme housing estate in the middle of Manchester and many of the slabs and towers surrounding them were impossible to heat if all you had to live on was an income from the social security system, a student grant or not much more. Turnover rose, flats were left empty and squatting spread; so did theft, vandalism, violence and other disorders, and the people living there came increasingly to consist of those who had nowhere else to go – lone parents, people released from institutions of various kinds, homeless families... the story is too familiar. Morale in the public services working in the area unravelled: repairs were not done, rents not collected, refuse not properly cleared – even the letters were rarely delivered on the upper decks of these blocks. Things might have been better if the designers and developers of this huge estate had asked the people who were to be rehoused there what kinds of home they wanted. Citizens who do not clearly distinguish between the different departments of government would have compelled decision-makers to think about poverty and environ-mental problems. Things might have been better if the new building materials and methods used had been better understood and the work better supervised; and if the proposed gas-fired heating systems had not been replaced at the last moment by electric underfloor heating – cheap to install but very expensive to run – because of the gas explosion which destroyed the Ronan Point tower block just before work began. But only a very well-informed and far-sighted environmentalist could have guessed at the vast increases in energy prices due to come shortly afterwards. Now, after much pain, years of belligerent campaigning by the tenants, a lot of research and massive public expenditure by central and local government, a new Hulme is taking shape which local people have played some part in creating. There are some more jobs for them, and they play a part in managing their own homes through the housing associations and a cooperative which have taken most of them over. Poor people living in the estate have been rehoused there, rather than driven out; public services have improved, heating is far more efficient at much lower costs, and the whole place is becoming more attractive to live in.[8]

On a less dramatic but far more extensive scale, Glasgow has been addressing similar problems. After the Second World War, from which it emerged almost unscathed by bombing, this city had some of the worst and most extensive slums in Europe. Massive building of council housing was demanded by the people – many in large families living in two-room tenement flats, sharing toilets and cold taps with several other households, plagued by vermin which could not be eradicated, while in some flats other people's sewage boiled up through the plugholes of kitchen sinks. During the 1960s and 70s, the city achieved the largest planned clearance and rehousing programme the world has ever seen. But a price was paid for that. As a result of this pell-mell rebuilding, Glasgow had by 1991 more damp homes, poorly insulated homes, and households dissatisfied with their homes and heating systems than did any other authority in Scotland.[9] Since then, most of Glasgow's capital expenditure on housing has been devoted to putting these things right. Its Housing Plan for 1996 starts by stressing the implications of growing poverty and of 'green issues' for housing policy, and goes on to lay out a six-point strategy starting with '1. Regenerating the City', and '2. Eliminating Condensation and Dampness'.[10]

As we switch from the regeneration of a near-derelict housing estate to the renewal of a whole city on terms which will make it both a more sustainable and a less poverty-stricken place we move to an increasingly strategic scale of discussion. If Glasgow is to be 'recentralised' it must be attractive to all kinds of people – rich and poor, old and young, and people of various cultures and ethnic origins. That aim has implications for the quality of health services, schools and cultural opportunities, the cleanliness and safety of the streets, the mix of housing tenures available and much else. So ambitious a plan has to deal with these and many other subheadings of the anti-poverty agenda as well as the Agenda 21 issues.

Many other examples of the interlocking nature of these two agendas could be offered. Both, for example, are concerned to develop good public transport systems which enable people of all classes and ages to get about the city, and reduce the pollution and congestion caused by private motor cars. Glasgow's Wise Group and its associated enterprises, now also working in many other places, have trained and employed several thousand people, previously unemployed, who have worked on the insulation of homes, environmental improvements and similar projects – contributing both to sustainability and to the reintegration of people who have been excluded from the mainstream economy.[11] Those who have sought to develop a 'complementary economy' of what are sometimes called 'third force organisations' – housing cooperatives, LETS trading systems, local community enterprises, credit unions and the like – which can maximise the use of voluntary labour, minimise transport and building costs, and provide greater satisfaction to their users than more conventional enterprises are working in both causes. Many other examples of these shared interests could be given but it is time to turn to some of the broader conclusions of this discussion.

Conclusions

Those most concerned about social justice have sometimes argued that we must have a growing economy to produce the resources to lift people out of poverty. Forty years ago, Anthony Crosland was one of them.[12] And if economic growth damages the environment, some of them added, so be it: justice must come first. Such people have misunderstood both problems.

It is of course politically easier for governments to raise the incomes of the poor if growth enables them to do that without reducing the incomes of the rich: by levelling up rather than levelling down. Crosland was speaking as a professional politician in saying that. But unless levelling of some kind goes on, growth by itself will not reduce poverty. It will only change the forms it takes – as Chapter 1 of this book made clear.

Poverty does not consist of having an income which falls below a particular level. The essential feature of poverty is hardship – meaning pain, humiliation and all sorts of things which destroy talent, blight human potentialities and prevent people from creating and shaping their own lives. Amartya Sen describes these collectively as 'capability failure'.[13] Such hardships are more common among people living below certain levels of income and less common above that level. But the income level at which they begin to bite varies from country to country. The European convention that people living on incomes which are less than half the average for households of their kind in their country is a useful way of expressing that fact, and of comparing the extent and severity of poverty in different countries and different social groups. Some people have criticised that convention, saying it is really a measure of inequality rather than poverty. Of course it is a measure of inequality: that is the point of it. For hardship is eliminated, not by raising everyone above particular income levels, but by eliminating massive inequalities. In a developing economy which steadily transforms the luxuries of previous generations into the necessities of their successors, massive inequality creates new hardships among those deprived of the new necessities: safe piped water and flush toilets long ago; education and electricity today. We can reduce Britain's growing inequalities and the hardships they create partly by actions which make incomes more equal, and partly by providing good services which everyone uses: schools and health services good enough to give no major advantage to those who buy their way into private education and medical care; a public transport system good enough to get people out of their cars; cities good enough to retain their richer people instead of sending them fleeing to distant suburbs.

As its people become less driven by greed and fear to seek growth at all costs, such a society would be both more equal and more sustainable. Politicians who assert that the voters would reject this vision may have underestimated their fellow citizens. The latest Report on British Social Attitudes shows that people who send their children to private schools are not less, but more, likely than most 'to see education as the top priority for extra public spending'. They may, say the authors of this Report, be 'reluctant members of the private sector...'. Perhaps, 'had state education been better, they would have preferred to save the cost and inconvenience of educating their children privately'. Likewise, a majority of those with private health insurance favoured extra spending on the National Health Service.[14]

The drive to resist and reverse socially divisive trends in our society and the drive to play our part in creating a sustainable world which does not destroy the resources which future generations will need must sometimes come into conflict, but they are more wisely understood as differing ways of formulating what has to be one vision of the future. Resolving conflicts which arise between them is a necessary part of the task of clarifying that vision. In future, no-one should write a plan of action or a book about either cause without considering its implications for the other. Richard Wilkinson's remarkable book, *Unhealthy Societies*, which I have quoted in earlier chapters, concludes by bringing these themes together. It should be a text for our times.

Already, the strategies being developed by civic leaders and officials concerned with these causes have a good deal in common. Both groups agree that they must take a long-term view and formulate a vision of the future of their city, their county or their country. They are dealing not only with specific, solvable problems but with a new approach which has to inform policy-making and public discussion at all points. Both agree that they cannot succeed just by wielding bureaucratic power. They have to listen to their fellow citizens and involve them in policy-making. Much of the action required under both agendas has to be taken at a local level, and will call for a partner-ship between public, private, voluntary and community initiatives, and between authorities acting at local, national and international scales. Both agree that aims need to be clarified and progress towards them monitored and regularly reported to the public. The perfor-mance reviews now being carried out by local authorities as a part of their duties under the Citizen's Charter should include objectives drawn from anti-poverty and Agenda 21 programmes and show the progress made in working towards each of them.

The people concerned with each of these causes may believe that these strategies were their own invention, but they are in fact talking about the more open, participative forms of governance which are to be seen developing in many fields where a broadly based mobilisation of public concern is required to get things done. 'Healthy cities' and 'community safety' projects have called forth similar initiatives.

There are differences between these movements too, from which those concerned with inequality may have something to learn. The professions concerned with Agenda 21 and the agencies in which they work have the advantage of being backed by stronger international leadership, expressed through the United Nations, the European Union and other bodies. The Green Party seems at the moment to be dying, but under Britain's present electoral system a political party seeking seats in Parliament may not have been a fruitful strategy: better to gain supporters in the parties which might win power. Meanwhile the movement continues no less vigorously, carried forward by citizens who are on occasion prepared to march, to lie down in the road or to chain themselves to trees and lorries in support of green causes. The poverty lobby has fewer supporting troops.

Why people so committed to the health of the universe and the survival of its creatures seem reluctant to do anything about one third of our own children who are growing up in poverty, or about the million and a quarter people who have been out of work for more than a year is an interesting question. To the poverty lobby it may seem that the 'greens' have a less contentious and politically simpler task. They can identify clearly-defined 'winnable issues' and target the people who take decisions about them. A small number of their activists may risk their lives by boarding an oil rig on the high seas to stop the Shell company dumping it in deep water, or by lying down in front of lorries carrying calves to France. But the mass of supporters who win the day for these causes are obliged only to write to their MPs, to buy their petrol from filling stations without the 'Shell' sign, or to eat pork rather than veal. No powerful popular interests have to be explicitly confronted – as has to be done when people protest about low wages or unemployment. No increased tax burdens have to be called for – as has to be done when people ask for the restoration of social benefits to young people or pensioners. It is always easier to stop one simple thing from happening – like stopping the building of a bypass – than it is to make a lot of complex things happen – for example, all the things which would have to be done in order to lift children and their parents out of poverty.

But the main handicap of the poverty lobby and its supporters may be of a different kind, arising simply from the fact that they have less hope than green campaigners, less confidence that they can change the world. There may nevertheless be things which they could learn from them: to pick specific, winnable issues, for example; to identify the decisions they want and the people who could take them, and then target those people; to take the private sector as seriously as the public sector, because it often has more clout; and to specify measurable objectives – concerning the welfare of children and young people, I suggested in the previous chapter – and monitor progress towards them. Egalitarians concerned with poverty should respect the enthusiasm of the greens and make common cause with them whenever they can. For, in the long run, the just city and the sustainable city have to be the same place. The fair city it might be called.

Notes

1   For example, the International Council for Local Environmental Initiatives, *World Cities and their Environment – the Toronto Declaration*, Toronto, ICLEI, 1991; and *Strategic Services Planning – Sustainable Development: A Local Perspective*, Toronto, ICLEI, 1994. European Commission, *Towards Sustainability: A European Community Programme of Policy and Action in Relation to the Environment and Sustainable Development*, Brussells, Commission of the European Community, 1993. United Nations Economic Commission for Europe, *Guidelines on Sustainable Human Settlements Planning and Management*, Geneva, United Nations, 1996.

2   For further information on local Agenda 21 policies, see the Special Edition on this subject of *Local Government Policy Making*, **22**(2), October 1995, particularly the articles by Stella Whitaker (guest editor), Derek Bateman, Martin Fodor *et al.* and Ian Worthington *et al.*

3   Tim Dwelly (ed.) *Living in the Future*, York, UK National Council for Habitat II, 1996.

4   Hugh Stretton, *Capitalism, Socialism and the Environment*, Cambridge, Cambridge University Press, 1976, p. 3.

5   Geraint Parry *et al.*, *Political Participation and Democracy in Britain*, Cambridge, Cambridge University Press, 1992.

6   This point, first made by John Benington, was developed by Peter Marris in *Community Planning and Conceptions of Change*, London, Routledge & Kegan Paul, 1982, for example p. 126.

7   For an account of the massive differences in heating costs to be found in different buildings, and their social consequences, see Brenda Boardman, *Fuel Poverty. From Cold Homes to Affordable Warmth*, London, Belhaven Press, 1991. For a local analysis of the costs of the combined consequences of poverty and unsustainable house designs, and a discussion of policies to deal with both problems, see Glasgow City Council, *Glasgow's Housing Plan*, 1996.

8   Capita *et al.*, Hulme Study, London HMSO, 1990; and Tim Dwelly (ed.), *Living in the Future*, York, UK National Council for Habitat II, 1996, p. 54.

9   Scottish Homes, *Scottish House Condition Survey: 1991 Survey Report*, Edinburgh, Scottish Homes, 1993. (The 1996 survey is to be published in 1997.)

10 City of Glasgow, *Glasgow's Housing Plan*, 1996.

11 David Pollitt, 'Wising up to employment', *International Cities Management*, May–June, 1996, p. 22.

12 Anthony Crosland, *The Future of Socialism*, London, Jonathan Cape, 1956.

13 Amartya Sen, *Inequality Reexamined*, Cambridge, Mass., Harvard University Press, 1992.

14 Lindsay Brook *et al.*, 'Public spending and taxation', in Roger Jowell *et al.* (eds), *British Social Attitudes. The Thirteenth Report*, Aldershot, Dartmouth, 1996.

Chapter 10

For Baffled Citizens

Introduction

Books of this kind are usually written for people who have a foothold of some sort within their country's system of governance. They are politicians, officials, members of the 'public service professions', voluntary activists, church leaders, journalists who write about them, or students preparing for work of these kinds and their teachers. These are the people for whom publishers produce books – particularly the students and teachers: they or their librarians are most likely to buy them.

That is natural; and why should authors complain? Books would never get written or published if there were not *someone* out there who might buy them. But it means that we are all enmeshed in an industry which may too easily confine our thinking. It's like 'The House That Jack Built'. These are the authors who write for the publishers who produce the books which students have to read because their teachers use them to set the examinations which confer the qualifications to work in the professions they wish to enter. So all of them may be tempted to believe that these professions – politics, administration, community work, social work, the church and so on – are the most important things in the world and the only instruments we have for making it a better place. Which is not true.

This chapter, like much of this book, is written for people who stand outside that system of governance. It starts by exploring how changes in policy come about and who plays a part in the story, and goes on to ask how the ordinary, unorganised citizen can get into the act.

Making the world a better place

How can the world be made a better place? Often by developments which owe nothing to governments: by inventing and producing useful things, by devising better, less exhausting ways of making them, by creating enchantment through music, painting or poetry. The same independent sources of action can also make the world a much worse place. So stopping things from happening can be as important as making things happen.

Even the things which do call for changes in public policy may not originate within the big battalions of the state. Here are some examples already in the history books.[1]

- The recognition that in an urban, industrial society a single wage often cannot provide adequately for the upbringing of the children upon whom the survival of that society depends – a realisation which led to the introduction of family allowances, now renamed child benefit, in 1946.
- The growth of concern about air pollution, leading to the passage of the Clean Air Act of 1956, one of the first British measures to write such concerns into an effective law.
- The acceptance of the idea that anyone, anywhere, should at any stage of their lives be entitled to the most advanced education their society can offer, and the founding of the Open University in 1969, which was an assertion of that conviction.

These and many other examples of social reform show that important new ideas seldom originate in the political parties, the trade unions, the civil service, big business or the other big battalions of a modern society. They usually begin among small groups of slightly cranky people who may be drawn from any or none of these worlds: people committed to an idea, working on it in their spare time, writing papers for each other in little magazines, seeking out expert help among like-minded folk – 'networking' as we might now say. The backing of the big battalions is needed before anything much can be done, but that comes later; usually many years later, when large numbers of people have taken up the same ideas.

The reformers often have a base of some sort where they meet. They may earn their living there, but their influence does not depend on any authority conferred by that institution. The Fabian Society, Toynbee

Hall – an east London settlement – and the London School of
Economics and Political Science frequently served that purpose during
the first half of the twentieth century – none of them, at that time,
powerful organisations. Before that, other centres played similar parts in
the network, the Charity Organisation Society was one of them. More
recently some of the independent 'think tanks' have taken over the role.

One may glimpse something of the drive required for this
reforming task and the unpompous way in which it was pursued in
the life of Octavia Hill who was one of Britain's greatest social innova-
tors during the last quarter of the nineteenth century, playing key
parts in the creation of housing associations for working people, the
founding of the National Trust and the development of the hospital
almoner's profession (known later as medical social workers).[2] When
she was invited to give evidence about her housing work to the Royal
Commission on the Housing of the Working Classes which reported
in 1885, the noble Lord who chaired that body welcomed this little
woman and thanked her for coming. Then, to start her talking, he
asked her to explain how she set up her housing associations: 'I
suppose you form a committee of some sort?' The transcript suggests
there was a pregnant pause before her first brief sentence to the
Commission: 'I never formed any committee'.[3]

I am not suggesting that others can emulate Octavia Hill, Eleanor
Rathbone (who played a key part in developing the idea of family
allowances – or 'family endowment' as she called it) or Michael Young
(whose many reformer's battle honours include the Open University).
I am recalling that the story of social reform usually begins, not within
political parties or the committee rooms of big bureaucracies but in
small groups of people talking to each other. Later come bigger
meetings, propaganda and the mobilisation of more widespread
support. That may eventually bring the big battalions into play.

This pattern continues today. For 10 years and more, small groups
of women were talking about their place in society, setting up shelters
for battered wives and their children, asserting their own rights to
more sensitive medical care and presenting their arguments through
fringe publishers. It was much later that the Equal Opportunities
Commission was set up, universities started teaching 'womens'
studies', mainstream publishers produced books for them and the
whole 'gender industry' began to roll.

In Britain, somewhere in the middle phases of such a story, there
often comes a time when charitable foundations provide funds for

research and experimental ventures which enable people to clarify their ideas and develop them into workable forms. The Gulbenkian Foundation's support for community work and community arts, the Rowntree Foundation's support for research and experiment in housing and the Nuffield Foundation's support for new thinking about teaching methods and curriculum development left their marks on these fields. The campaigns for the prevention of racial discrimination, for the abolition of capital punishment and for the provision of safe and legal abortions followed a similar, slow course. Meanwhile others – for a basic citizen's income for all, or for the legalisation of voluntary euthanasia, for example – are at an earlier stage, their advocates still regarded as somewhat cranky and their prospects still uncertain.

Human beings can make a difference. Indeed, nothing changes unless human beings make it happen; and the bigger the change the more likely it is to have begun among small groups of people arguing among themselves in obscure bars and sitting rooms long ago. Some have asserted that it has become harder to push onwards through the middle phases of this process which build mass movements that ultimately compel the powerful to change course. Fewer people in Britain are going to political meetings or to church; trade union membership has declined and the unions themselves have grown more businesslike, less like a movement; pubs are less widely used as we learn to buy our drinks in impersonal supermarkets and take them home; and the motor car, which saves us the trouble of standing in bus queues, also deprives us of opportunities we used to have for meeting our neighbours. Meanwhile, power itself is seeping away from national governments and entrenching itself in more remote, less accessible, less comprehensible global networks.

Yet, although the channels of communication have changed – relying now increasingly on telephones, television, E-mail and the Internet – people can still mobilise in their thousands to give the world a brief but powerful shove. The rejection of the poll tax, the abandonment of deep sea dumping of oil rigs, the European Union legislation we have been promised which is to regulate the transport of live animals… all of these are recent examples of successful popular political action, beginning at street level and making – in two of the three cases – an international impact. Even apparent failures, like the dispersal of those resisting the building of the Newbury bypass, may teach the wider society and its politicians a lesson which makes such projects less likely in future. Such movements are likely to grow stronger. Their supporters are more frequently working together – turning out to man the same barricades.

The problem, from the standpoint of this book, is not that ordinary citizens have become powerless. It is that concern for the poor and the excluded has become harder to mobilise, even when the victims include one-third of our children, and every citizen suffers to some extent from the effects of the hardships which these children and their parents experience. There are more unemployed people – here and all across the European Union – than farmers. But compare their political clout! Evidence about the growth of poverty among our youngsters has been presented in report after report, but it is easier to mount a protest about the export of young cows. Perhaps for the reasons outlined in Chapter 4 of this book, the climate of public opinion on these matters has turned very cold. It seems at times that no-one cares.

So what can unorganised citizens who have no role in the agencies of governance do if they feel a sense of outrage about these things? It is very tempting to despair. Despair, once we have sunk into its cold embrace, enables us to go happily on our way – like a tourist who has decided that the beggars and the prostituted children of another country are no concern of his.

The active citizen

Can we avoid becoming tourists within our own country? Many resist that temptation, starting from wherever they happen to be – from the bottom upwards, as it were. Millions work as volunteers for the local Citizen's Advice Bureaux, for churches and 'faith groups' of various religions, for local branches of Shelter, Age Concern, or Oxfam, for their local schools, for disability groups and many other bodies. Helping people who are having a hard time is always worth doing. It often does us more good than those whom we try to help: keeping us in touch with things going on in a harsh world; giving us humbling glimpses of the courage which some people show as they cope with conditions that would destroy most of us, and reminding us of what our country does – with the voters' assent, and thus in our names – to its more vulnerable citizens.

But no matter how hard we work in these ways, there will, next month and next year, be as many people coming for help: more, very likely. We have made no dent whatsoever on the statistics of poverty and pain. Indeed, our efforts may have offered the powerful a slightly better excuse for neglecting vulnerable people by enabling them to say that some voluntary organisation is looking after them. So what more can we do?

The work of such organisations often gives them a window on the world which shows what goes on in its harsher areas. That experience – it may be of the numbers of people in a particular place who are contending with debts, or in fear of homelessness, or battered by their partners, or unable to keep their homes warm – can be collected, summarised, put into printed and videoed forms, and communicated to the world through local news media, always hungry for a local story, through local politicians and in other ways. Better still, some of the people who are having a hard time can be enabled to tell their own stories in ways which gain far more attention than mere statistics. When people tell their own stories they begin to gain some control over the use made of their pain and are less likely to be treated as case studies in someone else's news story or research report.

The figuring done in this way can be taken a step further to reveal and explain the implications of policy changes. If VAT is imposed on fuel, if child benefits continue to dwindle in value, if unemployment rises or falls by 10 per cent, if social benefits for youngsters are withdrawn or increased, these will be the probable effects on the numbers of families in debt, on the number of homeless youngsters, on crime, suicides and so on. Such evidence and argument must be presented with scrupulous fairness so that the people responsible for them gain a reputation for getting things right which encourages others to rely on them. There will be research workers in the local university, and perhaps also in the local authority, who can help amateurs to achieve and maintain these standards. Experts in both may be better equipped than small voluntary groups to publish the results and gain media attention for them, but volunteers should insist that the professionals do not take over and distort what they want to say. It should always be remembered that those who are excluded from the mainstream of society may see the local authority and the university as more a part of their problems than a part of the solutions for them.

For a long time, most of this work may be confined within particular agencies concerned with particular needs: housing and homelessness, perhaps, or specific diseases or physical disabilities. But if people push on they may come to recognise that their concerns are shared by other groups, and poverty and powerlessness may be common themes running through the experience of these groups. In particular places, these problems may be related to unemployment, the collapse of local industries and the need for new skills. Beyond those issues lie further questions, partly political, about the causes of economic changes and the responses a society should make to them. People who get together with others who are dealing with similar issues to share ideas, attract media attention and seek commitments from politicians and other power-holders begin to gain a political education which gives them a better understanding of their society's power structure.

The conferences mounted in many cities in recent years on poverty, social justice, unemployment and similar issues have been a response to this conviction that shared concerns need to be mobilised. 'Poverty alliances' linking such groups have been set up in some cities and regions. The Scottish Poverty Alliance – originally Strathclyde's – has been one of the most effective. These alliances have often been supported by local authorities which fund what they know will sometimes be an opposition to themselves because they feel that their most vulnerable people need independent advocates. 'My job', said one official to me, 'is to turn moaners into complainers – and perhaps, one day, into campaigners.' Constructing and maintaining an alliance between professionals, who know all the statistics, the rules and benefit rates, and the authentic representatives of those who actually experience the problems is an essential but difficult part of this task. Power always tends to seep back into the hands of the professionals who come to be seen by the poor themselves as yet another band of experts – on their side for a change, but giving them no greater control over their own fate than they got from old-fashioned bureaucrats.

Reformers in a cold climate

There are more conferences today than ever before. They have become a central feature of tourism and the catering trade, keeping hotels and universities in business when they might otherwise have had to close. They can be a useful way of educating their generally middle-class participants. But their influence on public affairs is usually negligible. When a large number of people gather to talk about poverty or unemployment, their concern about the issue may be genuine enough, but at the end of the day they go back to their jobs and their comfortable homes and nothing happens.

Conference rituals come down to us from a tradition which flourished more robustly in the past than it does today. Before the spread of television, political meetings drew larger audiences and made a greater impact. Those were times when government departments and local authorities had no research workers, no economists or statisticians. Thus independent researchers who worked for a few years in a particular field of public policy – housing, for example, or crime – became more expert about some aspects of their subject than anyone else. Governments might pay no attention to their policy recommendations, but they needed at least to know what they were saying. This was the society which gave rise to the traditions represented by the Fabian Society and, before it, the Charity Organisation Society – independent bodies publishing pamphlets about social problems, mobilising and educating the liberal, London-centred, middle class, and occasionally exerting a real influence on public policy.

Today, when the Rowntree Foundation holds a big conference to discuss its major report on income and wealth,[4] or the National Association for the Care and Resettlement of Offenders holds another to discuss its report on *Crime and Social Policy*,[5] most of the evidence presented in both comes from official statistics assembled and published by government departments. Those departments have larger teams of researchers, economists and statisticians, bigger computers and more data than any independent research group. If government ministers want to know about poverty or crime they can consult their own officials any time. For politicians today, poverty and crime are not problems on which they require fresh evidence. Their only 'problem' is how to gain favourable media treatment for their own responses to the issue. If those responses are applauded by tabloid newspapers, poverty and crime (or homelessness, ill-health, educational failure and other issues) are not 'problems'; they are assets.

If conferences and reports rarely make a lasting impact, can public interest be mobilised in other ways? The campaigns about the disposal of oil rigs, the transport of calves and the building of bypasses have already been mentioned. But demonstrations about more complex issues likely to call for a major redistribution of resources and powers, such as cuts in social security benefits and rising unemployment, have generally been a failure. It is in this frustrating climate that some people have resolved to find other ways of gaining some action about issues which none of the main political parties seems prepared to tackle seriously.

An example

The Citizen Organising Foundation (COF) is one example of such an initiative. Although its members would not claim to have changed the world, their principles are worth studying. They owe something to Gandhi, but a great deal more to the American Industrial Areas Foundation and Saul Alinsky, one of its founders.[6] He learnt his political skills in the trade union movement and transferred them to the broader arena of urban politics, working particularly in places where there were deprived ethnic minorities. COF was formed by people who wanted to do something about the problems discussed in *Faith in the City*[7], the report made in 1985 by a Commission set up by the Archbishop of Canterbury, and it was at first funded mainly by the Churches' Urban Fund created by that initiative. They focus on particular areas: the first two were Merseyside and Bristol, followed later by east London, the Black Country, north-east Wales, and Sheffield. Funds are raised from foundations and other sources to appoint a full-time organiser for each area, but that person's job is to recruit, train and support local leaders to do the work, rather than to do it themselves. They seek members initially from the congregations of various faiths – including Muslims and other non-Christians – but are now extending into other groups: residents' associations, student unions and so on. They find that even the most successful meetings generate no commitment to act. Only when people talk to each other, one to one and several times, does that kind of conviction begin to build up, so creating an effective local group is slow work. They also ask for a regular payment of 'dues' – Alinsky's American trade union term – from all their supporters, but they do not insist that every member of a congregation or any other group associated with them should join and subscribe.

The questions on which action is to be taken are chosen by the membership. They must be convinced about their importance. After exploratory meetings with local power-holders, they pick 'winnable issues' for which they want a specific decision. The person responsible for that decision is then identified and 'confronted'. Large numbers can be brought to bear, with the local media in attendance. Much of this movement's work has been focused on local issues: some small, like the building of a pedestrian crossing at a dangerous local intersection; others larger, like the regulations governing the admission to this country of the relatives of earlier migrants. One of Hanson's companies was persuaded – by a large public attendance at a shareholders' meeting, backed by television cameras – to convert an empty building which he intended to demolish so that it could offer work spaces for enterprises in an area of high unemployment. The same Bristol group persuaded the Bristol and West Building Society to lend money to housing associations working for the homeless, and, when at first brushed off, they sent hundreds of their members to queue at the Society's offices to open accounts with £1 each, thereby bringing business to a halt. The Building Society is now one of the group's local supporters – which illustrates another of COF's principles: it should have 'no permanent enemies and no permanent friends'. Their projects are not all so confrontational. Since then, they have begun to work with the local authority on bringing about the renewal of a large and very deprived inner part of the city.

This brief account suggests some of COF's weaknesses as well as its strengths. They depend heavily on priests and other church leaders to bring their congregations in, which is a quick way of mobilising troops. But each priest's successor may take the same people out again. In America, the churches provide a robust and prosperous foundation for social action. Most people belong to one. But in this country they are weaker, poorer, and to give them a central role may alienate some potential supporters. It will be very important to extend the core of support initially provided by the churches to include more secular groups.

The 'principles' I have described are tactical rather than strategic, and could therefore degenerate into a programme for winning battles, rather than making a better community or a better city. The political marketplace thus created may, at the end of the day, be no more attractive than the commercial marketplace. If the actions mounted are to add up to a humane, coherent and continuing force – a social movement – more fundamental guiding ideas will be needed. COF's national leaders are aware of that problem, and regular meetings of local organisers and leaders are organised to develop strategies of this kind.

More secure sources of funding will be needed to pay their organisers if COF is to extend its work much beyond the half-dozen centres where it is now operating. Dues paid by their own members have never provided more than a quarter of the funds needed for this purpose. They may have to reconsider their present rule that no public money be accepted for their work, but, if they do, their independence will have to be firmly defended.

I could have picked other examples of local collective action taken by people who have a concern about social justice which extends beyond a single issue or the interests of a single group. They would include some of the LETS schemes, already mentioned in Chapter 6, which are being set up in many places – most successfully in Manchester. But it may be more helpful to note some of the lessons to be learnt from movements of this sort. They have recognised that, no matter how carefully justified by rational argument it may be, the pathway to social justice has to lead through conflict. The liberal dream of pain-free progress to a happier world is a confidence trick. They have been able to attract into purposeful social action a lot of people with no previous experience of politics, public service or community work. These are the kinds of people – so often missing from other demonstrations – whose families and friends will ultimately shape the proposals which politicians feel they can risk putting to the electorate. Starting from no assumptions about the location of power, they have been prepared to take the private sector as seriously as the public sector: indeed, they are convinced that, for most purposes, the private sector generally has a good deal more clout. That too brings a useful perspective to bear on many social questions. They have tried to work constructively with the public sector, to seek support from the private sector, to consult expert professionals in the universities and elsewhere – but without surrendering to any of them their own responsibility for deciding what to do.

Conclusions

It is no part of my purpose to convince people that ordinary citizens, working together, can transform the world through sheer, benevolent enthusiasm. However, I have shown that when people get together with sufficient determination they can make an impact on events. The women of Dunblane, who have got handguns banned by law, started their campaign with no political experience and no powerful friends. The political parties and the big battalions of the public and private sectors must ultimately be involved before important changes can be brought about. But the impetus for change rarely originates among them.

When major changes are needed – a successful 'war of position', rather than a guerrilla 'war of movement'[8] – we have to remember that a regime only disintegrates when it has to, that is to say, when it is utterly discredited. That rarely happens without turbulence of some kind. But there must then be a convincing and widely known alternative, already tried out at least in experimental ways, if anything good is to happen. If the hard work required to mount those experiments has not been done, turbulence leads only to disaster. The Marxist story – that social reform always requires conflict – and the Fabian story – that it requires research and experiment – are both true. Regimes which decay without enabling their opponents and potential successors to formulate publicly debated alternatives, tried out in practical experiments, too often lead to chaos. Eastern Europe is littered with examples.

Meanwhile the rest of the world does not stand idle. Other people are preparing plans of a very different kind for the day of turbulence. The abolition of democratic local government, the abolition of trial by jury for many offences, the abandonment of some neighbourhoods to the rule of local gunmen, soldiers and an armed police force patrolling the streets... all of these have already been tried out in the province of the United Kingdom where a previous regime was most resoundingly discredited and no broadly acceptable alternative was prepared. The result – direct colonial rule from Westminster – is politely described as a 'democratic deficit'. Only by putting together fairer ideas about the way to run our society and by trying them out whenever we get a chance shall we ensure that, when the day of turbulence comes, there will be enough people around who are determined to make our country a better, not a worse, place and have some ideas about how that can be done.

Notes

1   These and other innovations in social policy are traced in Phoebe Hall *et al.*, *Change, Choice and Conflict in Social Policy*, London, Heinemann, 1975.

2   E. Moberly Bell, *Octavia Hill, a Biography*, London, Constable, 1942.

3   Royal Commission on the Housing of the Working Classes, *First Report*, 1884–5, London, HMSO.

4   Joseph Rowntree Foundation, *Inquiry into Income and Wealth*, York, Joseph Rowntree Foundation 1995.

5   NACRO, *Crime and Social Policy*, London, National Association for the Care and Resettlement of Offenders, 1995.

6   Saul Alinsky, *Reveille for Radicals*, Chicago, University of Chicago Press, 1946.

7   Archbishop of Canterbury's Commission on Urban Priority Areas, *Faith in the City – a Call for Action by Church and Nation*, London, Church House, 1985.

8   Gramsci's discussion of these concepts is explored by James Joll in *Gramsci*, London, Fontana Paperbacks, 1977, p. 97.

PART III

Towards Conclusions

Chapter 11

By What Authority?

Introduction

This book is full of words like 'should' and 'must' in sentences prescribing action of various kinds. Behind these lie assumptions about the good society which we could create and the bad things in our present society which we should correct. By what authority does anyone make such judgements about a society and the people who live in it? Readers who have come this far probably have some sympathy with the sense of outrage I feel about the injustices which divide our society. But others are blind to the hardships, humiliations and anxieties suffered by many of their fellow citizens, or they have no hope that anything can be done about these things. Some are wholly unconcerned about poverty. They may think there should be more inequality, not less of it. What right has anyone to tell them that they are wrong? What kind of a statement would that be?

These are questions which have puzzled some of the world's greatest minds for thousands of years. I shall only explain the way in which I, along with many others, would now answer them, beginning first with judgements about specific fields of policy and then turning to the wider society we live in. Drawing conclusions in the final section of the chapter, I discuss some of the political implications of this standpoint – implications which will be explored further in the final chapter of this book.

Moral authority in specific fields

Taken by themselves, the words 'good' and 'bad' – as in 'She's a good woman' or 'He's a bad man' – are little more than appreciative or hostile noises. They tell us something about the speaker's feelings, but not much more. 'Good (or bad) at what?' we would have to ask in order to get some fuller understanding of such assertions. But say that she (or he) is a good mother (or father), a good doctor, a good farmer, a good Christian, a good plumber – or a bad one – and your words convey a great deal of meaning. Why the difference?

By adding nouns to the adjectives we bring four important things into play.

1   First, an *institution* of some sort – motherhood, the medical profession, the farming industry, Christian churches and communities. 'Institution' is a woolly word, describing everything from very small and vaguely defined units such as 'the family', to large and more clearly defined groups such as 'the medical profession' and ill-defined areas of society such as 'the farming industry'. But it will serve our purposes for in all these cases it identifies a group of people who have some shared interests and distinctive ways of interacting which are based on interlocking roles and status, and often on shared feelings and ideas. The word 'family' brings to mind parents, children, possibly grandparents – the cast and the relationships between them vary from one society to another. The pattern in each case has a structure of some sort which is moulded partly by neighbouring institutions. Thus the 'shape' and character of our medical profession depend partly on the character of our hospital system and health services, the nursing profession and the behaviour of patients. The institution takes different forms in other countries where these neighbouring institutions differ from ours.[1]

2   Associated with an institution there are one or more *practices* or ways of working – parenting and childrearing, medicine or medical work – which go on in and around it. When evaluations of individuals or groups are made, it is often their performance in this work that is being assessed.

3   In the course of time, practitioners develop, sustain and continually modify a *tradition* or culture of some sort which sets standards and defines good and bad practice. These standards have a moral character; people who understand the practice are shocked when they are disregarded. That is what adds the passion to our arguments about the workings of the family and the Christian churches. Much the same feelings can be found among the

insiders within every institution. Plumbers and other skilled tradesmen express moral outrage, not just technical disapproval, when they encounter the work of 'cowboys' who fail to maintain the standards of their trade.

4   In an evolving world, institutions, practices and traditions will all be changing in response to changes in economic and social circumstances, and changes in knowledge, technologies and ideas. There will therefore be *conflicts* about the best ways of responding to these changes. Arguments about lone, surrogate, and gay and lesbian parenthood illustrate some of the conflicts now to be seen around our changing ideas about the family, just as arguments about abortion, euthanasia and 'genetic engineering' arise from changing practice in the medical profession. The meanings of phrases such as 'good parent' and 'good doctor' are disputed and changing. Likewise, growing public concern about animal welfare, and about the impact made upon the environment by the heavy use of chemical fertilisers and pesticides is changing what it means to be a good farmer. Eventually such conflicts have to be resolved and the definition of good practice may then settle into an agreed form. But new conflicts will succeed the old ones because no perfected, unchangeable, universally valid practice and tradition are ever attained. The concepts used in this account are most clearly set forth in the works of Alasdair MacIntyre.[2]

The prevalence of conflict means that we scarcely ever find a complete and uncontested definition of good practice. In a vigorous field of work there is always an argument of some kind going on. But these conflicts, which worry people who seek a universal and permanent definition of the 'good', are in fact a healthy sign of life – provided the argument is constructively settled in ways which enable practitioners to adapt to changing circumstances and move on.

Changes in our judgements about practice in such fields may originate from many quarters. They may start from changed economic conditions – changes in the labour market and the housing market, for example, which encourage or compel mothers to stay in paid work and thereby change the meaning of good motherhood and fatherhood. Or they may be prompted by advancing technology – which enables doctors to keep patients alive for much longer, makes the point of death increasingly a matter for human decision and therefore raises questions about euthanasia. They may start from new knowledge, followed up eventually by changes in the law – as in the case of the research which revealed the dangers of tobacco and led to new rules criminalising smoking in many public places. Or public debate and changes in the law may play leading parts in changing moral values – as they slowly are in helping to outlaw racism and to separate drinking from driving.

Often several of these influences will be at work. The slow acceptance that women must have equal opportunities with men is being pushed forward by changes in the economy which bring them better opportunities for work while eliminating many jobs previously done by men, increases in housing costs which make it harder for families to get a home if they do not have two incomes, advances in technology which reduce the burdens of housework, the growing confidence of women themselves and many other factors. Once they have taken hold, these influences bring about changes in public morality – new ideas about what it means to be a 'good wife and mother' – and changes, therefore, in what it means to be a 'good husband and father', 'a good son or daughter' and also a 'good employer'.

To use words like 'good' and 'bad' properly in such cases you must get mentally inside the world of those involved in the institution and understand its practices, traditions and conflicts. But you also need to be able to stand outside that world and assess its values in the light of conditions in the wider, changing society we all inhabit, and make your own judgements about the evolution of the tradition involved. That right and obligation to make our own moral choices in the light of concern about a wider world must never be forgotten. Once it is abandoned we shall drift into believing that it makes as much sense to talk about the 'good' concentration camp guard (another institution and practice) as the good mother.

Before moving on to consider the wider world we should note some of the points made thus far. Coherent, defensible standards of behaviour arise within an institution, from its practices and traditions – that is to say, among people living and working together who develop shared interests and aspirations, and shared expectations of each other.

That may suggest that standards and values can be developed privately, as it were, within the confines of one institution and its practices. Not for long. To withstand criticism they must be consistent with those which people apply in neighbouring arenas of discourse. A controversial example will clarify the point. Some people assert that abortion is murder and always wrong. Their standpoint is more convincing if they assert, equally passionately, that society should help parents to choose when they wish to bear children (with safe means of birth control), should help them to raise and care for the children they bear (with good health services, generous child benefits, subsidised housing for those who need it and so on) and should treat other forms of killing, such as the death penalty, as murder and ban them too. Someone who rejects what many would regard as closely related values has the difficult task of justifying what seems like inconsistency. I do not suggest that we can achieve general agreement about issues such as abortion, only that we can learn from each other and clarify our standpoints by exploring how our values relate to those which people apply to other relevant issues. Ultimately we each have to create and defend our own standards, but not in isolation from other people or other arenas of discourse.

Moral standards and rules of behaviour, being embedded in a constantly changing economy and society, are themselves constantly changing and open to critical discussion. Part of the task of advocating or defending such standards has to consist of showing that they fit the society in which they are embedded and will change that society – or stabilise it – in desirable ways. That kind of discussion has to take place within communities of some kind – among groups of people (ranging from a family to a whole nation) to whom the standards matter. Many people have to share the same interests and aspirations, and to feel that their prospects and the prospects of those whom they care about depend on the outcome of the discussion.

It follows that people who participate in very few vigorous institutions – perhaps because they do not go to work or belong to trade unions, clubs, churches or political parties; their neighbours change so frequently that they do not know who they are; and they cannot afford to go to pubs or to other places where they meet a regular group of friends – will find it harder than others to develop and adapt robust moral standards. Or their standards will be regarded as deviant because they are shaped by institutions and experiences – in illicit trades, prisons and elsewhere – which other people do not share.

The wider society

This analysis is already moving into the wider world – as indeed we must if we look deeply enough into any institution. There is no clear-cut boundary to be drawn between evaluation conducted at these different scales. The example of debate about abortion made that clear. An anecdote may remind us that anyone who pulls at a thread hanging loose within one institution will ultimately find the whole fabric of society at the end of it. Talking with a doctor friend who works in a large general practice in Dublin, and knowing that Irish doctors generally take their postgraduate training either in the United States or in Britain, I asked if his American- and British-trained colleagues worked in the same ways. 'Oh no', he replied. 'Those who have worked in the British Health Service are always thinking about priorities – which patients should go to hospital first, and how scarce resources can best be used. Their American-trained colleagues just try to do the best they can for whoever is sitting before them in the surgery.' His account does not tell us which practice is best. Speaking as tax-payers, health service managers or a Minister of Health, we would probably prefer the British pattern. But if we, or our nearest and dearest, fall ill we may prefer the American. Richard Titmuss researched and recorded the differing practices and traditions which the British and American health systems developed in dealing with blood donations – the former relying on unpaid volunteer donors and the latter relying mainly on market mechanisms and their commercial motives; the former helping to create 'social man', the latter helping to create 'economic man'.[3] Institutions and practices bear the imprint of the wider society in which they are embedded and contribute their own influences to that society.

Two such traditions rarely operate side by side for long. More often, they grow up separately in different countries, or one institutional pattern gives way to another, and changes follow in the values and standards which govern practice. Most people then come to accept and work within the new tradition, not because it is in some universal sense the best but because it fits their circumstances and they can see no alternative. Soon we are faced with a self-fulfilling prophecy. What exists is accepted because the social structures which made other systems and their moral values feasible have disappeared.

Anyone who wants to bring about – or to resist – major shifts in the character of a modern society has to work for – or resist – a broad pattern of changes to institutions and their practices. Appeals to moral principles and prime values – 'liberty', 'community' and so on – will sometimes be helpful in providing a sense of direction, mobilising and focusing energies, but the real human networks created and the relationships between people which they foster will in the long run exert a more powerful moral influence than sermons, no matter how eloquent they may be.

To pick the directions in which a society should be moving we need to understand its character and the trends already to be seen within it. It will also be helpful to compare these patterns with those of other countries at a similar stage of development. It is a journey that is being made, not a final destination that will ever be reached. Looking at where we have come from, where we have got to and where we are heading, and comparing our progress with that of neighbouring societies, we can formulate priorities and strategies which offer some guidance for the next stage of the journey. But it is still a choice that we have made – a choice which can be criticised and which will have to be defended – not a moral trump card that we have played.

Criticisms of such a standpoint can take essentially three forms:

- an *analytical* or logical attack, arguing that we have been inconsistent within the terms of our own argument, or have failed to follow the normal and widely accepted rules of logic;
- an *empirical* or factual attack, arguing that the facts used to support our argument are erroneous, misinterpreted, or omit other important facts which should be taken into account; or
- a *moral* attack, rejecting the argument as wicked or morally unacceptable.

All three arguments, or any combination of them, must be treated seriously, so that we arrive at decisions with as full an understanding as possible of the possibilities open to us and their implications for the future, and a clearer grasp of the points at which we differ from our opponents. But the decision will always remain provisional, open to further amendment as the traditions in which it is embedded evolve. We have done the best we can with what we had at the time, and no-one can do more.

Some people would reject this approach. Among them are those who rely on prime values such as liberty or dominant criteria such as human need. An excellent analysis of human needs, claiming that they provide universal and absolute standards to guide policy-makers, was made by Len Doyal and Ian Gough in *A Theory of Human Need*.[4] People who rely on prime values argue that they are so important that they must override everything else. Such ideas can provide helpful ways of clarifying the issues at stake when policy decisions are made, but there are no trump cards which will save us the trouble of further argument and thought. Who can prove that liberty is everywhere and always more important than 'equality', 'fraternity' or other candidates for trump card status? *Whose* liberty – whose needs – are most important, and whose less important? There will always be room for dispute when dealing with such essentially contestable ideas.

Some rely on God for the authority to settle such arguments. Religion may indeed offer them a tradition which helps to clarify problems and provide a guide through the maze. But infallible, unchanging prescriptions, valid for all times and places, cannot be found in this way. Throughout history the human race has created successive Gods to meet the needs of its changing societies.[5] The appeal to God does not settle the question; it reformulates it, making it one about what kind of God is preferred.

Others rely on constitutional principles, not to define the good society itself but to show how rational, unbiased citizens would set about drawing up its rules and principles. However, the social priorities which emerge from this kind of analysis conflict as sharply as those from any other school of thought. Two of the most distinguished modern examples of this approach are to be seen in John Rawls' book *A Theory of Justice* and Robert Nozick's *Anarchy, State, and Utopia*.[6] Rawls, in later years, recognised that his principles were not universal and timeless but socially embedded. 'What justifies a conception of justice is not its being true to an order antecedent and given to us, but its congruence with our deeper understanding of ourselves and our aspirations, and our realisation that, given our history and the traditions embedded in our public life, it is the most reasonable doctrine for us'.[7] That statement, leaving the debate open and capable of further development as '*our* history' and 'the traditions embedded in *our* public life' evolve, seems to me exactly right.

Those who approach the task of formulating a political philosophy by looking for a system of thought capable of prescribing universally valid principles are always uncomfortable with opposition. Their search for an authority which will be independent of the infinitely varied and changing character of each society means that any criticism that cannot be dismissed is a serious threat to their project. That is a grave mistake. Provided it can eventually be resolved constructively, lively contention within a tradition of thought and practice is a sign of health, not of weakness – evidence that it is capable of evolving in ways which may meet the needs of a changing society.

Those looking for universal, absolute values often dismiss the approach which I have adopted as a relapse into 'mere relativism'. Again, this is a misunderstanding. It is precisely because it endeavours to embed moral judgement in an understanding of conditions and trends in the society in which it is to be applied, and keeps those judgements open to criticism and amendment as times change, that relativism carries conviction. Approaches which have been described as 'historicist'[8] or 'pluralist'[9] have similar features, the former stressing that values change over time, the latter reminding us that they vary in different cultures at the same time. None of these provides a formula or a black box that turns out universal, authoritative solutions. All call ultimately for moral choices, but these are likely to be better informed and more carefully reasoned choices, more relevant to local conditions, not mere assertions of taste (like choosing between strawberry and vanilla ice cream) or dogmatic claims to unchallengeable authority (like asserting that your God is better than anyone else's).

Conclusions and implications

Some readers may feel that this excursion into philosophy has been a distraction. I hope to demonstrate its purpose as I draw this chapter to a close – first by summarising the main points made and then by considering their implications.

Moral principles and values are created, not discovered – created collectively by people who work together and reflect on what they do. They are to be found in the traditions which grow up around their work, and among the people engaged in it. (By 'work' I mean every kind of shared and purposeful activity, not only the things for which people get paid.) These traditions and the values they express are the most important products of the human groupings we call institutions. Principles and values identify the bad as well as the good – vice as well as virtue. Each helps to define the other, and both can be seen in a group or a society which has moral bearings of some kind.

Long-term unemployment excludes many people from some of the most important opportunities for learning these traditions – at work, in trade unions and in recreation shared with workmates. If they live in places where there are few opportunities for people to meet their neighbours and to get to know and trust them, shared traditions and standards get eroded still further.

People and the institutions they form are embedded in a constantly changing environment of needs, aspirations, technologies, knowledge and so forth. These changes create new opportunities and pose new dilemmas, compelling people to reappraise principles developed in previous times. Thus values are constantly changing too. Each generation decriminalises some of its predecessors' sins and criminalises other behaviour which their predecessors tolerated.

Such changes provoke moral conflicts which play a necessary part in the life of any institution robust enough to survive in a changing world. A tradition without conflict – like a church or a political party without schisms – is dead or dying. But unresolved conflict can be deeply divisive. The aim of those who care about an institution should be to resolve conflicts in constructive, healing ways, rather than to suppress or evade them. Those who play no part in these institutions are excluded from that continuing, and potentially creative, argument.

Public policies, like any other initiative that can change society in significant ways, may make new values necessary and old ones increasingly untenable. The most important effects of a new policy are often the moral ones – the values it strengthens and those it weakens.

Individuals are entitled – indeed, they have a duty – to stand from time to time outside the evolving patterns of moral values enshrined in the conventional wisdom of the institutions in which they participate – their family, their trade or profession, their church or party – to consider whether they should demand, or resist, changes in these values. If they resolve to bring about, or to resist, such changes, they will have to start by gaining an understanding of the lives of the people involved – to get inside their reality. While we are all entitled to preach at people, we are likely to exert much greater leverage if, with the help of our fellow citizens, we can change the social circumstances out of which values grow: not just telling people to be good, but making it easier for them to be good. The fact that people have to define – and, from time to time, redefine – what they mean by 'good' does not make that judgement any less important than it would be if it came down to them on tablets inscribed in heaven.

This standpoint, sometimes described as 'relativist', is not a weak one – something which people 'relapse into' when they lose faith in universal authorities. It provides a rationale and a framework which enable us to reason cogently about principles, and to validate them by showing that they are relevant and appropriate in particular circumstances. That enables us to formulate firm – although always provisional – moral standards and policies. There are no universally valid principles of social policy which apply at all times and places. We have to create them, rather than discover them. They will then evolve over time and will always remain contestable.

To be most convincingly defensible, such principles have to be rooted in the tradition and culture of many people, and relevant to the circumstances of the society concerned and the trajectory of its development. Studies of history and of the experience of other comparable countries are essential starting points for anyone formulating principles of this kind.

In Britain today an analysis of this sort suggests strong priorities for action: to arrest and reverse our growing social divisions, focusing particularly on the needs of children, youngsters and their parents; to give high priority to getting unemployed people back into decent jobs; to make public services more responsive and open, embedding them more deeply in the communities they serve; to rebuild capacities for civic leadership; and to link egalitarian social policies more effectively to 'green' environmental policies, seeing them not as competing priorities but as different ways of formulating a single vision of our country's and our cities' future.

But to pursue these priorities effectively will call for a much longer 'game plan' – for the rebuilding of institutions, practices and traditions which will enable the people of this country to work more effectively together, and to bring the most excluded people back into the mainstream. Those aims will often call for collective public action of some kind. Traditions and values have to be created collectively too. Take, as examples, some of the policies called for in this book: getting more jobs into the places where they are most needed and for the people who most need them; making dangerous neighbourhoods safer; monitoring what happens to children, young people and those who care for them; and formulating, for the places we live in, a vision of the future which combines a concern for social justice and equality, and a determination to create a sustainable, 'greener' world. None of these things will be achieved if they are left to market forces – any more than they can be achieved by *diktat* of the state. Most of them will call for participation by private enterprise, but that has to be mobilised with the help of civic leaders and public services.

Collective concern for those having the hardest time calls for collective action, and collective action will be needed to mobilise public concern. Neither can be achieved through programmes of action focusing only on the poorest people. As shown in Part I of this book, there are many in the middle reaches of society who are increasingly anxious about their future – the kind of people described by Robert Reich, Secretary of Labour in the Clinton administration, as 'an anxious class, most of whom hold jobs, but are justifiably uneasy about their own standing and fearful for their children's futures'.[10] Any party seeking power has to gain support from these people if it is to stand any chance of winning elections.

Collective concern and collective action call for effective public services staffed by credible professions. Battered though the reputations of some of them have been in recent years, the credibility and effectiveness of these professions are still vital requirements for a fair and democratic society. No-one else can ensure that everyone has opportunities to work and the skills required for it, that everyone gets good medical care when it is needed, that plans for urban development take account of social justice and sustainability. Yet we cannot simply reinstate the old, bureaucratic, top-down system of local government which we used to rely on. New forms of governance – more responsive, democratic and inclusive – are needed. That is a problem to which I shall return in the final chapter.

Notes

A fuller deployment of many of the arguments in this chapter was presented in David Donnison, 'By what authority? Ethics and policy analysis', *Social Policy and Administration*, **28**(1), 1994, pp. 20–32.

1 A fuller account of the meanings and derivations of this and other words used here can be found in Julius Gould and William Kolb (eds), *A Dictionary of the Social Sciences*, London, Tavistock, 1964.
2 Alasdair MacIntyre, *After Virtue*, London, Duckworth, 1981; and *Whose Justice? Which Rationality?*, London, Duckworth, 1988.
3 Richard Titmuss, *The Gift Relationship. From Human Blood to Social Policy*, London, Allen & Unwin, 1970.

4 Len Doyal and Ian Gough, *A Theory of Human Need*, London, Macmillan, 1991.

5 Karen Armstrong tells the story in her remarkable book, *A History of God*, London, Heinemann, 1993.

6 John Rawls, *A Theory of Justice*, Oxford, Clarendon Press, 1972. Robert Nozick, *Anarchy, State, and Utopia*, Oxford, Blackwell, 1974.

7 John Rawls, 'Kantian constructivism in moral theory', *Journal of Philosophy*, 77, 1980, p. 519.

8 Richard Rorty uses this word in *Contingency, Irony and Solidarity*, Cambridge, Cambridge University Press, 1989.

9 Ernesto Laclau and Chantal Mouffe, *Hegemony and Socialist Strategy: Towards a Radical Democratic Politics*, London, Verso, 1985.

10 Robert Reich, 'The fracturing of the middle class', *New York Times*, 31 August 1994; quoted in Peter Marris, *The Politics of Uncertainty*, London, Routledge, 1996, p. 172.

Chapter 12

Conclusion

Introduction

For 18 years the British have lived under a regime whose leaders have done their best to eliminate the word poverty from the English language, along with all talk about inequality and social injustice. They promptly abolished the Royal Commission on the Distribution of Income and Wealth; official statistics of income distribution and poverty have become scarcer and more expensive to buy; their publication, when they do appear, has often been timed to coincide with other news that is likely to distract attention from them; links between poverty and ill-health, and between unemployment and crime have frequently been denied; the Prime Minister and his Secretary of State for Social Security have said that poverty is only found in third world countries; and a Chancellor of the Exchequer has described unemployed people as a price well worth paying to solve the nation's economic problems.

These steps amount to a strategy of class war. For who was it that caused the economic problems which the Chancellor was trying to solve? Not the people who are their main victims – the people excluded from view by eliminating talk about poverty – but the people whose poor productivity, excessive wage demands, inadequate savings and excessive expenditure on imported goods sent the economy out of control. The rest of us.

This systematic attempt to change our language and thinking, and to destroy the idea that a society needs some sort of protective contract between its older and younger generations and its different social classes has failed. Influential independent inquiries have been set up by churches, charitable foundations and various political parties to study poverty, unemployment, the distribution of income and wealth, the social and economic causes of ill-health and the plight of increasingly deprived urban neighbourhoods. Their reports have so far had little influence on policy, but they have at least kept older words and ideas alive. It is still possible to talk about poverty, inequality and social injustice without sounding merely archaic. Indeed, more and more people are doing so. Local councillors and their officials have formed a National Local Government Forum Against Poverty and an Anti-Poverty Unit, and well over 100 local authorities claim to have anti-poverty policies of some sort. Poverty is back on the political agenda.

Most of the local authorities which have taken up this cause have Labour majorities – partly because it is becoming increasingly difficult to find any that don't. Never has the party so dominated the town and county halls. But that will not last. If it wins the next parliamentary election, past experience suggests that Labour's opponents will start to recapture local government 2 years later – before the end of the century. Thus, if the cause is worth fighting for, cross-party alliances must be built which keep alive public concern about the social divisions which afflict every town and county and carry forward the policies devised to heal them. Fortunately there are people who are concerned about human hardship in all parties.

A great deal has now been said about local anti-poverty policies and another handbook on the subject is not required. I mean no disrespect to handbooks – we all need them for many purposes – but it seemed more helpful to range further, saying more than the handbooks do about the strategy, the principles and the future development of these policies. However, I have accepted one of the limits usually found in the handbooks: I have focused mainly on what can be done by people working at a local level. That does not mean that nothing needs to be done at national or international scales. On the contrary, no really big change will be brought about until new policies – for employment, social security and local government finance in particular – begin to take shape on a nationwide and a European scale.

That will not happen, however, if we sit back and wait for it. For reasons which I explored in Chapter 4, our people lack the will to demand action on these issues. Some have lost hope that things can be changed; many have more pressing anxieties of their own. A new politics of poverty has to be constructed from the ground up. That will be a laborious, experimental task. People working at local levels will play important parts in this movement by trying things out, finding out what happens, reporting what they learn, and mobilising local alliances between public and private sectors, the community and its public services, Left and Right. It took half a century for the British people to move from the first stirrings of an organised labour movement and the first studies of poverty made by Charles Booth and Seebohm Rowntree, followed by Lloyd George's first pension scheme and William Beveridge's early work on labour exchanges, to the contract between the generations represented by the 'welfare state' which was created after the Second World War. That experience should mean that we can now learn a bit faster. But if not, we have nevertheless to learn. Societies which allow more and more of their people to be humiliated, impoverished and excluded eventually break up. Beveridge, writing in the midst of the democracies' life-and-death struggle with Fascism, began his book on full employment by reminding his readers that 'misery breeds hate'. If democratic politics and a capacity for honest work offer them no way out, excluded people ultimately turn to other strategies: strategies already well established in Northern Ireland and in some of Britain's more lawless neighbourhoods.

The rhetoric of reaction

Critics of the welfare state and all it stands for adopt the rhetoric of reaction which I briefly outlined at the beginning of Chapter 3. They say that progressive policies, despite their worthy intentions, either have effects opposite to those intended, or they achieve nothing at all, or they destroy fundamental and precious features of our society – theses of perversity, futility and jeopardy, as Albert Hirschman has called them.[1]

The whole of this book amounts to a refutation of the thesis of futility – the idea that nothing works. Britain's sharply hastened descent into greater inequality and social disintegration which set in after 1985 was largely brought about by deliberate policies of our government, and it has visible, measurable effects on millions of people – particularly our children and youngsters and those who care for them. The decline in reading standards traced in Figure 2.1 was probably one of these effects. There have been many others, some of which have been listed on page 24. Other countries, which held more firmly to the contract between the generations expressed in a welfare state funded by progressive taxation, weathered the economic storms which every Western society has encountered without throwing their more vulnerable citizens overboard. The Swedes, who were within living memory a largely rural people living spartan lives on the fringes of Europe, created an egalitarian society with generous public services which has achieved visible, measurable and remarkably equal advances for all social classes in health and life expectations, as Figure 3.2 shows. Differences in the health of different social classes used to be described as 'obstinately unchangeable'. We now know, from eight studies reviewed in Richard Wilkinson's book *Unhealthy Cities*,[2] that it is differences in the income, security and status of different social classes which are, for political reasons, obstinately difficult to change. Difficult, but not impossible. Make *them* more equal, or more unequal, and life expectations will change too.

As for the theses of perversity and jeopardy – the boot is on the other foot. Reactionaries who cut back expenditure on services from which everyone benefits and relied on economic growth to generate wealth that would filter down to the poorest, created a filter-*up* society in which the rich get richer and the poor get poorer still. Relying increasingly on means-tested social benefits, and driving down the wages of low-paid workers, they created new poverty traps and made it harder still for many people to support themselves by working. Relying on increasingly divisive housing and urban policies, backed by increasingly punitive penal policies to discipline victims of this system who make trouble, they have helped to foster crime and increasingly violent subcultures among those excluded from mainstream societies. It is a reaction which has had perverse effects and now jeopardises the whole fabric of society.

What are the alternatives? In the pages that follow I first review very briefly the main things said in this book, and then look to political possibilities for the future.

Review

Economic changes affecting all Western countries have checked or reversed the long-run tendency of these capitalist economies and the social movements created within them to create more equal societies.

For about 20 years, well-qualified people have continued to grow richer while those without qualifications have fallen further and further behind them. In Britain, there are signs that entry to the more privileged occupations is being closed off at earlier stages in life because these jobs increasingly require qualifications provided by a full-time system of education which excludes less successful students from the ladder early in life rather than encouraging people to climb the ladder at any stage of their lives.

Trends towards greater inequality first brought about by changes in the world economy have now developed a political life of their own. Society is divided in new ways, freeing the more successful from a sense of responsibility for their fellow citizens and exposing many in the middle reaches to growing insecurity and anxiety which are sharpened by the presence of poorer people on the excluded margins. Thus social solidarity unravels. The welfare state itself ceases to be a shared concern as more and more people buy their way into private pensions and out of council housing, and find schools becoming increasingly selective.

The people who suffer most from the growing hardships produced by these trends are children, young people and their families: the nation's most precious asset for the future. Those in poverty are increasingly concentrated in particular neighbourhoods while wealthier people concentrate in others. That makes poverty harder to bear and harder to reverse. It also erodes sympathy between different neighbourhoods and different social classes.

Most elderly people have so far been protected from these trends, but the growing insecurity of workers in an increasingly chaotic labour market ('flexible' is the smooth word for it) means that pension rights for the next generation will be uncertain. Meanwhile the state pension falls further and further behind average incomes and older people will henceforth be more likely to live in owner-occupied houses which they can no longer afford to maintain, rather than in rented houses with a landlord who is responsible for repairs.

The European Union draws a poverty line for each of its countries which distinguishes those who have to live on less than half their country's average income for households of their size and type. But this is not a clear-cut boundary. Many people move back and forth across it, although few of those below it move far up the income ladder. There is no separate 'underclass'. There is simply more pain and worry among people on the lower rungs of this ladder. The poor are much like everyone else, but having a harder time.

These stresses affect everyone in some way or other. They produce more mental and physical ill-health, more crime, more family breakdown, a growing prison population, massive bills for social benefits which compel governments to cut back other spending, higher insurance premiums for homes and cars, and increasing fear on the streets. Coupled with growing pollution and the general deterioration of our environment, these trends lead many to say that – despite increases in cash income – the average citizen's quality of life has been static or falling for the past 20 years.

Comparisons between different countries show that the growth of inequality can be resisted and even reversed, but to change these patterns will demand action at national and international scales as well as the local scale. People in the politically crucial middle reaches of society must gain greater hope for the future if a coalition is to be mobilised for wider social justice that gives a fairer deal to the most excluded. That cannot be achieved unless the private sector of the economy is generally successful and prosperous. These are the arguments deployed at greater length in the first three chapters of this book.

The political traditions which reformers can draw upon for mobilising a response to these divisive trends grew up in a different economy with social conflicts different from our own. Today's conflicts call for new responses. These were briefly outlined in Chapter 4, and then explored at greater length in the rest of this book. Socialism, I argue, has never been a fixed formula – a dogma from which no-one should deviate. It has been a resistance movement mobilised to defend people against the harsher impacts of capitalism. As capitalism changes, so too must socialism.

Much that has to be done can only be brought about if recognised democratic authorities give a lead and are determined to make it happen. The old, bureaucratic patterns of authority designed for command and control cannot be reimposed – and could not achieve what is needed if they were. Chapter 5 argued that the people who experience the problems to be tackled must gain a hearing, but there is no magic about 'community power'. It can only work effectively and fairly if it operates within a framework of civic leadership that is accountable to the wider communities of the city, the county and the nation.

Consultation with those experiencing the greatest hardships usually places skills, work and money at the head of the agenda. A strategy for local economic development, aiming to attract jobs and enterprises, to improve skills and self-confidence, and to provide childcare and other supports for people seeking training and work, is now widely understood and many authorities are pursuing it. Important though they are, these steps do not go far enough. Chapter 6 showed that jobs will be needed in the right places and for the right people; and for women as well as men. Neighbourhoods from which all the more successful people escape as soon as they can afford to do so must be made more attractive for all if economic development is not to leave them more deprived than before. Keeping existing enterprises in business and helping them to develop will usually do more for those with modest skills than attracting new ones. The complementary, 'social' economy of community enterprises, credit unions, LETS systems, housing co-operatives and the like can be an important adjunct to the mainstream economy. Many of those who live in the most deprived neighbourhoods are unable to do paid work: for them, advice and advocacy about welfare rights offer far more help. Together, these requirements call for intervention and expenditure by the state. The private sector, left to itself, will never bring people who have been out of work for a long time back into the mainstream economy.

Financially speaking, the net costs of such a programme are not very large when account is taken of the savings it would bring in expenditure on benefits, the higher tax revenues these new workers would contribute and the many other advantages of a fully employed society.

After jobs and incomes there come widespread concerns about safety and security. They have tempted some of our political leaders to bid for popularity by demanding militaristic 'crack-downs' and harsher penalties for offenders – which are generally ineffective. Chapter 7 pointed out that only 3 per cent of offences lead to a conviction in court. The police and the penal services play important parts in managing crime after it has occurred but they cannot prevent it. We must start by asking people what threats to their safety worry them most: the answers vary from place to place. For each a different strategy, involving different services, will be needed. Potential victims must be protected so far as possible. Where crime and 'incivilities' of various kinds are involved, we have to reach those responsible, and change the opportunities open to them and the social circumstances of their lives. If we cannot do that, our efforts at crime prevention will only displace it to other times and places. As for a more general attempt to raise moral standards – if it is to be taken seriously, it has to start at the top, with politicians, business leaders and others whose example influences many people.

For mainstream local services there are whole handbooks of strategies, with which Chapter 8 began. They deal with area-focused projects for economic and social regeneration, policies for reducing the living costs of poor people and for providing them with extra help of various kinds. Some authorities have been marvellously innovative in these ways. But such programmes are no more than a start, amounting to an attempt to make poverty less painful, rather than to reduce it significantly. For that we shall have to go further. The groups experiencing most hardship and stress need to be more clearly identified. That will usually focus attention on children, youngsters and their families, on certain ethnic minorities, and on people with particular disabilities. Their progress should be more carefully monitored in future. That will show where more fundamental changes are needed. These are likely to give a central place to economic opportunities, and therefore to education and training which too often do more to increase inequality than reduce it. These and other programmes will not develop effectively without committed civic leadership involving all public services, the private sector and the wider community.

Very similar strategies are called for by the other main priority for local action during the coming years: policies for the development of more sustainable communities which make a less damaging impact on the global environment. Chapter 9 pointed out that thinking about poverty and about the environment has sprung from different professions, agencies and motives. They are in danger of competing for resources and political attention. It explored the links between these concerns, arguing that they should be seen not as separate tasks but as different approaches to the common task of formulating a vision for the future of any city, town or village. In their urban structure, their housing, their heating and insulation systems and in many other ways the 'just city' and the 'green city' are the same place. Those campaigning in each of these causes have a great deal to learn from each other.

This book, like most of its kind, is largely written for people who are in some sense active within our systems of administration, politics and community action, or preparing for that. What about baffled outsiders, appalled perhaps at the things they see going on around them, yet at a loss to know how to respond? Chapter 10 tried to help them, partly by showing how important the contribution of outsiders has been in the past, and partly by suggesting ways of linking up with others and getting more effectively involved. Outsiders concerned about 'green' issues have in recent years been very effective at stopping major enterprises in their tracks. Activists working in more conventional ways have a good deal to learn from them.

Chapter 11 asked what right anyone has to tell their fellow citizens how their society should be run. This question led to an exploration of the ways in which moral standards evolve, revealing morality as something that is constantly being created, challenged and recreated – rather than discovered and then revered for all time. These standards are shaped by institutions, practices and the traditions that grow up within them. Brought together in broader public arenas, their traditions can enable people to develop shared values and a wider sense of civic responsibility. But such public arenas have been weakened in recent years. Meanwhile the public services and the professions working within them have alienated many people, and no-one should try to reimpose the earlier patterns of bureaucratic and professional power which still thrive in too many places. Nevertheless these services and professions still play a part, which no other agency can replace, in shaping a society's collective character – for better or for worse.

It is to these thoughts that I now turn.

Looking ahead

Many of the tactics for an anti-poverty policy are now well known, even if not widely pursued. It is the strategic questions which present more problems. These are some that have been posed in this book.

- How can policies concerned with poverty and policies concerned with the environment be effectively coordinated? What pattern of human settlements would meet both needs, and what transport systems would be required to support such a pattern? What other features of the character and tenure of its housing, the quality of its schools and health services, and much else would be required to ensure that the just city is also a green city?
- How can we encourage economic development on terms which get jobs to people who have been out of work for a long time and

to the places where they live? What work needs to be done in such places that these people can do or learn to do, and how will that be paid for? Will women get a fair share of these jobs? How can we ensure that this work does not displace other jobs which the market would have created? Since the private sector will never, for its own purposes, create jobs for these people, how can the state best intervene to bring that about?

- How can we reorganise secondary education and training so that they help those who now fail to do better, and preserve opportunities for people to resume their education, starting from any standard at any stage in life? How can these systems be meshed more effectively with employment and the needs of employers?

- How can we respond humanely and effectively to the fears of people who live in deprived neighbourhoods? What varying mix of public, private and community initiatives will be needed in different neighbourhoods to cope with traffic hazards, pollution, crime, graffiti, intimidating behaviour by youngsters who may not be committing any offence, and all the other things which people worry about?

- How may deprived communities living in bleak neighbourhoods where little of real excellence is to be seen be enabled to get together and present to others a sense of their own history and hopes – through drama, music, poetry, the painting of murals or in any other way they choose to celebrate their identity? Where may the funds and the audiences be found to support such projects on a continuing basis?

Further questions could be posed, but these will serve to illustrate what I mean by strategic issues. They have common characteristics. None of them can be tackled simply by directing people to do things, or by waiting for private enterprise to solve the problem, or by relying on the 'internal markets' set up to promote efficiency within public services. All demand close collaboration with the people experiencing the problems concerned, on terms which treat them with respect, respond to their needs and views, and enable them to do things. All depend on active participation by agencies in the private as well as the public sector. All involve a wide but varying range of public services, often extending beyond those provided by any one authority. Several of them require some help – funds, powers, expertise and so on – from sources outside the city or county concerned. In no case will the action go far without political leadership from elected representatives of the local community and others who may be described as civic leaders.

'Civic leadership', like 'community', is too often used as a spray-on word to coat everything to which it is attached with a warm glow of approval. But leaders are created and sustained by followers, and they have some choice about the people they 'play to' and those whom they neglect. If they want to encourage political action among the poorest and most excluded people they will have to develop programmes which address their needs. Many of these people, we have seen, are families with children: low-paid workers, lone parents, people without work, and ethnic minorities. It is the lone parents, in alliance with broader movements of women, who have been the most militant of these groups. People with disabilities and ethnic minorities, too, have gained political influence in some places. This has not prevented the government from launching attacks on the rights and benefits of all three in the course of 1996. The time has come to form alliances which will enable these groups to mobilise, linking them more firmly to each other and to sympathetic civic leaders, before they are attacked again.

Without trusted local services and the professions working in them we are powerless to tackle the strategic problems I have posed. There is a lot of evidence to show that local government, despite its faults and the low turnout often achieved at local elections, retains a great deal of credibility, particularly with working-class people. In a survey of 1,427 British households carried out in 1994 by ICM Research for Channel 4 Television, people were asked who should run each of a long list of public services: schools, rented housing, hospitals, health authorities, further education and employment training services. In every case but one, 'local councils' were the most favoured choice. Only for the police did 'Government-appointed committees' gain a higher vote. Other possible contenders, such as 'locally elected committees' and 'self-appointing committees', were all less popular. The preference for local authorities was generally highest among working class and poorer people.[3] The people who participate in politics in any way – perhaps simply by seeking information from those thought to have some power – are more likely to contact local councillors and their officials than members of Parliament and civil servants. They are more interested in the issues dealt with at local level, such as education and housing, than in those dealt with at national levels, such as economic policy and defence.[4] They are also more likely to write to the local than the national press.

When disasters and crises occur, such as the east coast floods of January 1953 which overwhelmed large areas and drowned many people, it was to local authority services that people turned first for help.[5] More recently, 'at the time of the Lockerbie air disaster, and the Hillsborough football disaster in Sheffield... people turned to the local authority not only to coordinate the emergency services... but also to help embody the community's sense of grief. The local authority as much as the Church appears to carry the latent yearnings of local people for a sense of belonging and of caring... when Coventry won the FA cup at Wembley almost the whole local population came down to the town hall to welcome the team home...'.[6] More recently, when four women, grief-stricken by the Dunblane massacre but with no experience of politics, set out to launch what became a nationwide protest about handguns, it was again to their council that they turned for advice and help.

But to respond to the issues discussed in this book local authorities will have to operate in new ways which have been well described by John Stewart[7] and John Benington.[8] Briefly summarising Benington's analysis, they will have to be capable of listening to their people, responding more promptly and effectively to the messages they receive, helping to build and rebuild economic capacity and community strengths, gathering and analysing information and responding to it, giving leadership to their own people and – on their behalf – addressing higher levels of government, both national and international. That will also call for a capacity to build alliances with civic leaders in other authorities experiencing similar problems and having similar interests.

Many of our neighbours in Europe are amazed and appalled by the British constitution which enables central governments, elected by minority votes, to recast, abolish or paralyse local government whenever they chose to do so. If, under a new government, this country re-examines its constitution and the civil rights it afford us, local government should claim an entrenched right to exist, with powers to do anything that is not forbidden by the laws of the land, and sufficient financial freedom to make those powers effective.

We are moving from a system of government conducted by public authorities to a system of governance calling for civic leadership within a broadly based regime. We may also be helping to sustain important moral values of earlier times and to create some new ones.

Together they may rebuild a contract between the generations and the social classes that will resist and reverse the social divisions now threatening to break up our society.

Notes

1   Albert Hirschman, *The Rhetoric of Reaction. Perversity, Futility, Jeopardy*, Cambridge, Mass., Harvard University Press, 1991.
2   Richard Wilkinson, *Unhealthy Cities*, London, Routledge, 1996.
3   ICM Research, *Results of a Poll on Democracy Conducted for Channel 4*, ICM Research, 90–92 Great Portland Street, London W1N 5PB, March 1994.
4   Geraint Parry *et al.*, *Political Participation and Democracy in Britain*, Cambridge, Cambridge University Press, 1992.
5   Hilda Grieve told the story in *The Great Tide*, Chelmsford, County Council of Essex, 1959.
6   John Benington, 'New paradigms and new practices for local government: capacity building within civil society', in Sebastian Kraemer and Jane Roberts (eds), *The Politics of Attachment: Towards a Secure Society*, London, Free Association Books, 1996, Chapter 11.
7   For example in S. Ranson and J. Stewart, *Management for the Public Domain: Enabling the Learning Society*, Basingstoke, Macmillan, 1994.
8   S. Ranson and J, Stewart, *Management for the Public Domain: Enabling the Learning Society, op. cit.*, pp. 158–64.

Bibliography

Alcock, P, Craig, G *et al.*, *Combating Local Poverty*. Luton: Local Government Management Board, 1995.

Alinsky, A *Reveille for Radicals*. Chicago: Chicago University Press, 1946.

Anderson, S, Kinsey, R *et al.*, *Cautionary Tales*. Edinburgh: University of Edinburgh Centre for Criminology, 1990.

Archbishop of Canterbury's Commission on Urban Priority Areas *Faith in the City – a Call for Action by Church and Nation*. London: Church House, 1985.

Armstrong, K *History of God*. London: Heinemann, 1993.

Atkinson, AB Seeking to explain the distribution of income, in J Hills (ed.) *New Inequalities*. Cambridge: Cambridge University Press, 1996.

Ball, J and Marland, M *Male Earnings Mobility in the Lifetime Labour Market Database, Working paper No. 1*. London: Department of Social Security, 1996.

Balogh, T *The Irrelevance of Contemporary Economics*. London: Weidenfeld & Nicolson, 1982.

Banks, J, Dilnot, A and Low, H *The Distribution of Wealth in the UK*. The Institute for Fiscal Studies, 1994.

Benington, J New paradigms and new practices for local government: capacity building within civil society, Chapter 11 in S Kraemer and J Roberts (eds) *The Politics of Attachment: Towards a Secure Society*. London: Free Association Books, 1996.

Benington, J *et al.*, *Local Strategies and Initiatives for an Ageing Population*. Warwick University, Local Authorities Research Consortium, 1995.

Beveridge, W *Full Employment in a Free Society*. London: Allen & Unwin, 1944.

Boardman, B *Fuel Poverty. From Cold Homes to Affordable Warmth*. London: Belhaven Press, 1991.

Britton, A *The Goal of Full Employment*. London: National Institute of Economic and Social Research, 1996.

Brook, L, Hall, J and Preston, I Public spending and taxation, in R Jowell *et al.* (eds) *British Social Attitudes. The Thirteenth Report*. Aldershot: Dartmouth, 1996.

Buck, N *et al.*, *The London Employment Problem*. Oxford: Clarendon Press, 1986.

Campbell, B *Goliath. Britain's Dangerous Places*. London: Methuen, 1993.

Carmichael, K *Ceremony of Innocence*. London: Macmillan, 1991.

Church, J and Summerfield, C (eds) *Social Focus on Ethnic Minorities*. London: HMSO, 1996.

Coates, K, Santer, J *et al.*, *Dear Commissioner. An Exchange of Letters*. London: Spokesman, 1996.

Craig, G *Poverty and Anti-Poverty Work in Scotland*. Glasgow: Strathclyde Poverty Alliance, 1994.

Crosland, A *The Future of Socialism*. London: Jonathan Cape, 1956.

Crummy, H *Let the People Sing! A Story of Craigmillar*. Edinburgh: Helen Crummy, 1992.

Currie, E *Is America Really Winning the War on Crime and Should Britain Follow its Example?* London: National Association for the Care and Resettlement of Offenders, 1996.

Deakin, N and Edwards, J *The Enterprise Culture and the Inner City*. London: Routledge, 1993.

Donnison, D *The Politics of Poverty*. Oxford: Martin Robertson, 1982.

Donnison, D By what authority? Ethics and policy analysis. *Social Policy and Administration*, 1994, **28**(1):20–32.

Donnison, D *Long-Term Unemployment in Northern Ireland*. Belfast: Northern Ireland Council for Voluntary Action, 1996.

Donnison, D What kind of new labour? *Soundings*, Summer 1996, 3. London: Lawrence & Wishart.

Donnison, D and Middleton, A (eds) *Regenerating the Inner City*. London: Routledge, 1987.

Downes, D *Employment Opportunities for Offenders*. London: Home Office, 1993.

Doyal, L and Gough, I *A Theory of Human Need*. London: Macmillan, 1991.

Dwelly, T (ed.) *Living in the Future*. York: UK National Council for Habitat II, 1996.

Family Policy Studies Centre *Children in Britain*. Family Report 2, London, Family Policy Studies Centre, 1995.

Finn, D *et al.*, Making benefits work. *Local Work*, **69**, February 1996. Manchester: Centre for Local Economic Strategies.

Fischer, C *et al.*, *Inequality by Design. Cracking the Bell Curve Myth*. Princeton: Princeton University Press, 1996.

Freeman, R and Katz, L (eds) *Differences and Changes in Wage Structures*. Chicago: University of Chicago Press, 1995.

Gaster, L *Quality at the Front Line*. Bristol: Bristol University School of Advanced Urban Studies, 1991.

Geddes, M and Wahlberg, M *The Value of Public Employment*. Coventry: Local Government Centre, Warwick Business School, 1996.

Gellner, E *Conditions of Liberty. Civil society and its Rivals*. Harmondsworth: Penguin, 1996.

Gershuny, J Post-industrial career structures in Britain, in G Esping-Andersen, *Changing Classes. Stratification and Mobility in Post-Industrial Societies.* London: Sage, 1993.

Goodman, A and Webb, S *The Distribution of UK Household Expenditure, 1979–92.* London: The Institute for Fiscal Studies, 1995.

Grieve, H *The Great Tide.* Chelmsford: County Council of Essex, 1959.

Grimes, A *Unemployment: A Modest Proposal.* London: Employment Policy Institute, Economic Report 10, May 1996.

Gudgin, G and O'Shea, G (eds) *Unemployment for Ever?* Belfast: Northern Ireland Economic Research Centre, 1993.

Hall, P *et al., Change, Choice and Conflict in Social Policy.* London: Heinemann, 1975.

Hayek, F *The Road to Serfdom.* London: Routledge & Kegan Paul, 1944.

Hayek, F *The Fatal Conceit. The Errors of Socialism.* London: Routledge, 1988.

Hills, J *The Future of Welfare.* York: Joseph Rowntree Foundation, 1993.

Hills, J (ed.) *New Inequalities. The Changing Distribution of Income and Wealth in the United Kingdom.* Cambridge: Cambridge University Press, 1996.

Hirschman, AO *The Rhetoric of Reaction. Perversity, Futility, Jeopardy.* Cambridge, Mass.: Harvard University Press, 1991.

Hough, M *Anxiety About Crime: Findings From the 1994 British Crime Survey.* Home Office Research Study 147. London: Home Office, 1995.

Hutton, W *The State We're In.* London: Jonathan Cape, 1995.

ICM Research *Results of a Poll on Democracy Conducted for Channel 4.* ICM Research, 90–92 Great Portland Street, London W1N 5PB, March 1994.

Irish National Organisation of the Unemployed *If You Think the Economy is Working – Ask Someone Who Isn't.* Dublin, 1996.

Jacobson, B *et al.* (eds) *The Nation's Health. A Strategy for the 1990s.* Oxford: Oxford University Press, 1991.

Jenkins, S Assessing income distribution trends: what lessons from the UK?, Working Papers of the ESRC Research Centre on Micro-Social Change, Paper 95–19, Colchester: University of Essex.

Joll, J *Gramsci.* London: Fontana Paperbacks, 1977.

Joseph, K and Sumption, J *Equality.* London: John Murray, 1979.

Jowell, R *et al.* (eds) *British Social Attitudes.* The 13th Report, Aldershot, Dartmouth, 1996.

Judd, D and Parkinson, M (eds) *Leadership and Urban Regeneration. Cities in North America and Europe.* London: Sage, 1990.

Laclau, E and Mouffe, C *Hegemony and Socialist Strategy: Towards a Radical Democratic Politics.* London: Verso, 1985.

Landry, C *et al., The Art of Regeneration. Urban Renewal Through Cultural Activity.* Stroud: Comedia, 1996.

Lang, P *LETS Work.* Warminster: LETSLINK UK, 1994.

le Grand, J *The Strategy of Equality. Redistribution and the Social Services.* London: George Allen & Unwin, 1982.

McArthur, A An unconventional approach to local economic development: the role of community business. *Town Planning Review*, 1986, **57**(1):87–100.

McArthur, A Jobs and incomes, in Donnison, D and Middleton, A (eds) *Regenerating the Inner City.* London: Routledge, 1987.

McArthur, A *et al.*, Credit unions and low-income communities. *Urban Studies*, 1993, **30**(2):399–416.

MacIntyre, A *After Virtue.* London: Duckworth, 1981.

MacIntyre, A *Whose Justice? Which Rationality?* London: Duckworth, 1988.

McCrone, G and Stephens, M *Housing Policy in Britain and Europe.* London: University College, 1995.

McGregor, A *et al.*, Creating community capacity for sustainable urban regeneration. *Scottish Journal of Community Work and Development*, 1996, **1**(1):55–66.

Mack, J and Lansley, S *Poor Britain.* London: George Allen & Unwin, 1985.

Marris, P *Community Planning and Conceptions of Change.* London: Routledge & Kegan Paul, 1982.

Marris, P *The Politics of Uncertainty.* London: Routledge, 1996.

Marshall, TH *Citizenship and Social Class.* Cambridge: Cambridge University Press, 1950.

Moberly Bell, E *Octavia Hill, a Biography.* London: Constable, 1942.

Murray, C *Losing Ground: America's Social Policy, 1950–1980.* New York: Basic Books, 1984.

Myerscough, J *The Economic Importance of the Arts in Britain.* London: Policy Studies Institute, 1988.

NACRO *Crime and Social Policy.* London: National Association for the Care and Resettlement of Offenders, 1995.

Nozick, R *Anarchy, State and Utopia.* Oxford: Blackwell, 1974.

Hancock Nunn, T *The Minority Report.* London: National Poor Law Reform Association, (undated).

Oldfield, N and Yu, A *The Cost of a Child.* London: Child Poverty Action Group, 1993.

Oppenheim, C and Harker, L *Poverty: The Facts.* London: Child Poverty Action Group, 1996.

Pahl, R *Divisions of Labour.* Oxford: Blackwell, 1984.

Parry, G *et al.*, *Political Participation and Democracy in Britain.* Cambridge: Cambridge University Press, 1992.

Patel, M International year for the eradication of poverty gains momentum. *Anti-Poverty Matters*, **9**, Summer 1996.

Pedley, R *The Comprehensive School.* London: Pelican, 1963.

Pollitt, D Wising up to employment. *International Cities Management*, 1996, May–June.

Power, A *Property Before People*. London: Allen & Unwin, 1987.

Power, A and Tunstall, R *Swimming Against the Tide*. York: Joseph Rowntree Foundation, 1995.

Ranson, S and Stewart, J *Management for the Public Domain: Enabling the Learning Society*. Basingstoke: Macmillan, 1994, pp. 158–64.

Rawls, J *A Theory of Justice*. Oxford: Clarendon Press, 1972.

Rawls, J Kantian constructivism in moral theory. *Journal of Philosophy*, 1980, **77**, p. 519.

Ringen, S *The Possibility of Politics*. Oxford: Oxford University Press, 1987.

Rorty, R *Contingency, Irony and Solidarity*. Cambridge: Cambridge University Press, 1989.

Joseph Rowntree Foundation *Inquiry Into Income and Wealth*, vols. 1 and 2. York: Joseph Rowntree Foundation, 1995.

Sassoon, D *One Hundred Years of Socialism*. London: IB Tauris, 1996.

Sen, A *Inequality Reexamined*. Cambridge, Mass.: Harvard University Press, 1992.

Smith, T and Noble, M *Education Divides*. London: Child Poverty Action Group, 1995.

Stretton, H *Capitalism, Socialism and the Environment*. Cambridge: Cambridge University Press, 1976.

Timmins, N *The Five Giants: A Biography of the Welfare State*. London: HarperCollins, 1995.

Titmuss, R *The Gift Relationship. From Human Blood to Social Policy*. London: Allen & Unwin, 1970.

Townsend, P *Poverty in the United Kingdom*. Harmondsworth: Penguin, 1979.

Trinder, C *Full Employment. The Role of the Public Sector*. London: TUC/Employment Policy Institute, 1994.

Tullock, G *Welfare for the Well-To-Do*. Dallas: Fisher Institute, 1983.

Tullock, G *The Economics of Wealth and Poverty*. Brighton: Wheatsheaf, 1986.

Webster, D *Home and Workplace in the Glasgow Conurbation*. Glasgow: Glasgow City Housing, 1994.

Wilcox, S (ed.) *Housing Review, 1996/97*. York: Joseph Rowntree Foundation, 1996.

Wilkinson, R *Unfair Shares*. Ilford: Barnardos, 1994.

Wilkinson, R *Unhealthy Societies*. London: Routledge, 1996.

Williams, C Social and spatial inequalities in the informal economy: some evidence from the European Community, *Area*, 1993, **25**(4):358.

Williams, C and Windebank, J Black market work in the European Community: peripheral work for peripheral localities. *International Journal of Urban and Regional Research*, 1995, **19**(1):23.

Wilson, WJ *The Truly Disadvantaged*. Chicago: University of Chicago Press, 1987.

Worswick, GDN *Unemployment: A Problem of Policy.* Cambridge: Cambridge University Press, 1991.

Official reports

Barclay, G (ed.) *A Digest of Information on the Criminal Justice System.* London: Home Office, 1991.

Barclay, GC *et al.* (eds) *Information on the Criminal Justice System in England and Wales.* London: Home Office, 1993.

Capita *et al.*, Hulme Study. London: HMSO, 1990.

Central Advisory Council for Education (England) *Children and Their Primary Schools.* London: HMSO, 1967.

Department of Social Security *Households Below Average Income. A Statistical Analysis 1979–1991/92.* London: HMSO, 1994.

Employment Policy, Cmd. 6527. London: HMSO, May 1944.

European Commission *Towards Sustainability: A European Community Programme of Policy and Action in Relation to the Environment and Sustainable Development.* Brussels: Commission of the European Community, 1993.

City of Glasgow *Glasgow's Housing Plan.* 1996.

Home Office *Criminal Statistics: England and Wales.* HMSO annual.

International Council for Local Environmental Initiatives *World Cities and Their Environment – the Toronto Declaration.* Toronto: ICLEI, 1991.

International Council for Local Environmental Initiatives *Strategic Services Planning – Sustainable Development: A Local Perspective.* ICLEI, 1994.

Northern Ireland Economic Council *Employment Creation in Northern Ireland.* Belfast, June 1994.

Office of Population Censuses and Surveys *Population Trends.* London: HMSO, 1993.

Public Schools Commission *Second Report.* London: HMSO, 1970.

Royal Commission on the Housing of the Working Classes, *First Report,* 1884–5. London: HMSO.

Scottish Homes, *Scottish House Condition Survey: 1991 Survey Report.* Edinburgh: Scottish Homes, 1993.

The Report of the Treadway Commission on Fraudulent Financial Reporting. Washington: US Federal Government, 1987.

United Nations Economic Commission for Europe *Guidelines on Sustainable Human Settlements Planning and Management.* Geneva: United Nations, 1996.

Warner, N *Choosing With Care. The Report of the Committee of Inquiry Into the Selection, Development and Management of Staff in Children's Homes.* London: HMSO, 1992.

Index